Friends You Can Drop:

Alcohol and Drugs

by
John Lawson

Quinlan Press

Boston

Copyright © 1986
by John Lawson
All rights reserved,
including the right of reproduction
in whole or in part in any form.
Published by Quinlan Press
131 Beverly Street
Boston, MA 02114
Library of Congress Cataloging-in-Publication Data
Lawson, John (John W.)
    Friends you can drop.

        1. Alcoholism. 2. Alcohol—Physiological effect. 3. Drug abuse.
4. Drugs—Physiological effect.
I. Title.
HV5060.L37   1986   613.8   85-71762
ISBN 0-933341-10-5 (pbk.)

Printed in the United States of America,
December 1986

For N. F. L.
who three times gave me life

John Lawson was born and raised in Providence, Rhode Island, the son of a physician, and graduated from Brown University in 1955. Since 1973 he has been active in the field of alcoholism and chemical dependency, and from 1973 to 1975 served as president of the Rhode Island affiliate of the National Council on Alcoholism. His experience in working with people suffering from addictive illness has involved individual and group therapy in a variety of modalities: a halfway house, a community mental health program, the Rhode Island Family Court Alcohol Program and, from 1980 to 1985, an internationally known residential treatment facility. He is currently living in Paris, France.

Contents

Introduction

Interest in the spectrum of human dysfunction caused by the addictive process has come to the fore only in relatively recent years, but it has sparked enormous and enthusiastic activity on both professional and lay levels. The 1970s and '80s have seen a springing-up of in- and out-patient clinics, a proliferation of therapy groups, booming sales of pills and capsules guaranteed to curb cravings and a vast output of literature setting forth theories on compulsive behaviors of all kinds, including how to bring them under control. "Addiction" and "addictive" have become catchwords to explain a variety of passions from nymphomania to loss of control after the first bite of chocolate, and as such, they have lost much of their true meaning and become a catch-all, as well as, in many instances, an alibi for self-indulgence and lack of willpower.

Willpower does not enter into establishing control over addiction in an effective therapeutic process that is carried out under the guidance of an individual who is knowledgeable about the phenomenon with which he or she is dealing. The syndrome from which the client or patient is suffering has far deeper roots, physical and/or emotional, which must be explored, understood and dealt with before the victim can achieve a lasting resolution of the problem. This will have to include a realization of the exact nature of his or her relationship with the addictive substance or activity, a removal of guilt about having had the addiction happen to him or her, and a clear understanding of what course of action will be necessary to prevent a reactivation of the addictive process. In the case of alcohol addiction, this involves first and foremost never reintroducing alcohol into the system and touching off the allergic-addictive reaction in the body chemistry that occurs only in alcoholics and that is so powerful and devastating in its effects that is ludicrous to compare it to the craving of a "chocoholic" who has allowed himself an orgy of bridge mix during an evening of television. The next day, the "chocoholic's" control will be re-established, in fact, remorseful, he will probably diet and go to bed chastened and hungry, but with self-esteem restored. The alcoholic who had put alcohol back into his system, however, would find himself once more in the iron grip of a compulsion against which he was powerless, and it would lead him once again into a nightmare of chaos and fear.

It is generally considered that there are five "true" addictions: alcohol (and the other central nervous system depressants, such as barbiturates and the "minor" tranquilizers), narcotics (opium and its derivitaves), food, gambling and work. The commonly held view is that the first three are "physical," and the other two "psychological," although physiological and psychological factors are involved in all five. All five present the same prime characteristic of loss of control despite increasingly severe sanctions of which the victim is all-too-painfully aware and of which he is deeply afraid. He or she needs to get at the root of the problem, realizing that the most strenuous efforts of will-power and self-control have failed, and to establish living habits that will enable him or her to live normally. The man who sees deepening alienation and friction at home as a result of his obsessive involvement with his work twelve or fourteen hours a day is as unable to help his behavior as the compulsive overeater who sees his weight top three hundred pounds, the alcoholic who is watching the fabric of home and job come apart because of his drinking or the gambler who has lost his house and his marriage and now has the loan sharks after him. Admonitions to "just stop it" and "get a grip on yourself" are about as useful as standing on the shore and telling the tide to stop coming in. If the afflicted individual knew how to stop what is happening, he would; no one wants to live with stress, disharmony and guilt. But he *doesn't* know how.

The central problem is that, for years, few people have had any real understanding of those in the throes of an addictive process, or sympathy with their unhappiness, although everyone knows, and thinks he understands, the word "addiction." Overwhelmingly, the prevailing view has been that addiction is a moral issue, and the man or woman afflicted with it has been judged accordingly. How often have we heard the word "disgusting" applied to the grossly obese or the habitually intoxicated, followed by the question, "How can they let themselves be that way?" The answer is that they are not "letting" this happen. It is happening *to* them, and all the willpower in the world can't put a permanent stop to it.

Certainly, there are few human afflictions older than alcohol addiction, and there is none that has been more misunderstood through the centuries. Even today, with public awareness focused on the massive proportions it has assumed in this country, where there are estimated to be between twenty and thirty million suffering from it, the amount of misinformation, myth and forklore surrounding it is overpowering. It is truly remarkable that the illness that ranks third in the mortality tables, coming after heart disease and cancer, should still be as shrouded in ignorance and misconceptions as it was in the Middle Ages and that its victims should be the objects of the same condemnation and rejection as they were then. Even more astounding is that until very recently the medical profession shared this attitude with the general public and that the average class time alloted to it in four years of medical school was one hour, during which the physical effects of the terminal phase of the illness were scrutinized and duly noted but nothing was done to affect attitudes or acquire understanding.

It is heartening that today, there is at least a growing concern about the threat that untreated alcoholism poses to the general public, especially on the highways, and it is to be hoped that from this awareness there will come increased motivation to understand the syndrome and to bring those who are sick with it to the help they need. It has become "the thing to say" to speak of alcoholism as an illness, rather than as a moral issue, but there is often a certain emptiness in such assertions when they are heard by professionals who have had not only close and intensive experience with the complexities of trying to help active alcoholics, but who have dealt as well with the total lack of comprehension on the part of the victims' families and friends concerning the clinical aspects of what has overpowered the patient. They are groping in the dark just as much as the alcoholic is, putting the blame for what has happened on him or on themselves, or both, and totally unaware of the real nature of his affliction. Moveover, they are almost invariably mistaken as well in their ideas about what will remedy the situation, and their well intentioned tactics only complicate and worsen it.

This basic primer on alcoholism (and its modern-day partner, dependency on other chemicals as well) originated as a newsletter which was sent to subscribers in twelve monthly installments. Its intent was to set forth in plain, lay terms the basic facts about alcohol addiction for people who needed the information because they were confronted with the disease in the course of their daily routine and wanted to feel that they were dealing with it on a sound, factual basis. There were some private individuals in this audience, but for the most part, it was composed of people whose daily work is in personnel offices, police and fire departments, social service agencies, schools and the like. Contact with alcoholism and other forms of chemical involvement is part and parcel of their daily routine, a fact that is in no way surprising in view of the epidemic proportions of the illness, and their interest in knowing more about it was founded on the frequency with which they encountered it on the job. There is certainly nothing rare or exotic about alcohol addiction. It is a commonplace fact of life. The paradox is that so little factual understanding of its exists, except on the part of those whose job it is to provide direct treatment for it. Certainly, it is encouraging to find that there exists in a growing segment of the population a realization that there is far more behind drunkenness than has been assumed throughout man's recorded history and that there exists an urgent need to discover what it is all about in order to begin to deal with it realistically and thus effectively.

The series was constructed on the premise that it would be best to start from scratch with the physiological origins of the syndrome, in order to establish the fundamental nature of it clearly, for one of the greatest misconceptions surrounding the problem is that it is brought on by emotional upheaval; it is essential for anyone who is attempting to deal productively with its manifestations that he or she have firmly in mind that what they are seeing has been caused by a malfunction of the body chemistry and that emotional chaos present in the alcoholic is the *result,* not the cause, of the physical addiction to alcohol.

There follows what is hoped to be a workable measure for determining whether or not one is dealing with true alcoholism: who *is* the alcoholic, and how can one tell if that is what is really present? From this, we have attempted to give a practical and down-to-earth discussion of the various ramifications of alcoholism. That particular problems of the female alcoholic are reviewed, along with the effects on the family, the results for children while they are growing up in an alcoholic environment and later on in life, the nature of poly-drug use and its effects, how to bring the patient to treatment, what an effective treatment process can be, and crucial issues facing the newly sober alcoholic in reentering society.

Response to the newsletter was the catalyst leading to its publication in book form. It is our hope that in that form, it can provide simple and practical information, as well as guidelines for those who find themselves confronted with a soul-destroying illness that has existed since man first learned to crush grapes.

1. Alcoholism: What Is It?

The alcoholism syndrome is one of man's oldest afflictions, cited in his earliest writings, a source of misery and lingering death that has remained a constant over the centuries. Other devastating, epidemic illnesses have been conquered and have moved into the realm of medical history: for a large segment of today's population, diphtheria and polio are not even fading memories, The Black Death ran its course and disappeared six hundred years ago. But alcoholism has remained, blighting the human condition, and its pattern today is identical to that experienced by its victims in the ancient world, the Middle Ages, the Renaissance, and the Industrial Revolution. It is timeless and knows no barriers. It was present in the palaces of the Caesars and in Dickens's slums. It went to the moon with one of the first astronauts to walk there. There is no immunization for it, and there is no cure. It continues to run rampant through every level of society and makes no distinctions: age, intelligence and position offer no protection. There is no such thing as being "too young" or "too old," "having more sense," or being insulated by wealth, or even by love.

The person with alcoholism can be anyone, at any point in life. Moreover, once there, it is there for good, irreversible and lethal. It is vitally important, both for the victim and for those concerned with his or her struggle, to realize that alcoholism, like diabetes, can only be arrested, put in remission. There is no such thing as a "former" or "ex-" alcoholic. These terms come from the almost universal misconception that when drunkenness stops, it means that the alcoholism is gone. Drunkenness is only the most noticeable manifestation of the active phase of the illness. Without alcohol in the system, the addicted person is indistinguishable from anyone else. But the condition is permanent and can be triggered back into life by a drink after decades of abstinence. It remains forever.

In basic terms, alcoholism is addiction to ethyl alcohol, or ethanol, which is the common component of beer, wine, and spirits. Roughly 10 percent of drinkers will develop it, and for this reason it is often termed a "selective" addiction. The remaining 90 percent will drink successfully all their lives, barring an occasional overindulgence, and they will drink as they please. They may be occasional or daily drinkers. They may drink lightly, moderately or heavily, according to how much they want and can tolerate. Drinking may be important to them, or it may be only a social gesture. Whatever their style, only one thing separates them from the alcoholic: they do not become addicted to alcohol. Great confusion is the result on both sides. Why can't that one out of ten "control himself" and "drink like other people"? The answer to that, as the illness becomes perceptible, is primarily physiological.

The Syndrome Begins

In the first of the three phases of alcoholism, there is no sign that there is anything abnormal in the alcoholic's physical reaction to the drug, no outward cause for alarm on his part or anyone else's. If anything, a person in the beginning stage of ethanol addiction will usually be remarkable for the quantity he can "hold," or tolerate, without experiencing the unpleasant sedative effects that succeed the initial stimulation. These are well-known to any drinker who has exceeded his particular tolerance level: slurred speech, confused thinking, unsteadiness, loss of inhibition bringing on embarrassing behavior, dizziness and nausea. Alcohol in moderate amounts will have a stimulant effect that accounts for its eternal attraction and for its permanent, accepted place in social interaction. People who learn to drink do so because of the pleasant, even euphoric, experience the drug can provide as long as they stay within their tolerance. That, of course, varies from one drinker to another. For some, one drink "does it"; for others, the pleasantness may be sustained through three, four or more. But experience quickly teaches the nonalcoholic, or "social," drinker at what point the drug's sedative effects will begin, and he will stop. This gauging of one's tolerance is basic to successful drinking, and the need for it is quickly grasped by the novice.

It is with respect to tolerance that the early-stage alcoholic begins to take a road not walked by the social drinker, and this walk takes place without anyone's knowledge. There is no sign of physiological or psychological malfunction; that may not be perceived for a matter of years, until the disease is solidly established. In the meantime, the victim's body is adjusting abnormally to an alcohol intake that steadily increases.

One of the primary organs affected by ethanol is the liver, which metabolizes it, producing a toxic substance called acetaldehyde. The liver enzymes in the alcoholic initially work more slowly than normal in eliminating acetaldehyde and compensate by multiplying. The alcoholic is thus able to handle increasingly large amounts of ethanol. However, the acetaldehyde level also continues to rise, and the alcoholic becomes caught on a merry-go-round of counteraction: more acetaldehyde produces more alcohol, which produces more acetaldehyde. For what is often a considerable length of time, his body will make adjustments in the cellular structure of the liver and of the central nervous system to accommodate the increasing alcohol intake. The rising acetaldehyde level has stimulated a physiological compulsion to keep drinking, and the body's tolerance to alcohol has kept pace with it.

This increased tolerance is an early sign of alcoholism. Ironically, it is generally perceived by the alcoholic and by those he associates with as just the opposite. He (or she) will be noted for an ability to drink copious amounts without "showing it," and this may be a source of some pride. Certainly, this man or woman would be the last person thought to be having a problem with alcohol and would indignantly deny it. An increasingly abnormal physiological reaction now has the alcohol being metabolized faster than in nonalcoholics, and the central nervous system has developed a tolerance that blocks drunkenness on amounts that would cause it in most social drinkers. At this point, the alcoholic feels he is doing what most drinkers do, which is taking a measured amount of the drug (if, in fact, he thinks of it as a drug) in order to induce a pleasurable stimulation and then, as it wears off, slipping back into his sober, normal state.

All drinkers are familiar with this little excursion from Normal (without alcohol in the system) to Pleasure and then back to Normal, and it is for most a highly predictable experience. An added plus the alcoholic may find is that his performance improves in the areas of concentration, memory and creative thinking. He feels better, more relaxed, and will say that he has more energy and that his thinking is clearer with the stimulation of alcohol. This will hold as long as he does not allow his blood alcohol level to *drop below* his tolerance point. This is because something unique to the alcoholic has begun to happen.

Maintenance Drinking

He has always realized that if he drinks beyond his tolerance, he will become drunk, like anyone else. This is one of the reasons he feels his drinking is "normal." However, unlike social drinkers, he has become aware, probably subconsciously, that when he drinks, he needs to keep his blood alcohol level at tolerance point. If he lets it drop, he will become drunk, shaky and agitated. His cells now have an addictive reaction to alcohol, and he starts to walk the tightrope known as maintenance drinking. Now the unpleasant sedative effects will occur not only when there is too much alcohol, but when there is not enough, and his drinking has had to become increasingly fine-tuned. Cells which are able to function well as long as the tolerance level is maintained have reached a point of addiction where they need alcohol to function normally. The alcoholic, of course, is not aware of this abnormal adaption in his body chemistry. He has only learned that when he drinks, he needs to keep drinking until he gets safely home to bed, that he can feel acutely uncomfortable as the alcohol wears off. He enters the middle stage of dependency without the knowledge that his body cells are drug-addicted. He may feel vaguely uneasy when he allows himself to see that his desire for alcohol is far more insistent than that of most other people, but that is something he can usually suppress or explain away: job pressure, the wife, the kids, the boss; the list can be a lengthy one. The maintenance drinker tells himself he "knows how to drink," and he tries to walk his tightrope carefully. He can often allay his uneasiness further, and dismiss any hints or criticism about his drinking, by seeking out other "real drinkers" as his chosen companions. With them, he can make a joke about the memory losses called "blackouts," about having to sneak drinks at home or during the day, about disguising the telltale signs when he returns from lunch. What he may not talk about is the increasing frequency of the blackouts, the half-pint in his desk or locker or under the seat of the car, and the moments when the uneasiness becomes fear. But he still sees nothing wrong. He knows he can handle it. The notion of having a "drinking problem," let alone alcoholism, is completely foreign to him.

The Grip Tightens

The middle stage of alcoholism is marked by the perception of others that something is wrong. The physical addiction is increasingly demanding, and the alcoholic is never going to return to the early road that led simply to euphoria and back, although he will continue to try and find it again. His body now reacts to even a short period of withdrawal, especially after a heavy intake, and the resulting hangovers become more severe, with agitation and tremors that are noticed by those who see him in the morning. He counteracts this with "medicinal" alcohol, and the addicted cells are appeased. The victim is still functioning, still doing what is expected at work or in the home, and the relief for the body cells may not come until a time deemed appropriate, such as after twelve noon (everyone knows only alcoholics drink in the morning). The day's work is done, the early-morning unpleasantness is pushed to the back of the mind, and the alcoholic may resolve once more not to let that happen again, to "take it easy."

It should be noted that the drink of choice will make no difference whatever as far as the addictive reaction is concerned. Whether the victim drinks beer or spirits, the cheapest vodka or vintage champagne, the body's response will be the same. To it, alcohol is alcohol, but it is part of the vast folklore surrounding alcohol that the form it takes affects what it will do. Anyone who has observed the struggle of an alcoholic to gain control over what is happening to him or her will be familiar not only with promises to "cut down," but also, in many cases, with a period during which the individual switches drinks. It may be decided that "it was those martinis," and that they should be replaced by "just beer" or "nothing stronger than wine." (In confirmation of the widespread misconception that beer and wine don't pose much of a threat to anyone, we see them advertised on television, while hard liquor is banned.) These efforts are doomed to failure by the very nature of the disease. If wine is being substituted for spirits, more of it will be drunk in response to the demands of the adapted body chemistry. By now, the disease is fully in place; it remains only for it to become progressively more severe, and it will not be checked by any temporary effort on the part of the afflicted individual, who will be experiencing the same symptoms with his lower-proof substitute and will eventually return to his original preference. He might as well;

he is experiencing the same effects. Total abstinence is the only way he is going to escape them, and that thought hasn't seriously entered his mind, although he may have experimented with brief periods of "going on the wagon," always followed by a return to drinking. He is physically addicted, and the notion that he can control alcohol's effect on him by self-discipline is pure fantasy (and wishful thinking). As he has no conception of what has actually happened to him, he will in all probability share yet another popular belief, which is that his exercising control is a matter of character and will power, and he will begin to experience deep shame and remorse over such failure to do so.

The alcoholic's unequal struggle with his illness in the middle, crucial stage of dependency becomes more and more apparent to those close to him, and promises start to be made and broken. The two-fisted drinker of the early stage is losing his tolerance because his cells are becoming damaged and can no longer handle the large amounts of alcohol he needs to ward off withdrawal symptoms. The absence of alcohol may bring on insomnia, sweating and the jitters. The deprived central nervous system will become hyperactive, and produce headache, dizziness and impairment of memory, and the sufferer with ingestion of alcohol. Thus the promises to himself and to others are broken, and dysfunction in interpersonal relationships is the result. Families react with hurt and finally with anger and disgust. The alcoholic is shaken by his morning image in the bathroom mirror, but even moreso by the angry outcry of his addicted cells and his need to relieve the agony of withdrawal and still the tremors in his hands. The "fun" aspect of drinking is long gone for the middlestage addict, and in its place there is a need and a craving for alcohol that is beyond the comprehension of the nonalcoholic. The gulf separating the two grows constantly wider, and the alcoholic feels increasingly isolated, not only from the world of the social drinker, but from those nearest to him and who mean the most to him. His obsessive need for the drug is taking him over more and more as the severity of withdrawal grows more painful, and this need will win out over all of his values.

Reaching this stage is not a rapid process. Alcoholism is a slow and subtle process that deludes its victims and has often been described as "the illness that tells you your all right." The alcoholic often does not recognize his gradual loss of control as such; it will usually be apparent far earlier to others, and he will have an elaborate system of alibis and excuses which he has come to believe. The onset of severe withdrawal symptoms after increasingly brief periods without alcohol may be so slow that he will come to accept them as part of life, the natural price he expects to pay for drinking. The decrease in tolerance will complicate matters, but it is very likely that he will retain the image of himself as having the large capacity of earlier years and excuse getting drunk on the grounds of being tired or having skipped a meal. The truth is that he can no longer manage the large amounts of alcohol he needs to relieve the symptoms he suffers when he stops drinking. He gets drunk more often, and he drinks at inappropriate times and places, so that the dysfunction may now be appearing at work, as well as within the family or with friends. Yet his rationalizing powers may well keep up with having a morning drink and with hiding bottles in the basement or the garage, or even at the workplace. He is conscious only of his need for relief and of his obsessive desire for alcohol, which he is less and less able to withstand. At all costs, he must stave off the jitters and anxiety that come when the acetaldehyde level rises and that cause the outbursts of temper characterized as "Jekyll and Hyde." His depression increases, as do his feelings of guilt and self-hatred as he is again and again unable to keep his promises to himself and others. The occasional uneasiness of the early-stage alcoholic, easily dismissed, now takes the form of a nagging anxiety that becomes his constant companion, makes him even more touchy and irritable, and requires more alcohol for relief. Even at this point, the alcoholic will delude himself that he is in control, that he knows how to drink and that his problems are caused by people, places and things, not by his "friend." The fact of the matter is that his "friend" is controlling him, not the other way around; he has lost control over his thinking and his behavior. Alcohol is guiding his thoughts and actions, coloring every aspect of his life.

People around him may now come to the erroneous conclusion that his drinking is being caused by psychological problems. Dysfunction at home or on the job may be blamed, and the alcoholic may be quick to seize upon this rationale. The services of a therapist may be sought, either to unravel his present difficulties or to probe as far back as early childhood. In actual fact, the cart is being put before the horse. Alcoholism is physiological in basis, and the alcoholic is subject to the same life stresses and problems as anyone else. What his disease does is to impair his ability to deal with them, and they are thus exacerbated and compounded. His mind is drug-affected, his emotions exaggerated, and his nerves rubbed raw by his alcohol abuse over a period of years. He is certainly experiencing emotional problems, but they are caused by his illness; they are not the cause of it. By not addressing the physiological nature of his suffering, and concentrating instead on painful episodes and feelings in the past, searching for pyschological causes of an illness that has gone out of control will often aggravate it further by deepening feelings of depression and guilt. To make matters worse, tranquilizers and sedatives are often prescribed to which the alcoholic can also become addicted. Valium appears to be the most common of these. The effect of these additional dependency-producing substances is simply to compound the extent to which the alcoholic's mind is altered, and they can be highly dangerous in combination with alcohol. Death resulting from an unintentional overdose of alcohol mixed with other drugs by an intoxicated person is by no means uncommon. Moreover, to become drug-free, the alcoholic will have to break the dependency on more than one substance. Anyone with extensive experience in dealing with alcoholics is well aware of the complications in treatment presented by the lasting effects of long-term use of these medications. Moreover, they appear to have little or no therapeutic value in enabling the patient to control his alcoholism. That can come only from an understanding of the physiological basis of the illness and a lifelong commitment to abstinence from alcohol.

Withdrawal

We have seen that the alcoholic has a physical craving for alcohol coupled with increasingly desperate attempts to avoid the results of withdrawal from it. The physical and mental pain of his hangovers worsens steadily. His addicted body subjects him to headaches, nausea, chills and sweats, and the longer he drinks, the more he will suffer when he stops drinking. He suffers as well from guilt, remorse, and fear, but these are overwhelmed by his physical need to replenish the burned-off alcohol. He may hate himself as he reaches for the first drink, but he will see no alternative. As his illness progresses, the symptoms of withdrawal will become even more frightening. The central nervous system, in chaos, may produced convulsions and hallucinations, while late-stage addiction may see the onset of delirium tremens (DTs).

Alcoholic convulsions are like grand mal epileptic seizures, with loss of consciousness and rigidity. They are produced by a number of factors when alcohol is withdrawn: very low blood sugar, a lack of certain hormones in the blood, malnutrition and build-up in the bloodstream of toxins and wastes. Hallucinations are also the result of central nervous system malfunction, and tend to be repulsive and frightening. Delirium tremens is their most severe form and will last for several days, during which the victim will be terrified by visions of snakes or rats crawling over him, or of water rising around him, or of blood and gore and corpses. In the weakened condition of the individual undergoing such trauma, medical treatment is vital to prevent cardiac arrest, brain hemorrhage or respiratory failure. The mortality rate when patients were strapped down in asylums and left to go through such protracted agony was about 25 percent, but modern medical techniques have greatly reduced the incidence of this kind of horror.

The pain of withdrawal, and the fear of it, coupled with the physical craving for alcohol, will keep the alcoholic drinking. We have seen that the alcohol will thus win out even at the cost of great emotional pain for the alcoholic and those close to him. The extent of human suffering caused by this illness is incalculable. But some alcoholics do recover, some lives are put back together. These people must survive the initial, acute withdrawal symptoms, optimally under medical supervision, and this process will usually run its course within seventy-two hours. Its severity will vary with the individual, depending in large part upon the extent to which the disease has progressed. It is after this acute period that recovery begins, but now the alcoholic also enters the protracted secondary phase of withdrawal.

To some degree, the acute symptoms will persist in a modified form. The majority of recovering alcoholics will continue to feel anxious, depressed and isolated. The craving for alcohol may not abate for weeks or months and may return without warning to torment and frighten the person struggling not to return to it. Sudden and unpredictable mood swings may also upset his equilibrium and that of his family, an echo of the "Jekyll and Hyde" syndrome of his drinking days. Abstinence may not relieve insomnia and vague, nagging fears. Again, the conclusion reached by the sufferer and by others is that he is suffering from psychological problems, and again, tranquilizers and sedatives may be prescribed. And again, the physiological source is missed. The damaged body cells have not healed; that will take time and care. They are still addicted, and although the victim has weathered the onslaught of the acute withdrawal phase, he is experiencing modified symptoms in the secondary phase and learning that breaking alcohol's grip is not that quick or easy. It is a very trying time, full of disappointment and frustration and frequently clouded by doubts as to whether sobriety is worth it, especially when he remembers the glow of alcohol, rather than the pain of it. Alcoholics Anonymous is an invaluable support always to the recovering alcoholic, and particuarly during this troubled period. There he can find understanding and empathy from fellow-travelers who have been through the same fire (or are going through it currently) and can share their experience, strength, and hope.

The alcoholic who is not fortunate enough to find his way out of the dark place in which his addiction has put him will pass on to the final stage of the disease. His tolerance will now decrease sharply because of heavy cell damage to the liver and central nervous system, and he will be drinking almost constantly to ward off increasingly agonizing withdrawal symptoms. It will no longer be possible for him to keep his illness hidden, and the extent of his physical and mental deterioration will become apparent. His drinking at this point will be focused entirely on relief, and if necessary he will sacrifice his entire value structure to obtain alcohol.

He is facing death from a variety of forms: cirrhosis of the liver, heart failure, pancreatitis, illness brought on by malnutrition and respiratory ailments and accidents of all kinds. Ironically, the least likely fate for untreated alcoholics is the one which stands out most in the public eye: dereliction. Ninety-five percent of those whose illness is not arrested will die first, or end up in some form of confinement. Yet it is the derelict who comes to mind when many people hear the word "alcoholic." To them, it is not a medical term, another "ic," like "arthritic" or "paralytic." The image the word calls up is that pitiful, terminal being, the "skid row bum." Moreover, the alcoholic is very likely to be blamed for what has happened to him. He is commonly perceived as lacking willpower, a glutton who has no self-respect and is heedless of the pain inflicted on others. All too seldom is the alcohol perceived as the villain and the alcoholic as the progressively powerless and frightened vicitm.

Attitudes

Such a view of alcohol is difficult for most people, because most people do not have alcoholism, and they do not think of it as a drug. It is in as common use as most household staples and is certainly not viewed in the same light as heroin or LSD. Attitudes toward it are important in considering alcoholism and alcoholics, because alcohol in the United States is an integral part of our social and cultural pattern, and a friendly part. It relaxes, lowers stress, builds confidence, provides solace and calm. As a social lubricant, Americans consider it an essential for entertaining at any level, from a formal wedding to a cookout with the neighbors. Millions depend on it for the easy camaraderie of the local bar. The business lunch is an institution. It is legal, easily available, and fits just about everyone's budget, in one form or another.

It is as this pleasant stimulant that the vast majority of drinkers have experienced alcohol, not as a soul-destroying darkness, and the alcoholic's behavior is seen as a perversion of an agreeable custom. The lady who takes an elderly aunt for a birthday lunch and orders them each a festive Manhattan is light-years away emotionally from the neighbor in the next block who has hidden vodka in an empty Clorox bottle in her laundry, and this is because she does not have alcoholism. She will drink her cocktail and have her lunch and think no more about it. She will feel the mild stimulation of the drink, which is why she ordered it, and she will experience exactly what she has learned to expect, nothing more. That evening, she will tell her husband that her aunt seemed to have a nice time, and he will tell her about the sale he made at lunch (with two martinis), and probably neither will mention the alcohol consumed. It is too commonplace to be mentioned, and in any case, they will be repeating the same ritual with a drink before dinner. These are social drinkers, the 90 percent of Americans who drink. They have no conception of what the woman down the street is going through. They would be shocked and uncomfortable with the knowledge, and repelled by the scenes that are taking place in that house with increasing frequency and bitterness. Naturally, they know that alcoholism exists, and they may or may not give credence to vaguely-remembered statements that it is a disease. But they have seen the derelicts downtown, and that has made a strong impression, stronger than the husband's fraternity brother and others who went to be "dried out," about whom they have tried to be very tolerant. When they think of alcohlism, it is the drunks downtown who come to mind.

These social drinkers have been raised with alcohol. They watched their parents and their friends drink it on social occasions, and observed as children that it was part of a good time, part of being grown-up. It was a big moment when they too, were given alcohol, a ritual rite of passage, and it made them feel adult and sophisticated. They are not strangers to drunkenness, either; no one in a drinking society could possibly be. But most of it was overindulgence, not alcoholism, although a number of cases of alcoholism have escaped their detection. They might even tell you that they can count the alcoholics they have known on one hand, but that isn't true, although they don't know it. What they are talking about is late-stage alcoholism, although they don't know that, either. Drunkenness to them is very likely to be amusing, something to laugh about later, although they have experienced some drunken people who were unpleasant or so sodden that they found them disgusting. It has been a mixed bag, typical of what social drinkers have known, and they have not spotted the hidden alcoholics along the way. Yet they have known some, as have most Americans by the time they reach young adulthood. But their knowledge of the disease is sparse and laden with myths, and as long as it doesn't suddenly touch them directly and inescapably, the most they feel towards it is a mild curiosity, which is very understandable. One tends to feel that way about any disease.

In the meantime, they are the targets of billions spent each year on advertisng for alcohol, advertising that makes drinking a bright and happy thing, or a status symbol, or a passport to romance. Alcohol advertising does not focus on drunkenness or divorce courts or people being fired. It does not focus on sickness. Rather, there is glamour or camaraderie or relaxation after a healthy day of climbing mountains or riding the range. It cannot be doubted that this bombardment makes an impression, and one that is far removed from the drunk downtown, just as he is removed from the social drinker. It makes an impression on the alcoholic as well, adding to his confusion about what he is experiencing with alcohol, and he too wants to be like the people in the ads. What is more, one of the reasons that abstinence is a troubling thought for him is that he doesn't want to feel cut off from the attractive world, and he feels that as a teetotaller he will be an outcast. Social drinkers and alcoholics alike share an awareness of what constitutes acceptable drinking behavior, and for both there is a stigma attached to aberrations such as habitual drunkenness, which most early- and middle-stage alcoholics try desperately to control. Both have grown up in a culture in which drinking is not only legal and highly acceptable but in which they feel a definite pressure to drink in order to be a part of the crowd, to join in most celebrations, or just to have a good time.

The attitude towards departures from this norm, such as alcoholism, is complex and often shared by observer and victim alike, as is their lack of comprehension of the syndrome as a disease. It is enormously helpful for the nonalcoholic to understand it as such, and vital for the alcoholic if he is to achieve and maintain sobriety. Progress is being made in this direction, although misconceptions and biases among the general public are still a hindrance to the alcoholic's recovery, and the following statements from the medical community endorsing the disease concept offer encouragement for the future.

The American Medical Association Statement on Alcoholism by the House of Delegates, American Medical Association (November 1956).

Alcoholic symptomatology and complications which occur in many personality disorders come within the scope of medical practice.

Acute alcoholic intoxication can be and often is a medical emergency. As with any other acute case, the merits of each individual case should be considered at the time of the emergency.

The type of alcoholic patient admitted to a general hospital should be judged on his individual merits, consideration being given to the attending physician's opinion, cooperation of the patient, and his behavior at the time of admission. The admitting doctors should then examine the patient and determine from the history and his actions whether he should be admitted or refused.

In order to offer house officers well-rounded training in the general hospital, there should be adequate facilities available as part of a hospital program for care of alcoholics. Since the house officer in a hospital will eventually come in contact with this type of patient in practice, his training in treating this illness should come while he is a resident officer. Hospital staffs should be urged to accept these patients for treatment and cooperate in this program.

With improved means of treatment available and the changed viewpoint and attitude which places the alcoholic in the category of a sick individual, most of the problems formerly encountered in the treatment of the alcoholic in a general hospital patient should be evaluated rather than have general objection on the grounds of a diagnosis of alcoholism.

It is recognized that no general policy can be made for all hospitals. Administrators are urged to give careful consideration to the possibility of accepting such patients in the light of the newer available measures and the need for providing facilities for treating these patients. In order to render a service to the community, provision should be made for such patients who cooperate and who wish such care.

In order to accomplish any degree of success with the problem of alcoholism, it is necessary that educational programs be enlarged, methods of case findings and follow-up be ascertained, research be encouraged, and general education toward acceptance of these sick people be emphasized. The hospital and its administration occupy a unique position in the community which allows them great opportunities to contribute to the accomplishment of this purpose. It is urged that general hospitals and their administrators and staffs give thought to meeting this responsibility.

American Hospital Association Statement on Alcoholism and the General Hospital (September 1957)

Alcoholism is a serious health problem. It falls within the scope of medical practice and it is often a medical emergency.

The alcoholic should not be denied the advantage of a thorough study of the cause or causes of his conditions and should not be denied the advantages of the best possible management of his case.

In 1944, a special committee of the American Hospital Association recommended that *"the primary point of attack (on alcoholism) should be through the general hospital. Because of the completeness of its facilities and of its accessibility, it is the logical place to which an alcoholic or his family would turn."*

There are still many hospitals that deny admission to all alcoholic patients despite the availability of improved methods of treatment and demonstration by experience that only a minority of patients with acute alcoholism are uncooperative.

Such a policy denies to the alcoholic patient benefits which would be available to him were his acute poisoning from another source, such as food, etc. It also denies to hospital attendants and house staffs opportunities for education in the management of the alcoholic patient.

The American Hospital Association urges general hospitals to develop a program for the care of alcoholics and having done so, to base the decision as to admission or nonadmission of the patient with a diagnosis of alcoholism upon the condition and needs of the individual patient.

This progressive step would keep pace with increased recognition of 1) the general hospital as a community health center, and 2) alcoholism as a medical problem requiring broad-scale attack if it is to be solved.

Position Statement of the American Psychiatric Association Concerning Responsibility of Psychiatrists and Other Physicians for Alcohol Problems (February 1965)

An adequate national attack on alcohol problems necessarily requires the application of the knowledge of many professionals reinforced by broad citizen support. Psychiatrists, together with general physicians and other medical specialists, have a continuing obligation and responsibility for contributing their relevant clinical knowledge and skills to the treatment and prevention of alcohol problems. It is urgent and imperative that psychiatrists and other physicians better prepare themselves for their proper role in attacking these problems on a national scale so that the medical contribution may become far more telling than it has been in the past.

Existing programs in the community for the management of alcohol programs are generally inadequate and need expansion and acceleration. General medical and psychiatric facilities, including general hospitals and psychiatric facilities, commonly discriminate against the patient with alcohol problems. Such meager services as they do render are offered in a spirit of therapeutic pessimism. What is needed are properly equipped and adequately staffed wards prepared to offer prompt and adequate treatment of acute and chronic physiological, psychological and social disturbances associated with alcohol problems, and community agencies concerned with the management of such problems. The principal of a continuum of services in the community applies here as well as to other kinds of disorders.

All prepayment plans for defraying the cost of medical care through insurance should cover the person presenting symptoms of alcohol problems who seeks treatment in medical settings on the same basis as for other illnesses.

Medically speaking, every person with alcohol problems should have the benefit of comprehensive diagnostic study including an assessment of his general health, his mental and emotional condition, and his social and economic adjustments. To concentrate exclusively on "the drinking problem" *per se* is to neglect the possibility of related diseases and various social and economic factors of possible critical import.

Treatment should reflect closely the results of careful diagnostic evaluation. As treatment progresses, furthermore, therapists should maintain continuous surveillance of the effects of that treatment and of intercurrent changes in the patient's condition. Critical review should continuously determine whether treatment is effective, appropriate and adequate.

The patient and his problems with alcohol are affected by his social environment but they also affect that environment. Treatment programs should take this into account.

Persons whose training is other than medical or psychiatric contribute substantially to the understanding and management of the patient. The treating physician should be willing to consult and collaborate with nonmedical individuals and institutions involved without assuming administrative or other nonmedical responsibilities in doing so. Such individuals include clinical psychologists, social workers, nurses, clergymen, vocational rehabilitation counselors, policemen, and others with qualifying education and background. Especially helpful with selected patients are organizations such as Alcoholics Anonymous. When collaborating or consulting with nonmedical persons and organizations, the physician will of course be always mindful of his medical obligations to his patient. He has neither legal nor moral authority to abandon those obligations.

Present research activities investigating the nature and causes of alcohol problems are both commendable and productive. They have not yet, however, reached levels commensurate with the magnitude of the alcohol problem and its threat to our society. Urgently needed are greatly increased public and private monies for research, expanded research institutes and programs, and large numbers of fully-trained personnel to conduct those institutes and programs. Procedures should also be developed which will greatly accelerate the adaption of research findings to the problems of patients and their promulgation to personnel involved.

We urge members of the Association to work with others in their communities for more adequate services for patients with alcohol problems in the context of this statement. We record our conviction of the need for undergraduate and graduate medical educators in general, and psychiatric educators in particular, to orient medical students in these constructive directions.

2. The Alcoholic

Theories abound on what constitutes alcoholism, on what causes it, and on the criteria to be used in making an individual diagnosis. In 1951, the World Health Organization defined alcoholism as "any form of drinking which goes beyond the traditional and customary 'dietary' use, or the ordinary compliance with the social drinking customs of the community concerned, irrespective of etiological factors leading to such behavior and irrespective also of the extent to which such factors are dependent upon heredity, constitution, or acquired physiopathological and metabolic influences." In 1960, Mark Keller, former editor of the *Journal of Studies on Alcohol*, described it as "a chronic disease manifested by repeated implicative drinking so as to cause injury to the drinker's health or to his social or economic functioning." In 1968, the American Psychiatric Association stated that "this category is for patients whose alcohol intake is great enough to damage their physical health, or their personal or social functioning, or when it has become a prerequisite to normal functioning." Finally, in 1977, the American Medical Association issued the statement that "alcoholism is an illness characterized by significant impairment that is directly associated with persistent and excessive use of alcohol. Impairment may involve physiological, psychological, or social dysfunction."

One can easily see the similarities, but the question remains of precise criteria for diagnosis in an individual who clearly needs help. Does this man or woman actually have alcoholism? Is the excessive and damaging drinking a reaction to a situation in his or her life, or is alcoholism reaching a stage in that individual where it is becoming outwardly apparent? We have already seen that in the early stage, which may go on for some years, most alcoholics are remarkable for their high tolerance, usually the last people for whom drinking would be considered a problem. It is like a cancer victim who appears vigorous and healthy while the malignancy, unsuspected, is developing and taking deep root. The reaction to both illnesses, when they finally surface, is shock and dismay, but with a vital difference: the person with cancer will be stunned, but will accept the diagnosis; the alcoholic will not, and will deny that the condition exists. A very basic, but very useful criterion for identifying alcoholism is that *the individual's drinking will continue despite steadily worsening problems socially, financially and emotionally.* Denial of the role alcohol is playing in the deterioration of such vital areas is a hallmark of the alcoholic, who will place the blame on "people, places, and things," as A.A. describes it. A.A. also describes the alcoholic as a "heartbreaking riddle" to those around him, but goes on to say that to other alcoholics (meaning sober ones) he is not. Recovering alcoholics understand, through looking back at their own experience, that it is in the nature of the illness that the active alcoholic is the last to see what is happening to him, that he has come to believe his own elaborate system of rationalization, alibi and denial. And alcoholics become very adept at this, confusing and intimidating those around them so that their drinking can continue without hindrance. They are skillful at placing the blame on a demanding and stingy boss, on office politics, on a spouse who doesn't "understand" them or with whom they can't "communicate," on problems with the kids and on and on. They come to believe it wholeheartedly, and the alcohol, more and more, becomes their "friend" as their situation worsens.

Exactly what that situation is may often be unclear to people closely involved with the alcoholic. The afflicted individual has often succeeded in making them feel guilty and responsible for it ("You want to know why I drink? Look in the mirror!" "Maybe I'd come right home, if I had one I wanted to come to!"), silencing their protests. There is often, as well, a denial system within the family, based on shame and fear. "He isn't that bad," they will hasten to say, "he's not an alcoholic, or anything like that." "He's tired," they will tell themselves. "He's under a lot of pressure." The problem is analogous to determining whether the chicken or the egg came first, and when the illness is beginning to manifest itself outwardly, it is often indistinguishable from problem drinking that could occur in a nonalcoholic. A row at home, marital discord, tension or even an explosive situation at work, can lead to someone seeking relief in drinking and does not necessarily mean alcoholism. A devastating loss or disappointment could also trigger drinking for a time, *after which that person's equilibrium will return.*

The Jellinek Scale

But alcoholic addiction is a persistent and progressive syndrome, and it is one which can be identified and tracked. The man whose landmark work in establishing the disease concept of alcoholism has made him the father figure of alcohol studies was E.M. Jellinek, D.Sc., a biostatistician who in 1952 published the results of a survey of over two thousand recovering alcoholics and gave the world what is known as the *Jellinek Scale.* The work focused on a pattern of progression, with a marked similarity of symptoms that was consistent, despite individual variations, to the point where it was possible to establish four distinct phases of the illness: the *prealcoholic, prodromal* (or *warning*), *crucial* and *chronic.*

In the prealcoholic phase, drinking is seen as socially motivated, and a growing increase in tolerance will occur. What was also perceived is that the prealcoholic will quickly discover a marked affinity for alcohol, be it as a social lubricant, a remedy for shyness, the essential component of a good time or an antidote for stress. Whatever the attraction, he or she will quickly gravitate to settings and people associated with drinking, and drinking will become more and more a focal point of that person's life. This phase may be brief or extend over a period of a few years before the onset of alcoholism. Here, by phase, are Jellinek's symptoms:

Prodromal Phase
Increase of tolerance
Temporary loss of memory ("blackout")
Sneaking drinks
Preoccupation with drinking
Hurried drinking
Avoidance of reference to one's drinking by others
Blackouts become more frequent

Crucial, or Basic, Phase
Loss of control (whether or not one will drink, quantity consumed once drinking starts)
Alibis and excuses
Strong comment/criticism from significant people (family, employer, friends)
Extravagance
Aggression, "coming on strong"
Persistent remorse
Periodic abstinence, "going on the wagon"
Change in drinking pattern (such as switching from hard liquor to beer)
Loss of friendship
Loss of position or clients
Significant people changing habits (e.g. children no longer bringing friends home)
Treatment of any kind—counseling, etc.
Holding grudges
Escapes (moving, changing jobs, etc.)
Protecting supply (stocking up, hiding bottles)
Morning drinking

Chronic Phase
Binge drinking (eighteen hours or more)

Ethical deterioration
Inconsistent, inappropriate thinking
Decrease of tolerance
Indefinable fears
Tremors
Motor problems (balance, gait)
Persistent feeling of desolation, emptiness

It should be noted that Jellinek's "scale" is not an absolute, in the sense that the symptoms do not necessarily occur in the order given, and not every alcoholic will experience all thirty-one of them. Moreover, nonalcoholic drinkers can have blackouts when they have too much to drink, and there are occasions when they may have a quiet "quick one" unobserved. Some nonalcoholics become loud and aggressive when they drink, and some decide to abstain for a while for a variety of reasons. There has also been a marked tendency in recent years on the part of many social drinkers to switch to wine in place of mixed drinks. These isolated similarities do not indicate a danger of alcoholism. Nor, obviously, are all of the things that happen to alcoholics cited on the scale. However, it is a very accurate outline of the progression of the illness, and it is in common use in many treatment settings when the initial assessment is being made. It is useful also for anyone concerned about an individual's drinking and who needs an indicator as to whether or not that person is actually suffering from addictive disease.

More of Jellinek's work with the disease concept, as well as other theories on the origins and nature of alcoholism, will be discussed later. For the moment, in considering the alcoholic and the largely consistent patterns of alcoholic behavior, it is useful to have the Jellinek Scale and to keep a few points in mind.

Again, it should be stressed that the alcoholic is the last to know that he is addicted to alcohol. In the prodromal stage, no one suspects it, and if he goes overboard and becomes drunk, followed by a hangover and possibly a loss of memory about the night before, this isn't viewed as anything out of the ordinary, because it can, and does, happen to people who are normally just social drinkers. The early-stage alcoholic has no conception of any physiological abnormality as far as his drinking is concerned, and if he does notice that his consumption is increasing, he will push away any disturbing thoughts about it. He may also begin to seek out other heavy drinkers to keep him company. At this point, it would take a sharp and practiced eye to react with concern to the way he "holds his liquor" or to spot his growing preoccupation with drinking. What the alcoholic may notice, but shrug off, is that he doesn't feel well when he stops drinking, but he won't think of that as a withdrawal symptom, and he will know instinctively how to remedy it. Like the cancer victim, he is unaware of early warnings or dismisses them.

The Road Grows Lonely

As his disease progresses, and he enters the crucial phase, others will become aware that something is wrong and will react in various ways. Some may comment on his drinking unfavorably; others, particularly family, may try to slow down his intake ("Honey, don't you think you've had enough?"); he may find others becoming distant, feel hurt or miffed that he was not invited to some special occasion; at work, he may find himself left alone at lunchtime or, far more significantly, not moving ahead as he had expected. At the same time, the toxicity affecting his brain will make him increasingly unable to see what is happening to him, and he will delude himself, often passing into paranoia or delusions of grandeur. Recovering alcoholics often speak of the "fantasyland" in which they lived with the aid of their "friend" and of their steadily accelerating flight from reality. He is unable to see what is causing increasing alarm or aversion in others: that alcohol is gaining control of him and affecting every aspect of his life, that his behavior is becoming more aberrant, and that his mood swings are becoming such that his reactions are no longer predictable and his growing psychological problems find expression in a "Jekyll and Hyde" personality split.

The alcoholic will deny that is using alcohol as a coping mechanism instead of dealing with life problems and situations in an adult way, and it is important to recognize that he believes what he is saying. His response to criticism of this kind may be a conscious effort to appear "normal," to "clean up his act," and prove, to himself as well as others, that he is in control of his drinking. It is at this point that he may decide to abstain for a while, and he may well succeed in doing so. For a while. Because he will return to drinking; he never intended not to, and he sees it as an unreasonable demand that anyone should expect him to give up what everyone else enjoys. It he does not do anything as drastic as going on the wagon, he may limit his intake in some other way, such as only drinking on weekends or after five o'clock, and this effort will also be doomed to failure. Another effort to bring his drinking under control by changing his pattern may be to switch to a lower-proof beverage, such as beer or wine. Again, it is unlikely that he will not find some rationalization for returning to his original drink of choice. Given the power of the addiction he is trying to combat, these struggles are pathetically feeble, but they are common to most alcoholics in the crucial phase. In the overall pattern of the Jellinek scale, the attempt and the failure are significant.

It is important to realize, too, what the alcoholic's relationship is with his "friend." He sees alcohol as a constant element in his life, perhaps the only one. When people disappoint or anger or frustrate him, he can obtain an instantaneous and predictable solace in drinking. Alcohol will give him relief from depression and anxiety, from feelings of isolation and of being misunderstood and unappreciated, and these deeply troubling emotions are becoming more and more a part of his everyday existence. He may vent these feelings angrily or reproachfully to others, but as he slides further into his addiction, he is very likely to keep them bottled inside him, in-

creasing his isolation, and begin to withdraw from people into a bog of self-pity and resentment. As he distances himself,
his reliance on alcohol increases, and he will use it to escape
either into fantasy or oblivion, to the point where he cannot
imagine living without alcohol any more than he could without
air or water.

People whom he sees as attempting to separate him from
his essential element become very threatening to him, and thus
it is that he may attempt to convince them that he is in control, as described above. At all costs, at home and at work,
he must be "normal," functioning well, able to "take it or
leave it." In a very real sense, those close to him become the
enemy, to be deceived and lied to, and he is very apt to react
with anger when his deceptions are discovered. Frightened and
guilty, he may erupt and then of course, seek comfort from
the ensuing scene in alcohol. His life becomes a more or less
constant escape from emotional pain—depression, fear, guilt
and resultant hostility—and he will see drinking as the only
thing that makes his existence bearable. His self-delusion is
complete. His confusion is such that he has no idea of the
bondage he is in, and his only instinct is to seek relief from
emotions that frighten him and that he doesn't understand.
Only when he has been detoxified, and a clear explanation
given to him and accepted, will he begin to see what kind of
a merry-go-round he had been on. It is a dazzling moment
of truth for a newly recovering alcoholic to realize at last that
what he was taking to make his emotional disturbances go
away was what was causing them in the first place, and that
it is within his power, and his power alone, to free himself
from them permanently. It all looks so simple at that juncture, but in fact, the process has been very complex and subtle, taking place slowly over an extended period and with that
unique quality of blinding the victim to what is only too apparent to everyone around him and causes them to blame him
for his tragedy.

This moment of truth involves the destruction of a vital and incredibly deep-rooted psychological component: the view of alcohol by the alcoholic as his "friend." To those who care about him, one of the most incomprehensible and heartbreaking things about an alcoholic is the tenacity with which he clings to the thing which is destroying him, a reality which goes against all logic. That is, their logic; not his.

We have already seen that as the disease progresses, withdrawal from alcohol causes increasingly agonizing symptoms. Therefore, it is not difficult to understand why the suffer has an urgent need for his drug and why he sees it as a painkiller. Understanding of the addiction also makes it clear that he has come to depend on it as a cure-all for equally painful emotional symptoms, and that he has pulled away from human contact. Alcohol is unquestionably his panacea as his isolation grows. He will become very devious and tricky in keeping his drinking pattern undisturbed, and hostile if that pattern is actually threatened.

There is a third aspect of the "friend" phenomenon which emerges consistently in alcoholics and which is a familiar block to those engaged in treating them. Despite the bondage in which he finds himself, and despite the pain and dysfunction it has produced in the vital areas of life, there is a persistent conditioned response in him which makes him equate alcohol with relaxation and fun. Pleasure remembered from his early drinking has a hold on him that is in many instances impossible to break. A large part of his continued drinking is seeking relief from pain, but a very significant element as well is the instinctive reaching back for a pleasure that he will never know again.

Tom

This brings us back to Jellinek's prealcoholic and prodromal phases, which seems a logical point at which to start tracking the progression of the illness in a "typical" alcoholic.

Let us select Tom from among the guests at a wedding reception in Tarrytown, New York. It is a pleasant community, comfortably middle-class, and Tom is home for the occasion from his freshman year at a small college in Vermont. He has come to the wedding with his parents and his younger sister, and he has known the bride and her family all his life. There are about a hundred guests, and they are on the lawn in back of the house, where there is a marquee and a dance floor. Tom is almost nineteen and trying to hide a shyness that overtakes him at large gatherings, although he is a nice-looking boy, and people find him agreeable and friendly. He has not had much experience with liquor, but he tries to assume a man-of-the-world attitude, becoming a college man as he sips a drink and studies the guests. He knows many of them, and his limited exposure to alcohol, mostly at college, has taught him that after a couple of drinks, he will feel confident in asking girls to dance and in making conversation with them.

Tom enjoys drinking and occasions where drinking is done. He has found that it relaxes him and heightens the enjoyment of socializing. Any anxiety he may feel with strangers or in new situations is quickly diminished, and he soon learned to enter in at the beer parties on weekends at college, finding that it speeded up the process of establishing a circle of friends and facilitated approaching girls he found attractive. A few experiences with having too much and getting sick have given him a fairly accurate gauge of his tolerance, and unless he's just out with the boys and making sure he keeps up with the best of them, he tends to be reasonably prudent. A nice boy, and certainly he's old enough to drink.

Three years later, by the time he's a senior, Tom has acquired quite a name for himself as a "heavy hitter" at college, and he enjoys that reputation. His grades are average, and there haven't been any problems, although there are some very funny stories that get told and retold, and he enjoys that, too. Tom is a nice guy who's always ready for a party, and people speak admiringly of his capacity, at times with something approaching awe. And the topper to it is that after all he's consumed, he's frequently been the one who's driven other people home. But his roommate sometimes feels a little uneasy. He's watched Tom drink a couple of six-packs while he's writing a paper at the last minute, and he's watched him do the same thing when he's just reading or watching television. Not all the time, of course, but it doesn't seem the same somehow as drinking at a party, and once or twice his friend has told Tom jokingly that he's going to become an alkie. That's as far as he felt it seemly to go, and after all, it wasn't as if there were any problem.

But there is. At twenty-two, Tom has alcoholism, but it won't surface for several years yet, although the way he drinks is changing. Once he's had a couple of drinks, he has trouble stopping. He still has control over when and where he drinks, but there have been a few times when his drinking behavior hasn't gone over very well with his date and two occasions when he couldn't remember past a certain point the night before. His friends made a joke of it, but when his roommate seemed concerned, Tom changed the subject with a finality that discouraged further comment. After that, Tom began to spend less time in their room, and a constraint, uncomfortable to both, developed in their friendship.

Tom's drinking is accelerating, but in small ways that don't attract any particular notice and that cause him no concern. He's all set to graduate, and if he stops in at his tavern for a couple of beers after this two o'clock class, isn't that all right? But sometimes he'll be there right on through the evening, and he's careful to pace himself and not to drink as fast as he'd like to. The situation with his roommate has troubled him and made him cautious; he doesn't want people talking about him. He has found that he is thinking more about drinking, sometimes during his morning class, and he has found it relaxing to go to another little place where he can have his ''couple of beers'' at eleven o'clock without an audience. It doesn't seem devious to him, just sensible. He just wants to have a little quiet time and relax, away from noise and people. By graduation time, he's doing a lot of his drinking there, away from the crowd he knows, and is telling people he doesn't feel like going out drinking. He makes a point of drinking very little in his room and is experiencing the satisfied feeling of the alcoholic who is keeping his drinking to himself. Subconsciously, he feels the need to present a facade and is developing his own strategy for doing so.

Tom has begun to find it difficult to go home, and his last Christmas and Spring vacations there were something of a trial. His parents' drinking is minimal, due in large part to his maternal grandfather's alcoholism, which is never mentioned, and there is no precedent for him keeping a supply of beer there. It has made him restless, although he has tried not to feel resentful, and he finally hit upon the solution of being out most of the time. He has found it possible to abstain for the sake of appearances, but on his last two visits, he found it uncomfortable trying not to wake his parents when he came in late at night. It was a relief to get a job in New York and to move there after graduation.

His first apartment is with two classmates, and he finds being on his own exhilirating. He makes friends at the large department store where he is a merchandising trainee and applies himself well there. His boss seems to like him, and Tom feels good about his prospects with the firm. He is free now to party as he likes, and he does so with enthusiasm. No one seems to notice that when Tom starts out to have a couple of drinks, it turns into a drinking bout. His tolerance is holding, but he is rapidly losing control once the physical demand for alcohol is triggered, and he begins to feel anxious and guilty the next day, especially as memory lapses begin to come more and more frequently. He is serious now about a girl he has met at work, and finds himself inventing alibis for her about his drinking. He sees her concern as an implication that he should cut down, or even quit altogether, and to appease her, he actually does stop for over a month. When he resumes drinking and there are repeated episodes of loss of control, he finds people and situations to blame it on and is so convincing that he believes his own excuses.

Tom does well at his job, and he receives a promotion and a transfer to a branch in Ohio at the end of his year's training. Encouraged by the approval shown him by the company, and pressured by his transfer, his girl decides to marry him, and they move to Columbus. Again, Tom does well, and he and Sue buy a house and have three children by the time he is thirty. Tom is well-known for his drinking, but there is no criticism at work or among their friends. The tolerance is still exceptionally high, and when he does occasionally get drunk while they are with other people, he is still a "nice guy" and people overlook it. At home, however, it is becoming a very different matter.

Sue watches her husband become a daily and compulsive drinker, starting the moment he gets home. She is fearful about the effect on their children and is beginning to feel inadequate as a wife. He consistently finds excuses to counter her reproaches—the job, the boss, the paperwork, the pressures. He is also remorseful and makes promises to her which he is incapable of keeping. Periodically, he abstains. He sets rules for himself: no more hard liquor (Tom has become a whiskey drinker), and he lays in a supply of wines; just two before dinner; nothing before five o'clock on weekends. All fail, and the alibis begin again. Sue finds a bottle of vodka hidden in the garage, and Tom explodes in a mixture of rage and guilt. There is a loud, ugly fight and Sue locks herself in the bathroom to cry while Tom shouts through the door that he is fed up with the store, with Columbus, with their house, their life together and with her.

Later, quiet and embarrassed, they sit down and try to "discuss the matter reasonably." Tom is miserably ashamed, guilty and fearful. His behavior baffles and frightens him, and he pleads with his wife to forgive him, again reiterating the pressures he had been under. Both grasp at that rationale and agree that Tom should seek professional help to deal with his stress and to explore what must be "underlying causes" of his tension and anxieties. As they talk, Tom feels an enormous wave of relief; Sue is being understanding and sweet, and nothing has been said about him not drinking anymore. He's bought some time, but he is controlled enough not to push his luck and get the drink he desperately wants. He's been forgiven. He's won. It doesn't occur to him that he's not thinking about his wife or his children or his future. He's thinking about a drink.

Tom goes willingly to a therapist. He has been worried about his drinking, and he welcomes the reasoning that it is a symptom of psychological stress. He has felt tense and strained, unless he was drinking, and he has found it easy to place the blame elsewhere. He hopes the therapist will be able to sort it all out, and while he is waiting for that to happen, he sees himself as having permission to drink. The threat of the alcohol being taken away has been lifted, and he feels elated. He no longer feels that he is to blame. Nor is his "friend."

During this period, the drinking does continue, and the family dysfunction rapidly worsens. Tom adds his wife to his list of resentments (isn't he *trying* to do something about it?). She's a bitch. She doesn't care. All she wants is a meal ticket. And he begins to think of flight, out of that job, out of this town, and compromises by going to a bar after work instead of going home. He enjoys talking to the people there and weaving fantasies to impress them with what a big shot he is. With their friends, he becomes aggressive and outspoken, even hostile, and people begin to distance themselves. ("What's gotten into him? He's getting to be an obnoxious drunk.") Sue, depressed and frightened, begins to drop out of activities she used to enjoy. She becomes evasive with friends and refuses invitations without telling Tom. She becomes protective of the children, who no longer have friends over to play, and tries to arrange activites for them away from home.

Tom's suffering is also becoming increasingly acute. When he is more or less alcohol-free, he is tortured by guilt and brings Sue and the children extravagant presents to express his love, then becomes angry if they are not enthusiastically received and feels unappreciated and sorry for himself. He experiences mood swings which can be touched off by the most trifling incident and which he is unable to control. His family, fearful of this unpredictable Jekyll and Hyde transformation, walk on eggs around him, and Tom feels increasingly isolated and resentful. He is also beginning to feel anxious about his job. He has noticed a coolness lately from his boss. He is sure that he is not imagining it, any more than he is imagining the snickers and whispers behind his back. He is certain that others in the office have complained about having to do his work when he has called in sick, or gotten Sue to do it (You'd think that they'd never called in with the flu! Especially that prize goldbrick Ferguson, but of course, the boss never sees *anything* wrong with him!). The day comes when the New York office liaison is taken from him. Angry, and with fear knotting his stomach, he goes in to ask why and is stunned by the unmistakable antagonism he meets. "You haven't been cutting it, Tom. I don't think I have to spell it out for you." Unspoken words hang in the air, and back at his desk, Tom begins to shake but doesn't dare go down to Charlie's for a quick one. Feeling all eyes upon him, he somehow manages to get through the afternoon.

Fear and resentment are now his constant companions. For some time, he has been drinking vodka in the vain hope that it is less detectable than other spirits, and now he begins to hide it in the house so that he can have what he needs when he needs it, especially in the morning when withdrawal is making his hands tremble. He shaves without turning on the bathroom light, unwilling to meet his red-eyed reflection, and carries with him eye-drops and breath fresheners. Tom is now a chronic alcoholic. The illness is fully established and is in the deteriorative stage. He is troubled by insomnia and constant tension. Food has lost all appeal for him, but alcohol is making him bloated and puffy. A vague, free-floating fear never leaves him, except when he has had enough vodka and his world regains a precarious equilibrium. It has taken nearly fifteen years of drinking for alcohol to do this to him and for his illness to be apparent to everyone who knows him. And yet no one, not even Sue or the therapist, has used the word "alcoholism" to him. He has minimized his drinking to the therapist, who will soon refer him to a physician for Valium if they don't start to make more progress. Tom has been a frustrating patient, week after week for nearly ten months, slippery and inconsistent. And Sue recoils from the word, although it is often in her mind. But Tom works hard and makes a good salary. They have a nice house and a fairly new car. She resolutely dismisses anything as degrading and shameful as her husband being an alcoholic. She would attack anyone who said so and defend her family loyally.

Tom has been seeing a psychiatrist for two months when he loses his job. He had shared his therapist's frustration and had dropped him when he began probing more deeply into the drinking thing. Shortly afterward, Tom had become alarmed at a sudden lowering of his tolerance for alcohol. He was bewildered by the fact that he became completely intoxicated on his normal intake, and there had been several embarrassing occurrences at business lunches. Terrified that his "friend" was betraying him and that the almost daily blackouts he was experiencing might be signaling the onset of insanity, Tom had picked a name from the Yellow Pages, and this time, he is being far more open about his alcohol involvement. The doctor has prescribed Valium for him and cautioned him about taking it in conjunction with alcohol. Tom is ignoring the warning and takes two to three times the prescribed dosage, hoping desperately that a tranquilizer will restore his balance. The result has been an intensification of symptoms, and even when he is relatively sober, he is frequently confused and defensive at work. He talks for fifty minutes weekly at his doctor, but does not receive much feedback. Nonetheless, he keeps his appointments because he does not know where else to seek help and his communications with Sue have broken down completely. Again, the word "alcoholism" has not as yet been mentioned. Even when he is fired, the word is not used; instead, he is advised strongly to get help for his "drinking problem" and the door closes. He is alone.

Fortunately, in many instances this last scenario does not take place. Numerous organizations now have Employee Assistance Programs to help troubled employees, alcoholics among them. Or else there is someone who is empowered to intervene in the situation, possibly before it reaches the late, deteriorative stage. In some cases, the employee himself, knowing that such help is available, may seek it on his own initiative. However the help comes, it may save a life and a family, as well as putting a valuable employee back on his feet by getting him into a sound rehabilitation process. We will be dealing later on with precise methods for this kind of intervention.

In Tom's plight, there are two possible outcomes for him. He will either continue to drink or at some point he will receive the treatment he needs to arrest his disease and begin the lifetime process of recovery. He has a chronic illness that will never leave him, but it can be put into remission and kept there for the rest of his life. If that does not happen, it will kill him, or he will end his days in some sort of protective institution. For the late-stage alcoholic, the need for help of the right kind is imperative. To simply dry him out, feed him tranquilizers, and have him counseled once a week is rarely enough. He must gain an understanding of his disease from competent professionals and help in accepting absolutely the fact that he has it and that any future attempts at "controlled" drinking are precluded for him because his condition, like diabetes, is one that is present in him permanently and irreversibly. He must learn to recognize the emotions that have fed the illness and learn to accept help in dealing with them from others. There are many changes in attitudes and thinking that will have to be made, and many of those processes are deeply entrenched. It is not a quick or easy proposition for an alcoholic to be rehabilitated, and it must be directed by people who know what they are doing and what they are dealing with. But alcoholics, even deathly sick ones, can be, and are, brought back to health and to useful, meaningful lives. The first task is to bring them to that help despite their illness.

3. The Alcoholic Woman

Estimates vary on the number of alcoholics in the United States today. The National Council on Alcoholism placed it at about ten million, and this seems to be an acceptable ballpark figure for most people working in the field, although there is speculation that it may be substantially higher. Alcoholism remains an enormous but often shadowy entity, often undetected or misdiagnosed, and it is unquestionably true that the vast majority of professional studies on it have concerned themselves exclusively with the male alcoholic, although women constitute at least half of the nation's population. The women's movement in recent years has been responsible for a marked shift of perspective as to who is the Alcoholic, and this has involved considerable readjustment in the viewpoint of the general public, as well as that of the researcher conducting demographic studies. It is very significant that between the years 1929 and 1970, there were only twenty-nine studies of alcoholism in women done in the English language, as if their presence were an intrusion into a traditionally male domain. What appears to be reflected is a tendency on the part of society to keep the female alcoholic or alcohol abuser in the closet; if her existence was not actually denied, she was very likely to be passed by with averted eyes, very much as the Victorians might have treated the spectacle of a fallen woman. It is interesting that this reaction has been a fairly universal one, extending even into what is generally assumed to be the purely objective realm of medical science, and it is evident that a drunken woman represents an ancient and very powerful taboo. The present-day acceptance of the *drinking* woman is in itself the result of changed perceptions of what a woman's relationship with alcohol should be and attests to the force of the feminist movement in altering her traditional role over the last ten to fifteen years. An unquestionable outcome of that process has also been that the plight of the woman afflicted with alcoholism has begun to be recognized and dealt with in an increasingly rational and accepting way, although the double stigma which that individual has borne for centuries is still a long way from being eradicated.

The Historical Perspective

As noted above, drinking has been traditionally considered a masculine activity and area of expertise. In many societies and in many areas, the two-fisted drinker has been the embodiment of the strong male, the man's man, and it has been unthinkable for a woman to join in, let alone match the male drink for drink. Exceptions to this have been rare and very limited in scope. In the ancient world, a female cult called the Maenads was allowed drunken celebrations to worship Bacchus, the Greek god of wine, and this was extraordinary in a civilization which otherwise kept women under very tight controls. Greek mythology also produced the wild and terrible Bacchantes, priestesses of the wine god whose drunken rites produced a horrifying mixture of promiscuity and murderous ferocity that clearly represents a concept of what women could be if their femininity were taken away by alcohol. At the same time, it is noteworthy that the ancient Greeks were the first to write of the fetal-alcohol syndrome and to cite the hereditary factor in alcoholism, so that in Sparta, women seen as likely to produce good stock were forbidden wine.

In the early, stringently upright days of the Roman Republic, a time in which a man held the power of life and death over his wife and children, a woman who drank was seen as a potential adulteress, and it was firmly believed that, "any woman who drinks wine immoderately closes her heart to every virtue and opens it to every vice." The law governing sobriety in women had as its basis the prevention of the ultimate outrage of infidelity, and in the accounts of men who put their wives to death for drinking, there is no element of censure, but rather a justification of their action as preserving their integrity. Curiously, as in Greece, women were allowed to hold drinking rites in honor of the wine god in Imperial Rome until men were allowed to participate and the bacchanalia became a drunken sexual orgy that was eventually halted by the Senate.

The message from thousands of years ago is clear: a woman intoxicated by alcohol is very likely to be promiscuous. That concept has remained intact until our own day and assumes various guises; it can be the hope of one man setting out for an evening's date and the fear of another whose wife of fiancee seems to be having too good a time. In either case, it is an integral factor of a double standard under which women have been obliged historically to live and which has deeply influenced society's perception of the female alcoholic on every social and economic level.

In the seventeenth and eighteenth centuries, when men, women and children shared the hardships of the New World, alcohol was viewed as a benevolent, kindly medicine and elixir, "the Good Creature of God," and was consumed freely and copiously. The manufacture of liquor was of great importance to the Colonial economy, and a study of drinking habits and attitudes of the period indicates that the typical American saw drunkenness as a "natural and harmless consequence of drinking" and was largely indifferent to it. Apparently women drank less than men, but they did so for the most part openly and without guilt, and it was quite respectable for a woman, often a widow, to own and operate a tavern. A parallel to this frontier sort of environment was to be seen in the Old West of the nineteenth century, when once again women shared the rigors of a life in which middle-class family patterns had not developed. However, from the end of the eighteenth century until about 1830, the Good Creature of God began to be replaced by the image of Demon Rum as the temperance movement grew and took hold in America. This somewhat schizophrenic view of alcohol has persisted into our time, in which it wears the faces of both friend and destroyer, but it was largely values rooted in family life and a middle-class lifestyle that promoted the temperance ideal.

The crusade for temperance was the most powerful secular movement of the nineteenth century. Its history paralleled the reign of Queen Victoria, and much of temperance ideology embodies the virtues of Victorian middle-class culture, especially the sanctity of the home and motherhood. However, in temperance thought, alcohol was made the scapegoat for every social evil, and none moreso than the threat it posed to the drunkard's wife and children. The saloon was the anti-home, and to attack it was to strike a blow against an enemy of women, a symbol of male domination, as well as against the demon that threatened the highest and most sacred Victorian ideals of uprightness, respectability and devotion to home and hearth.

Women were unquestionably in a dependent position, and this was further complicated by the pedestal on which they had been placed. Their role was to be madonnas, angelic, radiating sweet, feminine virtues and mother love, and their mission in the temperance crusade was to do battle for all the virtues of home. Frances Willard, president of the WCTU from 1879 to 1898, stated in 1905, "Were I asked to define ... the thought and purpose of the Woman's Christian Temperance Union, I would reply: 'It is to make the whole world homelike.' " However, Frances Willard was deeply committed to other issues as well, and the WCTU program has been well described as "a contradictory combination of Victorian middle-class moral vision, on one hand, and feminist goals and analysis, on the other." Certainly, it was strongly tied to the suffrage movement and to the emancipation of women from the dependency and stifling standards imposed upon them. In the last quarter of the century, the WCTU got women out of the home, gave them independence as organizers and speakers, responsibility in a powerful and significant movement, freedom from the role that had been forced upon them and involvement in a meaningful and invigorating fight. Small wonder that the liquor industry strenuously opposed the suffrage campaign. Frances Willard was a brilliant tactician, and while she was completely dedicated to ridding the world of the evils of alcohol, she was equally devoted to the feminist cause of liberation, and she used her slogan of "Home Protection" as an argument for getting the vote.

Prohibition became a reality in 1919, as did votes for women in 1920, and both are milestones in the history of women and alcohol. Prohibition provided a challenge that was taken up enthusiastically by both men and women, and the "new woman" of the 1920s found that drinking openly was one of many daring new behaviors that she enjoyed. The Victorian ideal of the "lady" was further broken down by the hardships of the Depression, which forced many women to work, and by World War II, with its reversal of many traditional roles. Frances Willard would have applauded the independence and action in many hitherto unconventional spheres shown by women since 1945, but she would undoubtedly have been dismayed by the departure in 1984 from her standards of the feminine virtues: the nurturing, gentle madonna of the home; the loving wife and tender mother; the lady. Her brand of feminism is a museum curiosity today, along with the other ideals brought forth by the founders of the WCTU in 1874, but its ghost continues to haunt women today and to be a tormenting element in the struggles of the woman addicted to alcohol.

A Gradual Emergence
That woman has been, until very recently, the shadowy figure mentioned earlier. To all intents and purposes, it has only been in the past decade that an awareness of the alcoholic

woman has seemed to dawn, not only on the general public, but on those involved in the study and treatment of alcoholism as well. As stated earlier, if one were to read through most of the vast store of material on alcoholism, the result would be an understandable conclusion that it is a problem of males, an area that is only occasionally invaded by an aberrant female. Traditionally, that female *has* been viewed as deviant; she does not fit the accepted stereotype of what a woman is supposed to be, and that stereotype still has, in 1986, a strong resemblance to the idealized conception of Womanhood that has remained more or less constant since ancient times and that finds a repeated echo in the literature of every age since then. The Victorian madonna of the WCTU was an extreme that invites ridicule today, but the laughter is very often mingled with a wistful regret for that gentle, nurturing being that seems lost to today's world. The alcoholic woman is seen as the antithesis of that ideal, and as such, she has been rejected without being known, not only by others, but by herself. We see as well a replay of the Greek and Roman assumption that an intoxicated woman is a loose one, and the historical concept of her has been that she is lower-class (very definitely not a "lady"), promiscuous and from murky surroundings. As such, it is understandable that she has not been of much interest to most people, including even those researching the illness, and *this* stereotype, as inaccurate as most of them are, has for years blocked investigation into female alcoholism.

The female alcoholic has the same illness as the male alcoholic. As is the case with the male, the victim has developed it without any intention of doing so. The culprit is alcohol, which has reacted upon the body chemistry in such a way as to produce addiction, and in most cases this has been a slow and undetected process that has gone on for considerable time before surfacing. As with the male, she is anybody. The women who develop alcoholism are young and old, rich and poor, bright and stupid. They barely completed P.S. 22 and they went to finishing school in Paris. They are lower class,

middle class, any class. Alcoholism is a selective addiction in
that it strikes only about 10 percent of drinkers, but it is not
at all selective about who that 10 percent is, at least as regards
intelligence, age or position.

By the majority of estimates, women are believed to comprise about one third of the nation's ten million alcoholics.
Variations of this figure are numerous, depending on what
sets of data are being used to establish criteria. Reports of
deaths from alcoholic cirrhosis will contrast sharply with
reports that women now seem to comprise about half the
membership of Alcoholics Anonymous, and both are equally
open to question as absolute measures of the male-female ratio
of alcoholics. Again, the area being dealt with is a very
shadowy one and no single demographic study can possibly
yield results that hold fast across the entire nation. There is
a great deal of guesswork even in the statement that the
alcoholic population is ten million; many professionals believe
that it is far higher. A conclusive figure on the number of
alcoholic women is even more unlikely to be arrived at because
of both the quantity and quality of data amassed over the
years. The bulk of existing studies reflects the aura of taboo
surrounding the subject and often gives only a cursory attention to it. One study on urban alcoholism, for example, dealt
with 1,200 men and 42 women; another, widely cited, re-
searched 3 women to support the premise that alcoholic women
are promiscuous.

However, some sound data has been produced since the
middle 1970s, which was a time of sudden interest in the issue
of women and alcoholism, sparked by the revelations of a
number of public figures, such as Mercedes McCambridge,
Jan Clayton and Joan Kennedy. Female alcoholism became
an "in" topic for the talk shows and the glossy magazines,
and the public was inundated with exposés of rampant addiction in the suburbs, among teenagers, among the elderly,
among housewives and on and on. (At the same time, it is
interesting to note, the magazines proliferated with liquor

advertisements aimed at women and stressing either the status and "equality" that various high-priced brands supplied or the low calorie aspect of light beers and dry wines.) Clearly, women were drinking, just as men do, and some of them were in serious trouble. In 1974 *Liquor Store Magazine* reported the results of a survey it had conducted which indicated that the ratio of liquor store customers has risen from 29 percent female in 1962 to over 50 percent. Seagram's distillers in 1978 rated *Better Homes and Gardens* among its five prime targets for marketing V.O. Also in 1978, Betty Ford went public with her alcohol and prescription drug problem, and it must be agreed that this was "a long way, baby" from the world of Frances Willard.

Findings began to appear that reflected serious exploration of the number of alcoholic women, but these took into consideration the unquestioned fact that although a much larger segment of that population was revealing itself and coming under scrutiny, there might well be an even larger proportion that remained concealed. The view of the late Marty Mann, founder of the National Council on Alcoholism and herself a recovered alcoholic, was that, "if you added up all the problem drinkers in the country, the hidden as well as the revealed, the sex ratio would be just about fifty-fifty." Women have been understandably reticent about coming forth with their alcoholism, in view of the double stigma attached to it in a woman. Some will, however, respond to the confidentiality of a medical setting, and there are numerous physicians who report seeing as many female as male alcoholics. A survey of private treatment centers came up with an estimate of about one-third of alcoholic patients being women, which coincides with the aproximate figure supplied by Alcoholics Anonymous. There will always be fluctuating and conflicting elements in studies dealing with an area as extended and yet as shadowy as alcoholism. What emerges solidly from *all* present data is that there is a very real alcoholism problem among women as well as men, that the number of female victims may approach, or even equal, the male statistics, and that the problem among women appears to be growing.

The Hidden Alcoholics

One extremely significant factor in the situation of the female alcoholic is the extent to which her illness may be concealed by her and/or by others. Historically, she has had less exposure to the world outside her home and has been provided for by her husband. Drinking alone at home during the day, she can draw the curtains and not answer the doorbell or telephone. Unless she has reached the acute, chronic phase in which her tolerance has decreased substantially and she has little or no control of when and how much she drinks, she is able to collect herself enough to function socially outside the home in a manner that does not arouse suspicion as to her alcohol involvement at her garden club or at dinner with friends. It will be the family who are uneasy or alarmed, and they will cover for her: "Sally has one of her headaches," or "Mom's taking a nap right now." For what is often a period of years, the family may present a united front to the world, ashamed and frightened at what is happening and desperately anxious for no one to know about it.

As long as this situation continues, the protected alcoholic will continue to drink in the majority of cases, despite the painful scenes that may take place within the family, behind closed doors. The same system of denial among family members that supports a man's alcoholism may also work to keep a woman's going. They may pull back from the very idea that their wife or mother is an *alcoholic* and minimize it among themselves, or pretend it isn't there, or grab hold of any encouragement that it seems to be getting "better" or even going away. Through an effort of will, she may be able to abstain or cut down (again, just as male alcoholics do) and to sustain the effort long enough to allay not only her family's anxiety but her own, after which the behavior will resume. As with any progressive condition, her alcoholism can only worsen, and the anguish of her husband and children deepen, particularly when hopes are repeatedly dashed.

It is, of course, impossible to gauge accurately the number of alcoholics living in this situation, and this compounds the problem of establishing a precise male-female ratio. The media have certainly seized upon this segment of the alcoholic population, and the housewife with the secret vice has become one of the stereotypes of magazine articles, and thus become for many the "typical" alcoholic woman who is sitting unescorted in a cheap ginmill.

The "typical" alcoholic woman is the woman who has alcoholism, as far as the nature of her illness is concerned, its threat to her well-being and her life, and the need for it to be arrested. As with all cases, for the alcoholic hidden in her home there must be confrontation, whether it comes from within herself, or, as more generally occurs, from significant others in her life. There must come a time when a line is drawn. Perhaps it will be she who will decide she can stand it no longer and will seek help. Or perhaps it will be her husband, who will decide he can stand it no longer and will present her with an either/or ultimatum. More therapeutically, an intervention may be arranged in which family members will present, with love and in a calm and rational manner, their concern for her and their insistence that she go for help. The latter scenario unquestionably provides *any* alcoholic with the greatest initial motivation to seek treatment and to have it work, supported in the decision by the caring of the most important people in that individual's life.

One of the most painful aspects of alcoholism for its victims is the low self-esteem, and even self-hatred, that it brings. Alcoholics entering treatment are almost universally characterized by guilt and shame. The remorse and fear they feel as they contemplate episodes in their drinking careers are heightened by the fact that they cannot now reach for their "friend" to dull the pain or to seek oblivion from it. Running from reality is one of the prime characteristics of alcoholic behavior, paradoxically with the very agent that has caused reality to be so frightening in the first place. And one of the realities that the alcoholic is least willing to face is the way she sees herself (or himself). The depression and anxiety that are standard symptoms of the illness cause her to feel frightened a good deal of the time—the vague, floating anxiety that the members of Alcoholics Anonymous have named "the fears." However, there are many times in which this fear is anything but formless. The memory of yesterday's occurrence or scene may be all too clearly remembered, and it may well bring with it deep embarrassment. As they succeed each other in the procession of her days, they pile up into a massive load of shame, and guilty remorse becomes a constant in her life.

The emotion may come simply from the fact that she was drunk the night before, that once again she was unable to keep her promise to herself not to let it happen. "What's happening to me? What am I becoming?" are questions that recur again and again to the alcoholic, and for a woman, they are particularly frightening and agonizing because of what she feels she is *supposed* to be. Once again, Frances Willard's madonna of the hearth reappears to reproach a sick woman, accompanied by all of the idealized imagery of women with which she is familiar. The concept of the "lady" has always been held up to her as a value and a guide to conduct. If she has a husband and children, she will also have a clearly defined sense of what her nurturing, comforting, feminine role should be. And she sees herself as far, far removed from being anything like what she was "brought up to be." These are concepts that have been drilled in, not only by the people who brought her up, but by society as a whole, and deviance from the feminine role that age-old tradition has assigned her carries with it a heavy burden of guilt.

The female alcoholic is thus doubly stigmatized, and she is well aware that her reaction is one shared by society, beginning with her own family. From youth, she has been aware of society's dictums about what "nice" girls do and don't do.

She knows that while a drunken man is tolerated because drinking is something men do, that he may even be considered entertaining or funny, the rule of thumb is that "there's nothing worse than a drunken woman." She sees herself as disgusting, not just unfeminine, and this is an emotion that she experiences again and again. It does her very little good within herself to present a front of apathy or defiance, to attempt to justify her drinking by citing her problems with people and situations and insisting that she is unfairly or insensitively treated. Nothing can excuse her in her own mind, and she increasingly feels that she is "just no good."

This is not to say that men do not experience similar guilt, remorse and battered self-worth. They do, of course, and very hurtfully. A man can also have an image of himself as the strong one in the family, the provider, the masculine factor, and this can be taken from him by alcoholism, just as a woman's identity can be. However, the double stigma does not enter in for the male as it does for the female. Drinking, after all, is still a masculine perquisite, and it is still all right, in many social situations, for a man to be intoxicated. He does not suffer the social stigma that a woman does, and as his illness progresses he does not suffer the same sort of self-stigmatization that a woman does, the same feeling of *unnatural* behavior. A man will feel embarrassment, even humiliation, as a result of actions while drinking; he can feel contrite and ashamed of himself for causing pain and unhappiness to his loved ones, but he does not experience the same emotion of going against the very essence of his being that alcohol addiction brings to a woman, of isolation from his essential reason for being. This is a uniquely female reaction, and a universal one in alcoholics, usually the first one brought up in treatment when they feel they can begin to talk about their feelings.

Feminism and the Alcoholic

The conflict in women caused by the strong surge of feminism over the past fifteen years has been blamed as one of the causes of increased drinking and alcoholism noted in that period. It must, however, be noted that one of the outcomes of the movement has been that women have come forward and sought help who would otherwise have continued to try and keep their alcoholism from being detected. It is not at all certain whether there are more alcoholic women or more who have reached a decision to do something about it and so are entering treatment facilities and joining A.A.

At the same time, it appears valid to accept the indicators that point to more drinking by women and to increased consumption by them; Seagram's distillers did not focus in on *Better Homes and Gardens* without substantial and well-researched reasons for doing so, and other manufacturers who began producing and promoting women-oriented fruit liqueurs and sweet cocktails were acting on sound market knowledge. Alcohol consumption by women has been rising steadily since 1945 and the war effort that saw enormous numbers of women entering the work force and beginning the reversal of their conventional role. Insisting on the right to drink, as well as to smoke in public, to go to restaurants, bars and nightclubs without male escorts, and to pick up the check were carryovers from the liberated days in the 1920s. Far more significant was the insistence of women on entering the workplace on a competitive level rather than a service one. Women began to invade traditionally male strongholds, going after executive-level jobs that, when they got them, involved drastic changes in lifestyle.

The working woman is exposed more to drinking situations, both socially and in the line of business, and she can very well feel as much or more stress in her work life, compared to her male counterpart. She may feel that she has to fight harder for acceptance and advancement than he does, and as a result feel threatened if she doesn't work hard to produce more and "prove" herself. She may feel stressed also at playing what has always been more or less a male role for which she has not had the same preparation as a man, and this strain may make her angry and resentful. And she may find that it's all a lot easier when she drinks with men.

This is hard enough for a single woman. For a married one, especially if she has children, there may be considerable conflict and confusion in roles. She may feel she is constantly taking off one hat and putting on another as she switches over from office to supermarket; she may be increasingly resentful over the fact that while she and her husband both work all day, his day appears to end at five o'clock and hers does not, although she feels just as tired, or moreso, than he does. She may resent more and more the evidence that seems to point to a belief on the part of others that she still has her traditional role which it is expected that she will fill, that having a job is her business, something *she* wanted to do, but that her family still wants a full-time wife and mother.

The result is that she may then become guilty about not filling that role to the standards she was brought up with and about the anger she feels toward those who want her to. This is certainly stress, but is not necessarily a blueprint for alcoholism. Nor is accelerated drinking. Nor is role conflict or an uneasiness about behaving in a "masculine" way when one has been brought up to be "feminine," which may be seen as a concomitant, or being successful in one's job. Alcohol causes alcoholism, not feelings. Many women work hard at two roles and experience a good deal of stress without becoming alcoholic, even though they may drink as much as many men and in the same settings, under the same pressure.

However, increased ingestion of alcohol poses a danger to anyone. For one thing, it can lead to problem drinking, as opposed to alcoholism. The woman who has had too much to drink can embarrass herself, or be stopped for drunk driving, or do something damaging to a personal relationship or to her standing at work. And this can happen to her on repeated occasions, without alcoholism being present. Stress from a variety of sources can certainly exacerbate this, as she gets into the habit of drinking to relieve it. This can be the case for a minority woman, for an elderly widow who feels increasingly alone and neglected or for a woman isolated in a rural area or small town who feels frustrated because life is passing her by. All can experience alcohol-related problems without necessarily becoming addicted to alcohol. It is important to make this differentiation. Alcoholism brings with it *loss of control*. It is no longer a matter of choice for an alcoholic whether or not she is going to drink or how much she is going to drink. She is the victim of a compulsive urge which produces an addictive-allergic reaction that takes control from her. Again, stress can certainly worsen the situation and keep it going, can increase the quantity consumed and break down controls at a faster pace. It is a question for many observers as to which came first, the stress or the alcoholism, and it is often difficult to separate the two, but it must be emphasized that alcoholism arrives on the scene independently, and that it will appear with or without stress.

To pursue this idea: it is mystifying for most people to see alcoholism in someone who shows them no reason for it to be present. They don't realize that there doesn't have to be a "reason" for it in their sense of the word. A woman may have "everything," as the world understands it, and still develop alcoholism. She may be beautiful, she and her husband may be deeply in love, her children may be perfect, there may be plenty of money and the good life, and she becomes alcoholic, and people are baffled. They are not at all baffled by the working woman who has a tough job, a difficult husband, children and a house to look after, and money troubles. When she becomes alcoholic, they can see all the "reasons." Yet the identical process has taken place in both women, independent of their life situations and of stress, or the absence of it. Clearly, the explanation is not exterior stress. Alcoholism is a complex process in which many factors play a part, stressors among them, but the root of all the ensuing problems lies in the initial process of physical addiction.

It was stated earlier that increased consumption is dangerous, and so it is. Alcoholism, like diabetes, can occur in anyone, at any age. Again like diabetes, there seems to be little question that there is a strong genetic factor involved, that it runs in families, and that the children of alcoholics are at higher risk of developing it at some point in life. However, massive doses of sugar can put anyone at risk of triggering diabetes, and the same is true of large quantities of alcohol. A woman who begins to drink heavily as a result of stress may well trigger alcoholism, particularly if the pattern continues over an extended period. An individual with a low threshold for stress may become a good target for alcoholism if she begins to drink for relief from tension and anxiety. And once the syndrome begins, it will follow its progressive course and worsen steadily. However, the blame should not be placed on the feminist movement, the sexual revolution or the lifestyle of the eighties. It should be placed squarely where it has always belonged: on the alcohol.

Implications for Treatment

It is crucial for a woman being treated for alcoholism to place the blame where it belongs. Almost invariably, she will enter treatment swamped with guilt, her self-esteem shattered, frightened at the damage that she perceives has been done to her life's structure, especially personal relationships, and very possibly filled with anger that this has happened to her and blaming God as well as people and situations. She may also be fearful that she is losing her mind, for that is a terrifying explanation that has often occurred to her for her actions. She will feel stigmatized by her condition, humiliated at being in treatment, and very possibly angry at the people she sees as having forced her to go.

It is at this time that she most needs reassurance from those close to her that she is loved, to realize that all they want is to see her well again, and acceptance of this may come slowly. The family need to be patient with her confusion and fear.

They may at times feel that they are dealing with a child, one who has been hurt and frightened and is reacting with anger, even while she desperately wants comforting and security. It must be remembered by them as well that while physical detoxification has taken place, and she is physically free of alcohol, her secondary withdrawal may continue to cause her insomnia, tremors, lack of appetite and fatigue. Moreover, the alcoholic depression and anxiety may take a long time to leave, and she may experience troubling mood swings that are best described as like a roller coaster. The emotions of a newly recovering alcoholic are very close to the surface, and she may have to struggle to control them without the soothing agent that is being denied her. She will need time and practice.

As she begins to interact with other patients, her peers, she will also begin to identify with them, to lose her sense of uniqueness and isolation. The parallels she will find in their stories with her own will begin to mitigate her guilt as she realizes that the behavior which so troubles her took place when she was *alcohol-affected* and that it does not reflect who she really is. She will have trouble picturing the other women doing the things they describe, and she will realize that that is true of herself as well, in their eyes. They are all seeing one another sober, and the realization of what alcohol has done to them will be a common experience. She will begin to see this commonality and to discover that while individuals vary greatly, each one being uniquely herself, their disease is the same, exactly as if they were all on a TB ward.

Her treatment should give her, ideally, sound insight into the nature of her illness and an acceptance that it will never leave her, that it can only be arrested through abstinence, and that the responsibility for that abstinence is hers alone. Thus, she will need to recognize those facets of herself which threaten her with relapse. She may need to identify her anger as a problem, or feelings of inadequacy, or frustration, or a lack of goals in her life, and learn how to deal with them sober. She will need to develop coping techniques to replace the alcohol, to learn that she can face things and deal with them. To do so, she will have to share those feelings with others, instead of internalizing them and presenting a facade, and this kind of honesty does not come easily to most alcoholics. The bonding that comes through this process is another beginning for her, and she can continue after being discharged to share that experience, strength and hope in A.A.

Again, it is vital for her to leave treatment knowing that what has happened to her is not her fault, nor is it the fault of anyone else. She must know that she has a deadly illness that is the cause of the suffering she has experienced, and that the responsibility is hers for making certain that it is not reactivated. And she must accept herself as a person, one with good points and flaws, a realist about herself. She will never be perfect; not the perfect lady, not the perfect wife and mother, not the perfect anything, because she is a human being. She has one of the most common illnesses that human beings are subject to, and she must accept it and learn to live with it, armed with the knowledge that it need never again block the way to anything in life that she is capable of achieving. Acceptance of herself and of her illness is the key that will free her.

4. Alcoholism and the Family

When the disease of alcoholism first emerges as a matter of concern to others, the focus tends to be immediately on the afflicted individual. This is entirely understandable, and quite proper. It is this man or woman who needs prompt attention and treatment, as would be the case with an accident victim or with someone who is exhibiting any kind of alarming symptoms.

However, in the case of alcoholism, the symptoms are frequently misunderstood; they are behavioral, and in the developing stages of the illness, those behaviors are commonly misinterpreted or ignored or excused by family members. Just as there is denial on the part of the alcoholic that there is anything wrong with his drinking, a strong current of denial will also be seen in family members. What has happened to the alcoholic is physiological, and psychological factors come into play with increasing intensity to complicate and excerbate his condition. He is more and more aware that drinking-related episodes are altering the way he is seen by friends and associates, and his reaction is usually minimization and rationalizing. "I wasn't that bad," he will tell himself. "I wasn't the only one. And after the week I put in, what do they expect when they don't serve dinner till nearly nine o'clock?" The excuses come easily: being tired, overworked, the unreasonably demanding boss or schedule, money problems, the nagging or demanding or indifferent wife, worries about children, conflicts at home or at work, physical ills, all of the components that can be loosely lumped under the all-purpose headings of "pressure" or "stress."

But the uneasiness grows, and it is shared by those around him. Someone who is drunk presents a condition that repels and often frightens others. For family members, a reason must often be found for it, if it begins to occur with any frequency, and they will often resort to the same kind of denial that the alcoholic is using, beginning with, "It isn't that bad." The initial reaction of those in the immediate family, those living with the alcoholic, may be anger, disgust, hurt and bewilderment at the altered state and the actions of the intoxicated person. There may be ugly scenes within the home that leave the family shaken and sleepless, or there may be nothing more than the simple fact that one of the family is drunk and is not functioning in his or her assigned role. The residue from an episode may vary, as well. There may be recriminations the following day; there may be silent, unspoken anger; there may be hurt, plaintive questioning that leads to apologies and promises on the part of the alcoholic; or there may be a determined effort on the part of all concerned to treat the incident as though it had never happened, to act out a little play for one another that will establish that nothing whatever is wrong.

Whatever the immediate reaction, the alcoholic family will experience fear. Initially, the fear may be for someone who is loved and is seen as troubled. For a wife who remains at home, this is mixed with anxiety that something may happen to the man on whom the family depends as a provider. Children will watch with apprehension the erosion of the mother or father figure from whom they have expected male or female parenting and nurturing. Mixed with the fear, there is often shame, and the family will pull together to present a united front to the outside world, denying that there is anything wrong, rationalizing and excusing, and often not even saying to one another what they are really feeling. To do so would be disloyal, and at all costs the family must preserve its solidarity. No one outside must ever know what is going on, and alcoholic families will frequently enter into a unspoken conspiracy to keep the truth hidden, not only from themselves but from the world at large.

Sometimes this is done so well that family members will delude themselves that what they are presenting to the world is what the family really is, and they will not only resist any attempt to address the situation, whether from members of the extended family outside the home or from friends, employers or other source, they may often react angrily and try to forestall any such interference in the future. Motivated by fear and shame, often covered up and unexpressed to each other, they will continue to protect the alcoholic and find excuses for alcoholic behavior. The will call work and say that he is too sick to come in; they will say he can't come to the door or the telephone because he is out, or ''napping''; they will excuse his absence at family gatherings, saying he has the flue or got called in to work; friends will be told about the terrific pressure he is under to ward off criticism if he gets drunk at parties; and they will make themselves believe the alcoholic's excuses, increasingly flimsy and implausible as they may be, rather than face the fact that his drinking is out of control.

As part of this denial syndrome, the family members will strive to maintain the family balance by shifting roles and taking on the functions of the incapacitated member. In the case of a couple with no children, the wife may have to become the breadwinner and manage the finances, but she will continue to defend the alcoholic, citing bad luck or office politics or a personality clash with the boss or ill health as the reason her husband is out of a job. In the process, she may even begin to find some gratification in her role of ''brave little woman'' at the same time she is explaining away her husband's drinking. If a mother is alcoholic, a daughter may take over her role and become the homemaker and disciplinarian of the younger children. In the same way, a son may take over the role of man of the house and become the strong, steady one on whom others rely. One way or another, the family goes on and continues to function while the situation inevitably worsens. The Family must be kept going. The Family must be looked out for.

The time will come when the family will have to recognize that there is a problem that cannot be denied any longer, whether or not the various members can bring themselves to use the words "alcoholism" and "alcoholic." Many will still recoil from those, with their image of skid row and its inhabitants ("He's not an *alcoholic,* or anything like *that,* but . . .''). But what? Well, there is a problem that's causing more problems, and that is finally recognized and attempts are made to control it.

Promises are often extracted from the alcoholic, promises that cannot and will not be kept, even though the alcoholic may want very much to keep them and makes them in all good faith. Activities and other diversions may be planned which it is hoped will take his mind off it, give him other interests, and that doesn't work either. The alcoholic may be showered with attention or given the cold, silent treatment, both without the desired effect. He may attempt to control his intake by changing, say, from hard liquor to beer and limiting himself to an agreed-upon amount, and he may make a sincere effort to stay within those boundaries. For a while. Inevitably, he will be unable to exercise the willpower required to withstand the irresistible demands of his addiction, and he will return, either stealthily or in open defiance, to his previous pattern. Whichever way he does so, when the fact emerges that the bargain has been broken, he will be armed with a battery of excuses and rationalizations to defend himself. Another, and usually desperate and angry, tactic used to try to establish control is get rid of the alcohol itself. Pouring bottles of it down the sink is an inadvisable action for two reasons. First of all, it may trigger rage in the alcoholic; it is a shock tactic, and such methods can be dangerous. Secondly, it is a waste of money. The alcoholic will simply replace it, either by going out to drink or by buying more. And once that has happened to him, he will take precautions to insure that it does not happen again. In no way will it stop him from drinking, even if he has to start hiding it (or hiding it better).

The family's attempts to control by these or other methods are, by the very nature of the affliction they are trying to either bring within reasonable bounds or eliminate altogether, doomed to failure. When that is recognized, their focus will again revert to the defense of the family system, and their reaction to the alcoholic may well be to push him out onto the periphery of that system. He is still present, but their ranks will close against him, even though the front will still be painstakingly presented to the world outside, insofar as that is possible. Alcoholics, particularly if they continue to provide the support of the family as breadwinners, continue to co-exist in the home. The rest of the family groups together defensively, and at best, an uneasy peace will be maintained between episodes as they try to hold on to some semblance of normality.

To the alcoholic, those closest to him will become the Enemy, the ones he has to deceive and lie to, and they become objects to be outwitted rather than people he loves. It is one of the most tragic aspects of alcoholism that this gulf is created, isolating an individual who is incapable of realizing that he is powerless in the grip of a substance that he sees as his source of solace and relief. He turns for relief from pain to the alcohol that is causing it, and he is unable to see the treadmill he is on, the vicious circle of his merry-go-round.

The family, uncomprehending, pulls away in hurt and anger. Recognizing their helplessness and the wall between them and the alcoholic, they will build a wall of their own as family life deteriorates and finally comes apart. Their attempts to function as a family along the traditional lines of their culture and heritage will be scheduled more and more to take place in the absence of the alcoholic. They will be most comfortable at a family meal when it is reasonably certain that he will be elsewhere. His appearance will be the signal for the others to be on guard, and there will be constraint or outright avoidance of him. The alcoholic may respond in kind and isolate himself in one particular place that becomes his own, and the family will leave him there gratefully. The presence of alcoholism over an extended period of time will cause the family system to collapse and will call forth survival instincts of its various members.

Behaviors will vary as this takes place. The spouse may take on all responsibility for the home and the rest of the family, become a "tower of strength," adept at manipulating to keep the structure intact. She will often feel inadequate as a wife and blame her failure for her husband's behavior. In that case, she may suppress her anger, hurt and guilt by appearing helpless and delicate, unable to cope, and trying to get others to respond to her self-pity. Children may attempt to free themselves by taking on a role, as well. One may struggle to improve the situation and present a facade of being on top of things, super-responsible and an achiever in his own right. To cover his anger, he may be the peacemaker and the source of strength. Inwardly lonely and confused by the progressively worsening home situation, he will establish a life of his own outside the home and try to excel in his activities to cover the inadequacy he feels because his efforts at home don't succeed in fixing the situation there. This child is likely to be the one who is most in touch with what is going on with the rest of the family, to be the most perceptive.

Another member may opt to be as inconspicuous as possible. This one will be quiet and withdrawn, and distance himself as much as possible from what is going on. He doesn't attract much notice and provides the relief of being the one no one has to worry about. Distancing is his defense against feelings of inadequacy, hurt and anger. Another defense system against those same emotions of anger, hurt and rejection may be defiance and acting out at home while seeking acceptance elsewhere. The anger this child feels at having to look for a support system away from home may be expressed by behavior that gets him into trouble at home. Yet another behavior may be to mask anxious feelings of insecurity and loneliness by being the family clown and providing fun and cuteness to relieve the situation. This is protective of that individual because no one takes him seriously and he is credited with only limited comprehension of the family's pain.

Implications for Treatment

All too often, what has been going on with the family is overlooked when efforts are being made to treat the alcoholic. It is often overlooked that the alcoholic's behavior has forced him into a position that has added to his difficulties. While it is unquestionably true that his wife may have had no choice but to take over the management functions that would normally be his, he has nonetheless been superseded. It is very likely that the rest of the family has formed a defensive alliance that has made him an outsider, and it will be difficult for him to break through that barrier and reestablish himself as part of the family system. They have been preoccupied with trying to function as normally as possible while living with his illness in the same house, and he may have to overcome years of resentment for making them live that way.

It is certainly unrealistic to see the struggle of someone trying to understand and arrest his alcoholism as a matter solely between him and the illness. There are too many emotional factors involved, factors rooted in relationships that are crucial to his recovery. It is, of course, essential that he understand the nature of his illness in order to gain acceptance of the fact that he has it. Good treatment begins there. However, those relationships must also be sorted out, the damage to them assessed, and both the alcoholic and the family prepared as well as possible for the sensitive process of his re-entry into the family system. The prognosis would be poor indeed for the newly recovering alcoholic who was expected to effect his own successful return to a family that understood nothing about his illness and that had been living, possibly for years, in conditions for which they saw him as solely responsible— and guilty.

Even a loving and supportive family has experienced feelings of hurt, inadequacy, anger and fear. And they have often acted on those feelings in ways that have widened the gulf between them and the alcoholic. Or they have acted on them in ways that have increased his dependency. It is not hard to understand that in a severely stressful situation, anger in an alcoholic's spouse that has been suppressed in order to keep the peace can suddenly erupt, and that it can be intensified by the resentment that spouse feels toward the person who is seen as responsible for feelings of inadequacy as a husband or wife. In feeling inadequate and a failure, they feel at least partly to blame for the other's drinking. Everything they have tried has failed (of course it has; they don't know what they're dealing with), and they are frustrated and frightened and fed up. Things get said in such situations, and separations grow wider. Both pull away, but the scene is added to the store in each one's memory bank, a storehouse that will have to be swept out thoroughly in the recovery process. For the marriage partnership to be restored to health, the spouse will have to have understanding of what happened to the alcoholic and to realize that there was no fault or failure on anyone's part, that the blame needs to be put squarely on the alcohol, where it belongs.

Fear on the part of a family member can also cause that person to unwittingly prolong the active alcoholism of another. Because they are afraid that if they don't cover for the alcoholic there will be severe repercussions, they will rush to the rescue and ward off the consequences of his drinking. This is the brother who tries to fix a DWI or goes down to the station with the bail money, the wife who calls in to say that her husband has a terrible stomach upset and won't be at work, the mother who "loans" the money for the rent or to clear up the bills, the father who goes to a friend to ask for a job for the son who's just been fired again. They mean well. They truly believe that they are helping and they are hoping that perhaps this will all somehow go away. It is anyone—relative, friend, co-worker—who steps in between the alcoholic and the consequences of his actions. Again, they mean well by acting as rescuers. It must be clearly explained to them that by so doing, they are enabling the alcoholic to go on drinking and giving him confidence that whatever bind he finds himself in, there will be someone there to get him out of it.

The Enabler

Of all the people in the drinking alcoholic's life, this is, ironically, the most dangerous one. It is someone who is concerned for him and wants to help, with no concept of "killing with kindness." It does not occur to someone, who acts out of fear that the alcoholic's drinking is going to catch up with him, that that is exactly what *must* happen if he is ever to recognize the reality of his illness and have any motivation to do something about it. Unquestionably, it is very difficult to stand back and watch disaster overtake an individual about whom one cares, especially when that caring person knows that he or she could ward it off, or to refuse help that is desperately pleaded for. By giving in, of course, the enabler must also see that he or she is taking the easy way out in many situations. It is much more comfortable to write out yet another check than to withstand the kind of emotional pressure that the alcoholic can bring to bear. Enablers can be made to feel very guilty if they do not continue to protect, either because they have refused to or because they have not acted on a generous impulse, and alcoholics are very much aware of this; it is one of their biggest trumps.

Closely aligned with the guilt that is brought into play on enablers is fear. What will happen if the bail-out is refused? The landlord will evict or the bank will foreclose. The car will be repossessed. The children will have to withdraw from school. Wages will be garnished. There will be a summons from the

Personnel Office. The wife or husband will find out about something that has happened. There will be a lawsuit. There will be notoriety. There will be embarrassment or humiliation. The alcoholic will be fired or asked to resign or suspended or demoted to the shipping department or posted at his club. The list of unthinkable possibilities is infinite as far as what may be presented to the enabler, caused by active alcoholism in someone who matters to him. All too often, the possibility is too terrible to contemplate, from the enabler's point of view as well as the alcoholic's, and the latter will be gotten off the hook, to continue on in his destructive pattern. The crisis that might have brought him to a realization of the hold alcohol has on him and of its potential for further pain has been averted.

The motives of the enabler are usually beyond reproach. He or she is sincerely trying to head off a clearly perceived calamity for the alcoholic, and in addition to guilt and fear, a third emotion is often present. The enabler is often very hopeful that this may be the last scrape in which the alcoholic finds himself, and this is reinforced by the alcoholic's remorseful promises. What is saddest about this repeated scenario is not the inevitable collapse of the enabler's hopes, however. Retrospect (and it is very true that hindsight is 20-20) will show, when the enabling system finally breaks down, that much damage could have been prevented if the alcoholic had been forced much earlier to face, and to cope with, a painful situation that his illness had brought about. By the time his rescue system does fail him, the hole he may have to climb out of may be much deeper than it would have been if he had been forced earlier to a realization of the influence alcohol was having in his life and of the hold that the drug has on him. By the time his self-delusion is finally replaced by a realistic view of where alcohol has taken him, he may have lost the things that mean the most to him and face a long struggle to try to regain them. It is sadly true that only pain will finally motivate a victim of alcoholism to look honestly at where he is and at the role his "friend" has played in his life. To forestall that moment of truth and keep the alcoholic from having to face reality is truly to kill him with kindness.

Nonetheless, any professional who has had to deal with the overall picture of an alcoholic's situation has had considerable experience with the enabling cycle and with trying to make family members see what they are doing to the sick individual and to themselves, as well as to recognize the inescapable fact that their efforts are based on wishful thinking. The alcoholism is never going to stop causing distressing situations until it is addressed and dealt with. It never just goes away. Shielding the alcoholic will prolong the active phase of the disease; he will not stop drinking just because peace has been restored by getting him caught up on his rent. His promises mean nothing. All enablers eventually learn that there is no such thing as the "last time I'll bother you like this," until they take a firm stand and make the alcoholic face whatever the situation is. For most people who have taken on the enabling role, this is one of the hardest things they will ever have to do, and they frequently need professional support to understand what they must do and to follow through on it.

Once again, fear is the predominant emotion. They are afraid because of what is going to happen as a result of their refusal. They are afraid that they will turn the alcoholic irrevocably against them (his angry and accusing reaction when he sees that this time, he is not going to get what he came for may make this seem a very real risk). They are afraid of the guilt they will feel if he loses his job because they wouldn't cover for him or his house because they wouldn't give him his mortgage payment, "just this one last time." Finally, they may be afraid of what he may do when everything comes crashing down on him, and most alcoholics will not hesitate, in their desperation, to play upon this last fear in order to get what they need. "You'll never see me again!" can have a variety of meanings, all of them effective in beating down a concerned person's determination not to give in. Again, that person may need consistent and persuasive support not to waver or give in and to focus on breaking the cycle that is keeping the alcoholic sick. An alcoholism professional, an informed Employee Assistance person, and Al-Anon member, a recovering alcoholic or a combination of these can give that support to someone caught on the enabling treadmill and help him or her, as well as the alcoholic, to break free of it. Help from a source *outside* the family is often the most effective. The person coming for counseling will feel that he or she is receiving direction from someone who is knowledgeable and has experience in handling the kind of dilemma being presented. In addition, the counselor is not involved personally and has no emotional investment in any of the persons concerned. His or her objectivity is an important factor in presenting an appraisal of the situation and a course of action that will be accepted by the family member seeking guidance. In the emotionally charged atmosphere of turmoil that has been surrounding someone who finally goes outside the family for help, a calm and reassuring presence can provide not only relief, but an element of hope and trust that will promote willingness to begin a difficult course of action.

Some Case Notes

In the experience of this writer, many families share the self-delusion of the alcoholic in believing that if things could just be straightened out and whatever is "bothering" him or her could be eliminated, the excessive and destructive drinking would stop. In this belief, many families turn their attention to relieving the strain the alcoholic is under, and the result is enabling behavior. At the same time, families will re-group and take on new roles to protect themselves and to preserve family structure while presenting as unified a facade as possible to the outside world.

What is lacking is an understanding of the real needs of all parties concerned and of the progressive syndrome in one member of the family that is affecting them all in such a way that meeting those needs becomes impossible. Each in his own way, all members of the family are focused on the sick one in their midst and reacting to that individual. They are doing so, in the vast majority of cases, without any clinical understanding of what is afflicting that dysfunctional member and affecting their own behavior and interaction with one another. A curious phenomenon about alcoholism is that almost all people think that they know just what it is and just what needs to be done about it. Many view it as a moral issue and feel that is a manifestation of self-indulgence, irresponsibility and supreme selfishness in the drinker. And they react accordingly, even while tolerating the alcoholic's presence in the home because that person is mother/father/husband/wife/child and cannot just be put out into the street. What can be done is to isolate that person, and this is frequently the solution in their view.

Manuel

An instance along this line is recalled in which the alcoholic was a Portuguese man in his early sixties, a native of the Azores. The family's culture prohibited strong action being taken against his illness, because that would have been seen by them (and their community) as an assault on an old man who was a father and grandfather and who owned the house in which the family lived. Instead, he was relegated to a room in the back of the house in which he was willing to remain as long as alcohol was provided and food brought when he wanted it. A pail of water was placed as an ashtray next to the sofa on which he spent his days dozing and watching television. His eldest son, a construction worker, lived in the house with his wife and teenage children and made it possible for Manuel and his wife to remain there.

The family tried to live their lives as "normally" as possible. Manuel's wife ministered nervously to him and lived as much apart from him as she was able to. The son became head of the house, and his wife took on all domestic responsibility, crowding out Manuel's wife and relegating her to the status of a poor relation. Disruptions occurred when Manuel emerged from his room and attempted to join the family or to assert his authority, and the strain under which the family lived caused acute dysfunction, especially in the daughter-in-law and grandchildren, who felt they were denied not only a home of their own but a place to which they could safely ask friends. The son was adamant in fulfilling what he felt was his duty to make it possible for his parents to stay on in their house, and family scenes were frequent and increasingly painful. Manuel, not alcohol, was seen as the villain and became the object of fear, revulsion and hatred, and his beer supply was kept plentiful in the hope that it would sedate him and keep him out of the family's way.

Resolution of the situation came when the seventeen year-old granddaughter became pregnant and screamed the news defiantly at her parents before running out of the house. The girl had been progressively withdrawn and sullen at home and at school since she was fifteen, and now the family was drawn into counseling. What emerged in that process was a realization on the part of the parents of what had been going on with their daughter as a result of the alcoholism with which she lived. She had interpreted her father's insistence on keeping his family in Manuel's house as greed and as not caring how they felt. She had suffered deeply from being ashamed to ever bring a friend to her home and thus feeling different from her peers, as well as fearing that she was laughed at and looked down upon because "we keep an old drunk in the back room." Her anger and sense of rejection and hurt had led her to distance herself from the family and to seek acceptance and caring elsewhere, while becoming moody and antagonistic at home. Deeply shocked, and guiltily aware that they had misread their daughter's signals to them, the parents moved to bring Manuel into treatment. Counseling had made them aware not only of the root cause of their family's dysfunction, but also of the fact that Manuel was a sick man, not a perverse or immoral one. With guidance, they were able to make him feel their concern while bringing sufficient pressure on him to induce him to enter a treatment facility.

Manuel responded well to treatment. As he gained understanding of his alcoholism and what it had done to him and his family, he also began to see the possibilities for him in sobriety of regaining control of his life, of reestablishing love and mutual respect, and of seeking out activities for himself that would make him interested in living again. The family participated in his treatment and welcomed him home as father, grandfather, and head of the house.

Lynn

Lynn was married at twenty-two to her high school sweetheart and proceeded to have four children by the time she was twenty-eight. At thirty, she had to go on welfare because her husband, Bob, had become an unemployable alcoholic and she was solely responsible for four young children under seven. When she was not careful, Bob would get the welfare check and spend it at the bar, and when she confronted him and threw his lies and excuses back at him, she ran the risk of getting beaten, often in front of the children. She lived in terror of not being able to provide for her children, of seeing them cold and hungry, and yet she would not appeal to her family, two hundred miles away, for help. Lynn loved her husband and clung to the image of the handsome Irish boy with the winning smile who had charmed and won her back in high school. Her family had mistrusted him, and she resolutely refused to "give them the satisfaction" of admitting they had been right in cautioning her and then actively opposing her when she announced that she was going to marry Bob. They had been married defiantly in city hall, and Bob had painted a glowing picture of the new life they would have in the city where his "good buddy" was now living and would find him a job at the plant where he worked. There had turned out to be nothing doing at the plant, and Bob had drifted from one low-paying job to another while the babies kept coming. He laughed at her fears, always promising something big just around the corner, but as his drinking accelerated, the winning smile compensated less and less as anxiety replaced her faith in his promises and she found herself increasingly alone in the apartment with the babies.

Lynn was well aware of the widespread alcoholism in Bob's family. It had been one of the repeated arguments used by hers in their opposition to her marriage. She knew also that there would be no assistance forthcoming from her in-laws. By the time she applied for welfare, Lynn was desperate, but Bob welcomed it and used that income as a rationale for only working sporadically. When Lynn appeared at a community agency for alcoholism counseling, she had been referred there by Legal Services, because after two years of fighting over the welfare checks and being repeatedly abused by her husband, Lynn had filed for a legal separation and had a restraining order to keep Bob out of the house. She had no substantive knowledge whatever of alcoholism. She had never heard of Al-Anon and thought that Alcoholics Anonymous was a religious movement. Her only grasp of alcoholism as a disease was her feeling that Bob's illness was the family "taint" coming out, and she was fearful that it might be transmitted to her children unless she was able to give them a good home and education so that they would have good jobs and not be interested in drinking.

Most strikingly, Lynn continued to hope that Bob would "straighten out." The picture she painted of him was still the boy in high school, not the ravaged, prematurely graying man with the glassy eyes and tremulous hands who once accompanied her to the agency and never returned after seeing there were no additional funds to be applied for there. To date, Lynn had had nine restraining orders, because she kept letting Bob talk her into giving him a place to stay for the night. She was unable to turn him away when he appeared in the cold or rain, pleading and cajoling and reminding her that he was the children's father; in the morning, he would laugh at her and demand money, daring her to get him out again after in-validating her court order, and would settle in until she ob-tained a new one and had a sheriff enforce it. Therapy for Lynn involved putting an end to the self-deluded game she was play-ing with Bob and taking realistic stock of the situation she and the children were in. She needed to understand her hus-band's illness and to realize that she was powerless to affect it unless he wanted to stop drinking. Since that seemed unlikely, and she had no leverage to use on him, she needed to let go of her fantasy that somehow the drinking would stop and the shining boy she had fallen in love with years before would return to her. Lynn had shown a survival instinct, and the counselor was able to use that, and her strong desire to give her children a secure environment, to enable her to make a final break from Bob and to address the issues that she could be helped with in the here and now. Backed by emotional sup-port from someone she liked and trusted, Lynn obtained a divorce and uncontested custody of the children; later, she was able to move back to her native city, where her family helped her to get re-established. Bob disappeared, and the sadness of her marriage to him will always be with her, but she was fortunate in finding the direction she needed to establish sound priorities based on a realistic assessment of her and her children's situation and a recognition of her inability to af-fect her husband's alcoholism when he was unwilling to ac-cept help for it himself.

Claire

Claire was forty-four when she came for counseling at the insistence of her sister, Anna. She had taken time with her ap-pearance, and it was possible to see an attractive woman with an engaging personality, although on that morning she was bloated and bloodshot, and there was liquor on her breath. She described herself as a binge drinker, and was clearly un-comfortable when Anna took over the interview and offered her analysis of Claire's situation. Anna described her sister as energetic and "on top of everything" when she was sober, but "a mess" when she was drinking and completely controlled by her husband, who also proceeded to tyrannize their son and two daughters, all in their teens.

Claire was a beautician and had risen to assistant manager of a prestigious salon until her drinking had caused her to be fired a year and a half before. Since that time, her periods of sobriety had become less and less frequent, to the point where she had also relinquished her role at home and the children took on her responsibilities there, supervised by her husband. Claire stated that her husband had never liked the idea of her working, that he had considered it a reflection on him, and Anna added that the husband had also disliked the independence it gave Claire and the fact that he was clearly jealous of any man she might meet while working downtown. It was Claire, Anna insisted, not Don, who was the attraction as far as the couple's social life was concerned, as well as the one the children really cared about, and at this point, Claire began to cry and told Anna to shut up. It was plain that she felt guilty about her husband and had a low image of herself as "no good" because of her drinking.

Two days later, Don made an angry appearance at the counselor's office and stated that he had just found out what his wife was "up to." He described her also as "no good" and wanted to know what she had told the counselor about him, adding that if it weren't for him, his wife would be on the street and that "his" children wouldn't have had any upbringing at all, and threatening that he would "do something about it" if the counselor continued to talk to her. There was obviously fear mixed with his anger, and in subsequent conversations with Claire (who insisted that her visits be kept a strict secret), it became apparent that Don was frightened of losing her and that she made him feel socially inadequate. Discussion of her drinking history established that Claire was addicted to alcohol, that the first drink set off protracted, round-the-clock drinking which she was powerless to control, and that her periods of abstinence initially involved a tremendous struggle within herself, although after a few days, this eased, and she was able to remain sober more or less comfortably. The key to her relapses was found when one day she spoke of her resentment toward Don for restocking the bar after she had gotten rid of all the alcohol in the house. "He does it every time. He says we can't live like it doesn't exist, and we've got to be able to offer people a drink, but it makes it tough."

It did, indeed, and it became clear to the counselor that Don was well aware of just how tough it would be, as long as Claire was alone in the house all day. The pattern that emerged was that when Claire began to feel like herself again and started to make plans for going back to work and into the world she enjoyed so much, the bottles would reappear. Claire, however, pulled back from the suggestion that her husband was deliberately sabotaging her sobriety in order to control her, and visits to the counselor dwindled and ceased. Anna remained in contact and reported that her sister was losing ground steadily in her efforts to control her alcoholism and that the family was becoming increasingly dysfunctional, with Don playing the despot and the children often in open rebellion against him. Attempts to re-establish contact with Claire found her evasive and usually intoxicated, while the children were abrupt and denied that their mother "or anybody else here" needed help. It was not until a few years later, when Claire was hospitalized with pancreatitis, that a counseling relationship was again established, this time with a social worker at the hospital who was successful in persuading her to get alcoholism treatment after discharge. She did so, and reappeared one day at her old counseling agency to report on the new life she was making for herself. She was now on her own, with a job she liked and living in her own apartment with the one child who was still in school. Alcoholics Anonymous was giving her the support and understanding she needed, and she had now been sober for ten months. Her nineteen year-old daughter was with her and smiled happily when her mother put her arm around her and said, "I never could have done it without my kids. When that Mrs. Drew talked me into going to rehab, and they saw I was really serious about it, they were behind me all the way. I felt so lousy about myself, I don't know if I would have stayed there if they hadn't kept calling and coming to see me and found out what they needed to know about what I've got." No mention was made of Don, and Claire's focus was entirely on her life as she was seeing it that day, positive and filled with optimism as she looked ahead. Sound treatment had made it possible for her to take responsibility for her disease and, with the support of her children, to establish the priorities she needed.

A Question of Survival

Alcoholism raises the very basic question of survival for the alcoholic, for family members as individuals and for the family unit. For this to be possible, all concerned must acquire an understanding of the disease and of what its impact has been. By thus recognizing and isolating the cause of individual and family dysfunctions, it is possible to gain a clear perspective on what is needed to establish normal functioning. The alcoholic must learn to fully accept and live with his illness, once it has been arrested. Family members play a crucial part in that recovery, and they can do so only when they clearly understand not only the syndrome, but how it has affected each of them, for they are also victims of alcoholism and enter into a recovery process along with the alcoholic.

The family unit may not survive completely intact. The alcoholic may not recover, in which case the rest of the family must learn to take care of their own emotional health and get on with their lives. Or there may be changes in the family structure, as in Claire's case, and the family must adjust to the new grouping. Not all relationships may survive, and this must also be accepted and adjustments made, in order for individuals to survive and get on with their lives. Many families, however, do come out of the ordeal intact if they are given understanding support and direction based on accurate knowledge of the disease. Without that, it is all too likely that they will flounder, that issues will not be resolved and that wounds will not heal. Alcoholism is a fatal, progressive disease, not only for those in whom it takes root, but for marriages and for family systems. Its effects in all those whom it touches must be understood and addressed in each individual in order for that person to be healthy in a family that is striving to surmount the experience of active alcoholism in one of its members, and those who have sought and found the help they needed have proven that such a victory is possible.

5. Children of Alcoholics

With the increasing awareness, in both the public and private sectors, of the enormous problem presented to society by alcoholism, there has come an accompanying realization that the illness is a far-reaching and many-faceted one. Alcoholism does not confine its effects to the afflicted individual alone. Its impact on the economy runs into the billions through work loss, poor performance, mistakes on the job, accidents, unemployment and compensation claims. After heart disease and cancer, it is the third largest public health problem in the nation. MADD (Mothers Against Drunk Driving) and other forceful public interest groups have at last brought pressure to bear on legislators to take action on the horrifying fact of 26,000 deaths a year on our highways caused by drunk driving. Alcoholism is, of course, a familiar specter to social workers, and it is encouraging to see the rapidly growing realization on the part of health professionals in all areas that alcoholism permeates nearly every one of their disciplines as well, from fetal alcohol syndrome to malnutrition in the elderly. The list is a lengthy one, and to those who are closely involved with any of the various manifestations of the disease, it is heartening to find that the long-awaited public interest and response appears to be a reality, and that the scope of the problem is beginning to be understood.

Interest has focused, quite naturally, on the alcoholic him/herself as the primary person to be treated, and rightly so. With increased sophistication in assessing the effects of the disease, there has in recent years also been a recognition of the damage done to children living in an alcoholic home, and to the far-reaching implications for those children after they become adults, as well. Robert G. Niven, M.D., Director of the National Institute on Alcohol Abuse and Alcoholism and a former director of the Adolescent Alcohol and Drug Abuse Service at the Mayo Clinic, made the following comments in the summer of 1984:

It is estimated that there are currently 7 million children of alcoholics under the age of 20 in the United States and many more million adult children of alcoholics. Studies to date on this population have focused predominantly on describing a variety of psychological impairments or on assessing the risk of alcoholism experienced by such children. Psychological problems attributed to such children have been numerous and varied. These include the presence of both major and minor types of psychopathology, impaired self-esteem and reality testing, impaired academic or vocational performance, and susceptibility to a large number of acting-out behaviors including delinquency, running away, and alcohol and drug abuse.... There is very strong evidence that alcoholism is an inherited disease. Impressive evidence now indicates that heritable factors influence susceptibility to alcoholism as well as to a number of physiological and biochemical responses to alcohol consumption. Furthermore, research has documented that environmental and hereditary factors interact to produce the alcoholic state in some individuals. The demonstration that sociocultural influences are critically important in the majority of genetically predisposed individuals suggests that changes in behavior and social attitudes by and toward individuals at high risk can alter both the course and the prevalence of alcohol abuse and alcoholism. It may soon be possible to identify potential alcohol abusers through sensitive and accurate physiological, biochemical, and behavioral predictors of alcoholic vulnerability.

With increased understanding and acceptance of alcoholism as a disease entity over the past ten years, the plight of the child of an alcoholic parent or parents has become a matter of growing concern to professionals in the field and to those working in interacting areas. It has become an accepted fact that the children of alcoholics often develop alcoholism themselves, or marry alcoholics, or both. In addition, these children present a great commonality of traits and behaviors which not only characterize them as children, but continue to have a strong influence on their lives as adults. Whether they themselves develop alcoholism or not, and it is estimated that as many as three out of five alcoholics had an alcoholic parent or parents, and whether or not they marry an alcoholic themselves, they show a very marked similarity of reaction to the environment in which they passed their childhood and adolescence, and it is becoming clear, as a result of growing research and documentation, that they will struggle with similar psychological and emotional problems after they are grown and on their own.

These children grow up and learn to survive as best they can in an atmosphere pervaded by the alcoholism of one or of two adults, their parents. The drinking patterns with which they live can vary widely. Perhaps drunkenness is a daily occurrence, and perhaps it is sporadic, coming as a binge after a period of abstinence. The drinking may be done in the home or outside, or both. The child may have been exposed to it since infancy, or he may be older when it begins to develop in his mother or father. Whatever the manifestation around which he must try to make a life for himself, there are certain invariables that all of these children know. Tension is an ever-present factor even if there are periods of calm when there is no drinking. The family is always waiting for the next episode, with the certainty born of constant repetition that it will come. It does, and it follows a more or less predictable and painful pattern in each household. There may be arguments between alcoholic and spouse in which the child may become involved, or there may be verbal of physical abuse, or the alcoholic may just pass out and have to be put to bed. Whatever the pattern, the result is that the child is bereft of a sense of security, of feeling solid ground beneath his feet when he comes through the door of his home. Anyone dealing with a child living in an alcoholic home has a small person who each day must go up to that door and not know what is waiting on the other side, either when he goes in or in the hours to come, and it is very likely that the child has been dreading that moment all day, whether at school or involved in other activities. The consistent, dependable security and support of a normal family system that are so vital to health development are foreign to him, although he is well aware that his peers are not similarly deprived.

The Assault on Self-Esteem

The result is that the child feels set apart, different, and that he has difficulty forming close ties. Almost invariably, he will not speak to anyone of the problems at his house. Indeed, he will go to great lengths to prevent anyone discovering his shameful secret, terrified of rejection and possibly scorn and ridicule. "No one must know" is the first rule, and so he not only feels unique, he is unable as well to ask friends to his home where they might see what he is so desperate to conceal. As a result, he will feel that he cannot go too often to someone else's house to play because of the awkwardness of never having them to his, and so he is likely not to form close friendships, either from the point of confiding in a friend or from having his house as a meeting-place where he can have guests, or even have friends call him. This apartness and shame mixed with fear make a large contribution to one of the more outstanding characteristics of children of alcoholics; almost without exception, as children and as adults, they suffer from a lack of self-esteem. They tend to retreat and become loners, and anyone who is familiar with the psychology of children, and most especially of adolescents, is aware that the worst thing that could possibly happen is to be different from everyone else, to thus invite rejection and unfavorable attention, and this is what the child of an alcoholic home feels acutely and can never verbalize to anyone. Often, the only escape is to live in a world of make-believe, and this is also a solitary occupation, as well as one full of pitfalls. In his daily encounters with the realities of school and other young people, the sense of apartness is intensified and confidence is diminished, so that further withdrawal may seem the only option open to him. The most important thing is to keep his secret hidden.

The child will have his own conception of what is average or "normal," and he will base this on what he reads, or sees in movies or on television, and on what he himself imagines, based on what he hears others talking about and what he sees himself in other people's houses. In his fantasies, he will probably imagine his own home transformed into an idealized picture of what he imagines home and family life could be, if only drinking were somehow removed. As he imagines these things, he may try to project them to others by fantasizing out loud, painting to outsiders a rosy picture of family life as he wishes it were, and if this is a very young child, he may be caught at it and accused of lying. This can be very painful, especially if it is accompanied by ridicule and baiting from peers, and will cause the child to withdraw more.

Children are taught, in most homes, that telling the truth is what they ought to do. Yet in an alcoholic home, that message can be very garbled. For one thing, they have often seen that the truth about the sickness in their house is often not talked about. The family, trying to maintain some semblance of order, of what is "normal," will often try to go ahead with dinner or whatever other normal function they are engaged in together, as if nothing were wrong. The truth that their father or mother is drunk, or that there have just been ugly words spoken, is simply not mentioned, and the family will try to go on with what they are doing. It is not common for a child to relate that he never talked to his siblings about what was happening, never turned to a brother or sister for comfort, and did all his crying alone.

Children in alcoholic homes often see lying on the part of those who are normally role models. They will hear their mother lie when she calls her husband's workplace to say that he is too sick to come in that day, and lie about what the sickness is. They will hear other lying, too, in a variety of situations in which the fact of alcoholism must be covered up. Often, they will themselves be instructed to lie—to extended family members, to teachers, to friends and acquaintances of the family, perhaps to bill collectors or the oil man or the corner grocer when they are sent to buy something on credit. The messages that such a child receives from adults are very apt to be mixed ones, and he will be left to his own resources to figure out what is right and what is wrong.

The result is that they must often try to guess what their behavior and reactions should be when they are with children or adults outside their own homes. The fact is that these children do not have any experience of their own to tell them what is acceptable and what is normal. They will establish their own criteria from observing and try to imitate; they will try to give the right responses and have the right reactions, as they imagine they would come from the people they feel so different from. Much of their behavior is guesswork, and the old familiar fear of others knowing that they are "different" is never very far away as they try to behave and respond appropriately. Because they find it impossible to ask, they must conceal the fact that they often feel confused and at sea, so that what is normal social interaction for others becomes a slalom course for them, and one in which they must repress their feelings of anxiety and confusion. What they don't know is that many of their feelings and reactions are perfectly normal. Situations arise in which it would be perfectly appropriate for them to show dismay or anger or amusement, but they're not sure of that, just as they are not always sure about voicing approval or disapproval. Instead, they must try to guess what is the "right" thing to feel or express, and perhaps wait and see what the reaction of others will be. Children of chaos and receivers of mixed messages, they find they do not trust their own impulses and try to gauge their behavior by that of others. Self-esteem takes a terrible beating in the child with these feelings churning inside him, afraid to be himself and to act on the courage of his convictions because he isn't sure what his convictions are. The daily exposure to reality is very unsettling to one who lives, by preference, in fantasies of what his life *ought* to be, and there is a steady erosion of his self-concept, a daily exposure to uncertainty and anxiety. There is very little sense of self that would have come from consistent parenting and from a stable environment in which the child would have had reassuring structure in his life. He has been alone with his feelings, and therefore with his assumptions about who he is and where, if anywhere, he belongs.

Being Safe

The normal instinct of all creatures who feel vulnerable and alone is to withdraw and seek a safe place. For the child living with another's alcoholism, imagining a different life for himself is certainly understandable, and it is much easier to do so when one is apart from others. Friendship comes with definite demands on the friend, and when these cannot be met, the solution is not to have friends, or not to encourage friendship beyond a superficial point. The child we are looking at feels unable to include others in his life at home because of what is taking place there. He feels unable to let people into his life because he fears being stigmatized by association as the child of an alcoholic. He is uneasy with others who live in a world very different from his because he does not know what his behavior should be, how he should present himself. Thus, he pulls back and doesn't get close to any person or situation that he perceives as potentially threatening. There is no one out there, he feels, that he can really trust.

Trust is in short supply at home, as well, and he has learned that it is much safer for him not to attempt to trust that anything or anyone is really going to be there for him. If it is his father who is the alcoholic, it is very likely that his mother is too preoccupied to do more than see to it that her children are adequately provided with the necessities. She is often described as irritable and distant, too wrapped up in her problems to pay much attention to the emotional needs around her or to be consistent in her responses when those needs are violated. Even as she is trying to show, when she realizes that she needs to, that she loves a child, she will at the same time often be pushing that child away because of her obsession with her husband's alcoholism and what it is doing to the fabric of her own life. There will be no consistent, predictable response on her part to any emotion or situation that the child brings to her. She does not provide the reassurance that he needs when he is upset or seeking guidance, nor will she be there as a confidante to whom private matters can be entrusted. She will not be the interested audience who enjoys hearing about what happened at school and furnishing feedback. At least, she won't be that on a consistent basis, or nearly often enough for the child to feel that he can ever be confident in approaching her. The feedback he gets is very apt to be angry and carping, or unresponsive and remote, and he learns not to have any faith that the responses he wants and needs will be forthcoming. It is safer to avoid disappointments by not putting trust there, and the child withdraws. At the same time, there is a sense of sadness for the fantasy mother, the TV mother baking cookies in her cheerful kitchen while she waits to hear if Beaver got the part in the play.

He lives, moreover, in a house where he can never be sure of finding honesty. People don't speak openly of what is going on inside themselves, and it often seems to him that he is living in a conspiracy of silence. His mother is all too often untruthful or evasive, not like a mother, not even like a real friend. True, she may be trying to shield him, but he's going to find out about it anyway, so why doesn't she just tell him? Honest sharing is a casualty of the complicated, crisis-ridden environment produced by active alcoholism, and the family members must seek to protect themselves as best they can. The child will do it by learning not to trust and not to expect honesty. In turn, he often does not give others the expectation that they can turn to him for those things; in the alcoholic household, it is every man for himself. That is where safety lies.

The alcoholic, of course, is the greatest disappointment in these areas. Promises seem made to be broken by him, and lying has become a defensive second nature to him. The family has learned better than to believe it when he talks about trips they are going to take or ball games they are going to go to, just as they discount his versions of why this or that calamity has overtaken the household. It is a very painful thing for a small child to experience broken promises and eventually to come to the realization that he can never put his faith in the pleasant things that his father talks about. Exit the fantasy father as well, tossing a football with the kids or taking them fishing. What the hurt and disappointed child must come to grips with is a harsh reality, not just the absence of a role model that is essential in his development, but the inescapable fact that he risks a repetition of that hurt by trusting again. Not only is there an absence of nurturing and security in his house, there is a real necessity for him to somehow develop a self-reliance that will enable him to survive without trusting, without nurturing and without security. He cannot feel safe, except on his own resources.

Nonetheless, feelings persist, and they must be dealt with. Withdrawal from something that hurts is a basic instinct; it's what happens when people touch something hot, or when a laboratory rat gets an electric shock. Emotional withdrawal is instinctive as well, and this is what children of alcoholics do. They have learned not to try to share with those adults in the family to whom they would normally turn, because they can never be sure that the feelings they express would be validated and addressed in a way that would make them feel better. They are fearful of expressing them to outsiders because first of all, they obey the first rule of the alcoholic family, which is *never* to reveal the presence of alcoholism. In addition, they are uncertain of the reception such confidences would receive and unsure of whether or not that kind of sharing would be the right thing to do. Safer, always, to say nothing, and that is what they do. Repressing feelings is the prime coping mechanism of these children, and it is learned at a surprisingly early age, usually before adolescence. Isolation is the hallmark that often identifies them to the perceptive eye, and it is a truly terrible place for a child to be in. By denying feelings of hurt, anger, fear and rejection, the child will try to pretend that they are not there and that the situation that produced them isn't real. In this, he is often abetted by the rest of the family, and the defensive wall grows higher and thicker. They are trying desperately not to be overwhelmed and to achieve equilibrium on their own. In the process, a defensive mechanism can often become an ingrained trait, and what is very commonly seen in the adult children of alcoholics is repression of feelings to the point where they are denied altogether, and the individual will insist that they are not present. It is a very difficult sort of fantasy from the one that produced the cookie-baking mother and the football-throwing father, but its source is the same. Both are reactions against an illness that the child does not understand and against which he feels, and is, powerless. Silence, isolation, learning not to trust and denying feelings are all ways in which he tries to maintain his balance and survive. However "normal" they may appear, mixing with their peers and being involved in school activities, they are very unlikely to really get close to anyone, and they see clear reasons for that protective distance. What they present is all too often not who they really are, and to those who like them, this can be puzzling, and even disturbing, if they are discerning enough to sense it. This is a child who is preoccupied, no matter what else he may be doing, with problems that are beyond the experience of most of his peers and who is trying to stay afloat. And he is doing it with very little real sense of self or of self-esteem, following a lonely road on which he doesn't know he has a great deal of company.

Roles—The Achiever

One common reaction to awareness of the need to survive is a corresponding urgency to feel in control of one's life, not merely to be drifting in this or that direction with every wind that blows, and the issue of control and of demonstrating achievement is one that appears frequently in children of alcoholics. In a strong-willed individual, it is also a reaction against repeated denigration at home, habitual criticism or being victimized by the perfectionism the alcoholic parent(s) may inflict on a child. This is the quiet child who is never a problem in school, who is super-responsible and clearly motivated to do well. Everybody praises him, and his average is consistently high. You notice that he doesn't seem to be much involved with the other kids, but he's pleasant and always agreeable, the one you can trust with errands or little jobs in the classroom. His prime interest seems to be his grades, rather than excelling on the playing field, and you detect a sense of real *purpose* in him. Indeed there is. First of all, he wants approval to shore up his self-concept and make him feel worthwhile. He needs those strokes, and he needs a sense of belonging, neither of which he gets at home on a consistent basis. Sometimes when he's there he feels needed and is given responsibility, but all too often, he is put down and criticized or yelled at. The continuity of approval is important to him, and so is his realization that he is doing well, doing better than others, and that this is recognized and rewarded. Very possibly, he has given up on the idea of friends and being one of the gang, so he will set out on his own and prove himself. Seeing chaos and what he identifies as irresponsibility at home, he is establishing order in his own life and achieving something of which he can feel justifiably proud. He is separating himself from home and finding an escape from it. In so doing, he appears stable and mature for his age, certainly not as a child with problems, and this is gratifying to him, as well. He seems not to be prey to the volatile feelings characteristic of most of his peers, and his teachers may often express the sentiment that they wish they had a roomful like him. One description for this child is "hypermature," and while no one appears to find any sort of fault with his behavior—quite the opposite—he is nonetheless outdistancing himself in that he is an adolescent taking on the responsibilities and behavior of an adult. The praise and sense of achievement are welcome, but he pays a price in the form of confusion, conflict and anger at feeling cheated of his youth. "I never *had* an adolescence," he may report in later years. "With things the way they were, there was no way I had time to be a kid." It is a very real loss that they feel, and they are very apt to be angry about it.

The Manipulator

This is the "con," the one who always has an angle, and he is very likely to be modeling what he has seen at home. Alcoholics are very adept at manipulation—playing one person against another, robbing Peter to pay Paul, making others feel guilty, inventing plausible excuses and rationalizations, disguising motives—and children will model their behavior on what they see at home. It has been noted that he may view dishonesty as normal, as acceptable when someone is in a tight spot; lying has certainly been modeled, for him at home, and it is very likely that he has been instructed by one or both parents to do it himself. Not only that, but he has been lied to, very probably to the extent that he now takes it as a matter of course. In using the same manipulation and dishonesty that he has grown up with, he has no real idea of someday having to take responsibility for his actions, any more than the alcoholic does, so that when people finally realize what he is doing and his strategies collapse, he is genuinely at a loss when the consequences come home to him. His perceptions have been distorted by his surroundings, and he really has no sense of making his way as he has been taught to. A child who has been told by his mother to lie to his grandmother, or to a bill collector, sees nothing wrong with lying to a teacher, as long as it achieves the desired result; and he is completely unprepared for the furor that may ensue when he is found out. In fact, children of alcoholics are very apt to lie for no reason at all, just because they are so used to it, and this is a trait that often carries over into adulthood and causes them considerable stress. It is at variance with their strong desire for validation and approval, another characteristic that stays with them in later years as a result of the low self-esteem they acquired by being part of an alcoholic family. Manipulation and deceit, when they are recognized in a child, must be addressed promptly, and the consequences spelled out to him, as well as the view taken of them by society. Otherwise, the implications of continuing to order his life in this fashion can become increasingly disturbing, possibly leading to serious social, marital or even legal difficulties.

The Outsider

This is the child whose detachment and lack of achievement give rise to serious concern. It is safe to say that all children of alcoholics have a feeling of being "different," and this affects them in varying degrees, in large part proportional to how seriously their self-esteem has been damaged. In addition, some children worry a great deal more about what has happened and what may happen at home, and this preoccupation may distance them from other activities taking place around them in which it is expected that they will participate. To add to that, many children have a serious sense of urgency about the situation at home, feeling that they must be there to help, and they worry when they are away. Perhaps that fear is about an alcoholic mother who is alone in the house during the day, or it may center around small siblings toward whom they have strong protective feelings. The same worry could extend to having his mother at home alone if there is the possibility of an abusive father coming while there is no one else there, or he may be distracted about events the night before, and tired as well from being kept awake for hours by an ugly fight between his parents.

Whatever the reason(s), he is pulled away from what is going on that he is supposed to be part of. That is the reason he is gazing out the window instead of paying attention in class, and why his schoolwork is poor and why teachers are puzzled and irritated if they know he is capable of much better work. That is why he eats his lunch alone in the cafeteria and is off by himself at recess, and why he seems to rebuff friendly approaches by others or even behave in such a way that they are turned away from him. Again, it is very unlikely that this child will tell, even when questioned by an older concerned person, what is troubling him; the first rule of the alcoholic family is never to tell, even though inside himself, the child may be crying out for someone to help him. No matter; that rule is an inflexible one. Life is very unpredictable for this child, except that he feels the trouble at home is a sure thing. He just doesn't know what form it is going to take this time, but he knows it will come, and so his mind is elsewhere and he is incapable of being like the other kids. The outsider is the saddest manifestation of what life in an alcoholic environment can do to a child, and it is rendered even more so in that he shares one of the characteristic feelings of all alcoholics: he feels unique. He is unaware of the millions of others who are growing up under the same crushing handicap, and his loneliness is a small personal hell from which he can find escape only in fantasy. This is the one for whom the discovery of a support group, Alateen, can be a crucial turning-point. Here he will learn that his is a shared plight, and the realization that he is not alone can make all the difference in his life. An offshoot of A.A., Alateen is for children of alcoholics and offers the same support through shared experience, strength and hope. The times and places of meetings can be found by calling the A.A. listing in the telephone directory. For a lonely and troubled youngster, discovering Alateen can mean the discovery of hope and, perhaps for the first time in his life, real bonding with his peers.

The Clown

This child, badly frightened, has sought relief in play-acting and laughter. His mask is being cute, and it is a good one. He is very likely to be the youngest in the family, and as such, has come in for a somewhat larger than usual share of petting and attention, and he is anxious to continue receiving approval and validation. He has learned that he can do so by providing comedy and cuteness, a throwback to his baby years that continues on through his childhood and adolescence, and often beyond. This behavior furnishes a most effective screen to people outside the home for the "differentness" felt by children of alcoholics, and it gives the clown a sense of relief as well from the constant tension and anxiety that exists in his own house. It is an easy role to fall into, if he is good at it, because it bolsters his self-esteem to be wanted and welcomed by others as "fun" or a "hot sketch," and in most instances he will play it for all it is worth.

The security that this child gains from his positive reception may provide a balance for the insecurity that his family situation engenders, and so may be a help at school and in developing skill and confidence in social interaction with his peers. However, it may be accompanied by hyperactivity that can lead to discipline problems, especially when the child is very young and has not learned rudimentary social controls. Moreover, laughter is a good defense, an excellent way to interrupt a tense situation and to mask feelings of inadequacy and fear, but the clown pays one very heavy price for consistently presenting this facade to the world. He will find, limited as he is to the one response in times of stress, that while anyone likes him, no one really takes him seriously, and this, of course, is very hurtful and reinforces the low self-esteem and sense of isolation common to children in his situation. Since it is very likely to be his only modus operandi, he is at a loss when he *does* want to be taken seriously, since his only value is perceived by others as a social one. The clown is sought after only when it is party time, and he can be very lonely when it is not. He will also run across disapproval when his behavior is inappropriate, and this can sometimes become a very large problem for him indeed, especially with teachers and school administrators. He wants to be admired for his insouciance and his ability to laugh everything off, but there will be many occasions on which he will know that he is only being tolerated or that he is actually being rejected. As he grows older, this will be increasingly difficult for him, and the habit may be so ingrained that he will not know how to alter his behavior.

The Adapter

This child's response is perhaps the healthiest and most reasonable. Certainly, it is the least dramatic, or even noticeable. He has accepted the fact of his powerlessness over the situation at home, and has decided that the line of least resistance for him is simply to make as little fuss as possible, to be as inconspicuous as possible, and thus to go about his business with as little interference as possible. This is the most accepting of the children, and his way is unquestionably the easiest one. Whatever happens, he quietly shifts gears and adjusts his plans to the prevailing situation. To as great an extent as he can, he will pursue his own interests and detach from what is going on around him. For this reason, he may arouse resentment in his siblings, who might feel that he is showing indifference or even callousness, and certainly he is intent on survival with the least possible trouble to himself. However, it is hard to fault the adapter, who is acting on the very sound perception that to create a scene over unreasonable behavior on the part of someone who is drinking would be to place himself in a no-win situation. Therefore, he doesn't protest or argue. If he is blocked, he accepts the situation quietly. Rebellion is not his thing; biding his time is. His interaction in the family is minimal. He does not attempt to solve problem situations or to relieve tension, and his outstanding characteristic is that he draws little attention, either positive or negative. He is akin to the outsider in that he tends to remain pretty much on the outer edges of things, but this is not a withdrawal caused by pain. The adapter is playing it safe and patiently keeping an eye out for himself. In school, he tends to be average, without the trouble with grades that is likely to plague the outsider and the clown. Yet he is troubled, too, as is the rest of the family, and the repression of feelings, the detachment, and the guardedness that he has assumed to protect himself can also settle into a pattern that, as an adult, may make it difficult for him to be assertive when he needs to be or to enter freely into intimate relationships. The adapter is not a go-getter, and his coping mechanism may make it easy for others to impose on him and take advantage of him later on in life.

The Delinquent

At the other end of the spectrum is the child who acts on the hurt and anger he feels by misbehaving. He is likely to be the one who carries out his fantasy of running away from home. He is also the one most in danger of starting early to use alcohol and drugs, both as an escape and as an act of defiance. His may be the group of friends that worries the family as he gets into his teens, or even before, and in early childhood, he is likely to be the Peck's Bad Boy of the neighborhood. He is very likely to be the second child, as it is the eldest who most probably will have taken on the responsible, hypermature role of the achiever, and the chances are that the delinquent will recognize early on that he will never be able to take that role away from his older sibling. Therefore, he leaves the responsibility of family rescuer in the capable hands of the achiever and lets him be the one who tries to smooth things over, who looks after the more helpless members, and tries to keep the household running on some sort of even keel. Not for him the cares of working to maintain some semblance of normal, orderly functioning as a family or of leaping into the breach in a crisis.

Like the outsider and the adapter, he will withdraw as much as possible from the chaos surrounding him, but he will do it in a noisy, attention-getting way (even negative attention is better than none at all) that brings blame on him and enables the rest of the family to focus much of their frustration and anger on him. As with the other role-players, he does provide some measure of relief. The achiever is the only one they can point to with pride; the clown furnishes comic relief that breaks tension; the outsider is a good little fellow that nobody ever has to worry about, up there quietly reading in his room; the adapter is unruffled. And the delinquent lets them release the anger that can't fall on its true object, the alcoholic and the dysfunction he is causing.

The delinquent's position is the most dangerous. He is already the product of a sick household, and his behavior is alienating him from even that tenuous support system. In seeking attention, he has incurred rejection, and this tends to propel him more and more to seek out and rely on the company of peers who are also getting into trouble. It is they who will give him the approval and sense of belonging that he craves, and it will be less and less apparent that what he is doing is only reinforcing his already low self-esteem, an emotion which he will tend to cover with a mask of defiance and hostility. It is entirely possible that relatively harmless escapades may later on develop into outright antisocial behavior and that he may find himself in serious trouble. When that occurs, the reaction of the family will almost certainly be that he had disgraced them, and it is to be hoped that if he finally finds himself sent to counseling, it will be with someone who is able to see the hurt and poor self-image beneath the angry, sullen exterior. Unless there is a skilled intervention in his case, the delinquent is in real jeopardy of being lost, especially if in the process of his angry flight he has followed in his alcoholic parent's footsteps and has himself become chemically addicted.

Getting Free

Clearly, it is important for these children to get help, and
what is encouraging in contemplating their situation is that
there *is* help, and from a variety of sources. Patterns that have
been established as coping mechanisms to handle a situation
that is out of their control can be reversed, and the experience
of professionals who have dealt with children of alcoholics is
that results are usually rapid and dramatic.

The problem is how to get them to the help. All too often,
those observing their behavior do not realize what lies behind
it. Teachers deal with large numbers of children and are very
apt to be preoccupied. Coaches are handling children engaged
in strenuous activity and are primarily concerned with developing a winning team. Clergymen tend to see children who are
on their best behavior. Extended family members and friends
who are close enough to become actively involved in the family's problems are most likely to be focusing their attention on
the primary cause—the alcoholic. The children are overlooked
in the general concern over getting the alcoholic to stop drinking, after which it is generally assumed that everything will
be all right. Even though they are living at the center of the
storm, they are truly forgotten children.

The concept of alcoholism as a family disease is a relatively
recent development, even among professionals. Until quite recent times, in fact, it was largely regarded as a moral issue,
and those who saw it otherwise were voices crying in the
wilderness. In the prevailing view, the person the beleaguered
spouse ought to call upon was not a counselor, but a lawyer
(or a policeman). A growing number of lay people accepted,
in varying degress, the concept that alcoholism is a diagnosable,
treatable illness, but few see it in the light of one that affects
the entire family and that does so by not only attacking the
family structure but each individual in it, as well.

Upon reflection, it will appear logical that each member is
going to be affected, however. How could they not be? But
here, the focus tends to shift to the spouse, since it is he or

she who appears to be taking the brunt of the situation, he or she is in fact taking responsibility for the children. What is not recognized is that that person is probably unable to take that responsibility and that the children are being left to find their own ways of meeting their psychological and emotional needs, which can produce some very troubled children who may well grow into troubled adults.

The roles that have been described here are familiar to any therapist who has had repeated experience in attempting to help sort out the lives of these deeply unhappy people. They are highly predictable roles, all stemming from the same root cause. In families where there are only one or two children, a child may take on more than one role, shifting back and forth according to what is going on at the time, so that the clown may on occasion, for example, take on the part of the delinquent or the outsider. But they are all coping devices, used to handle fear, loneliness, lack of trust, emotions that cannot be openly expressed, rejection, low self-esteem, anger and frustration.

When a child is referred for counseling, let us say in school, it may be for behavior that is not recognized as stemming from alcoholism in the home, and it is very possible that the counselor may be frustrated by the child's lack of responsiveness. Remember rule number one: don't ever talk about the alcoholism at home. It should, however, *always* be considered as a possibility. There is more alcoholism in any given locale than there is the common cold, or any other illness except heart disease and cancer, and millions of children are secondary sufferers from it. Frequently, it is through a child being referred that an entire family can eventually be brought to help, once the truth emerges, and finally even the alcoholic himself, once the family has gained a sounder insight into the disease and has found a practical and effective means of dealing with it.

Referral sources specifically for alcohol counseling are available in most communities. Local mental health agencies, community action programs, courts, police departments, hospitals, group insurance carriers such as Blue Cross—all are good leads in tracking down competent people specializing in alcoholism. A.A., in its strict policy of noninvolvement with outside organizations, is not a source as a general rule, although individual A.A. members usually know where such counseling is available. Finally, it must be stressed that families benefit most from getting such help *as a unit,* sharing for the first time the feelings that have lain unexpressed among them and starting the healing process together. Alcoholism has separated them and placed each one on his path by himself. The road to recovery is a wide one.

6. Adult Children of Alcoholics

"Many of us find that we have several characteristics in common as a result of being brought up in an alcoholic household," begins the self-descriptive statement of an Al-Anon group of Adult Children of Alcoholics. "We came to feel isolated, uneasy with other people — especially authority figures. To protect ourselves, we became people-pleasers, even though we lost our identities in the process. Personal criticism is perceived as a threat. Often, we either become alcoholics ourselves, or marry them — or both. Failing that, we find another compulsive personality, such as a workaholic, to fulfill our sick need for abandonment. We live life from the standpoint of victims. We have an overdeveloped sense of responsibility and prefer to be concerned with others, rather than with ourselves. We somehow get guilt feelings if we stand up for ourselves, rather than giving in to others. Thus, we become reactors rather than actors, letting others take the initiative.

"We are dependent personalities who are terrified of abandonment and who will do almost anything to hold on to a relationship in order not to be abandoned emotionally. Yet we keep choosing insecure relationships because they match our childhood relationship with alcoholic parents. Thus, alcoholism can be seen as a family disease, and we can see ourselves as co-alcoholics — those who take on the characteristics of the disease without necessarily ever taking a drink. We learned to stuff our feelings in childhood, and we keep them buried as adults through that conditioning. In consequence, we confuse love and pity and tend to love those we can rescue. Even more self-defeating, we may become addicted to excitement in all our affairs, preferring constant upsets to workable relationships. *This is a description, not an indictment.*

"The solution is to become your own parent. By attending these meetings, you will come to see parental alcoholism for what it is: a disease that infected you as a child and continues to affect you as an adult. When you accept the disease concept, you will see your parents and yourself as co-victims. You will learn to keep the focus on yourself in the Here and Now and to free yourself from the shame and the blame that are hangovers from the past. You will become an adult no longer imprisoned in childhood reactions. You will take responsibility for your life and supply your own parenting. . . . We look now on our biological parents as the instruments of our existence. Our actual parent is a Higher Power that we call God. And if God gave us alcoholic parents, God also gave us the Twelve Steps of Recovery. We share our experience, strength and hope with each other. . . . We release our parents from responsibility for our actions today and thus become free to make healthy decisions as actors, not reactors."

Yesterday's child, living in the turmoil of parental alcoholism, speaks today as an adult who is trying to come to grips with the emotional residue of that experience. In such groups, he/she sees him/herself as a recovering person in much the same sense that A.A. members do, hence the term "co-alcoholic." Both have been affected by the alcoholism syndrome and are profoundly aware of the psychological scarring that it has left them with as they endeavor to lead healthy and fulfilling lives in the focus of the Here and Now. It is not easy. The view of life and of themselves that was instilled in the children interferes with their integration into the adult world and leaves them with a sense of confusion, isolation and uniqueness that closely parallels that of the newly sober alcoholic. The new A.A. member invariably suffers from guilt, shame and low self-esteem as he reviews his drinking past and contemplates the wreckage of the present. The child of an alcoholic home, now grown, has known those feelings for as far back as he can remember; they have always been part of the fabric of his life.

Both are victims of alcoholism. Each, in his own frame of reference, is trying to make sense out of what happened, to reconcile it with his own developing sense of self, and to establish a life pattern for himself that will enable him to know peace of mind and contentment now that the storm is over. In increasing numbers, the adult children have been turning to the same kind of support group that the alcoholic has had for decades, and for much the same basic reason: they have realized that they are an identifiable group of people who have suffered from the results of the same syndrome and are struggling with the same reactions to it. They share a common need to speak openly about their past pain and present difficulties. Perhaps most of all, they need the relief of knowing that they are not alone, not distanced from the rest of the world, and that they are just as human as anyone else. It is hard to feel set apart, to perceive society as a milieu in which one is a stranger who marches to a drummer other people don't hear, and alcoholism has that effect on its victims. They sense that their feelings and reactions are often different from those of "normal" people, and they question the validity of those feelings, despite the reality of them. "Should I feel this way?" is a question frequently heard at A.A. meetings, and it is echoed among grown children of alcoholics. The answer, of course, lies in finding out *why* the feeling is there. It is not a question of "should I?" when the fact is that one *does*. Victims of alcoholism need to be reassured about their humanness, to know that it's OK to have the feelings they do, and to find their way out of them in the company of others who have "been there" too. Alcoholism brings chaos, fear and isolation into people's lives, and it is important to know that those elements don't disappear by themselves once the drug has been removed from the picture. Alcoholism stays with people.

Children growing up in an alcoholic environment don't realize that they have a lot of company. They are not really aware that there are at least ten million alcoholics in this country, because their focus is on only one or two of that number whose sickness is permeating their lives, and this is more than enough for them to concentrate on. We have seen that they tend not to form close friendships because they need to protect themselves from the discovery by their peers of what is going on at their house. We have seen also that they grow up without the security of consistent, stable adults to whom they can turn with feelings and questions, adults who provide solid role models and act as buffers for the emotions and conflicts of childhood and adolescence. They catch glimpses of those role models from idealized television families or from visits to the homes of other children, but they themselves grow up in a conspiracy of silence in which they learn not to feel and not to trust. Their experience is one of learning to be a survivor; their environment is one of unpredictability and anxiety in which they don't know what to expect each day when they come home and open the door.

They have learned to try to sort out their own conclusions from the mixed messages they receive:

"I promise you/Maybe." The child has learned not to expect to have promises fulfilled, while at the same time he is supposed to give the grown-up credit for at least having thought of doing whatever it was. Not surprisingly, the adult has learned not to depend on people in order not to be disappointed, and he has also learned to seek immediate gratification, rather than to wait for anything. Go for it now, and avoid the anxiety of waiting to see if it is going to materialize in the future—this is his tendency, and it causes him difficulties with himself and others as an adult.

"Always tell the truth/As long as it's what I want to hear." The truth is not always palatable in the atmosphere in which he lives, and he sees everyone around him, including those who should be serving as role models, avoiding unpleasantness by being untruthful. When he knows that adults lie to him and to each other as a matter of course, their dictums about telling the truth become valueless, and the adult child will often have a pattern of lying, even when there would be no risk in telling the truth. It is a perfectly natural act for him, and of course, it causes problems.

"I love you/Leave me alone." The confusion this can cause in an adult who has grown up equating love with rejection is enormous. He has lived with two married people who are supposed to love one another and seen them bickering or actually tearing at one another on a day-in day-out basis. In their preoccupation with their own problems, they have little time for his, and he has frequently been pushed away and left on his own resources to solve them. His experience is one of isolation from those to whom he instinctively turns for nurturing, even while he is given the message that they love him. This is the only meaning of love that he knows, and he may well grow up feeling that it is the only kind there is, or that he will ever know. Even though he is told he is loved, he may always feel that at the same time he is in the way, and he may accept a relationship, or even a marriage, in which there is also an element of rejection. He may also demonstrate tremendous loyalty to people who don't merit it and persevere in friendships or love affairs which would have been terminated by people with a different set of standards. He does not have their sense of self-worth; he was not given the attention and respect that they received, and his existence and his feelings were not validated as theirs were. How could he have the same self-esteem as someone who grew up in an atmosphere of caring and acceptance from adults who set consistent standards of behavior?

"Everything's fine/Everything's wrong." The child has often been part of a play acted out by the family that is intended to present their home life as normal and orderly. They all know it isn't, but they feel they have to pretend, even to one another, and he has been part of the charade. His anxiety and hopelessness he is expected to keep to himself. He doesn't believe assurances that everything is going to be all right, but he knows he mustn't say that, either. Keeping quiet about how he feels while he joins the others in their pretending distorts his view of reality. He doesn't know how people really behave, people, that is, who aren't trying to ignore a charged atmosphere and a constant feeling of dread. The adult child isn't sure of his judgments in this area, because he doesn't know what "normal" is and thus often has a feeling of inadequacy or of actual powerlessness in his life. Thus, he may often feel depressed and insecure and may exhibit a tendency not to take action.

These are children who grow up essentially alone, and the feeling that they have is, "Who really cares about me?" Their perceptions of reality are distorted. They often grow up yearning for love and nurturing that was denied them, but feel that this may never be available for them, or perhaps that it doesn't exist anyway. Attention wasn't paid to the crucial issue of seeing that they feel good about themselves and develop a strong sense of their intrinsic worth as people, and so they lack this strength as adults. They have learned not to trust and to stuff and mask feelings, to try the best they can to look out for themselves and let others do the same. They have learned to lie as a matter of course and without guilt, as part of the survival pattern. By the same token, they will stifle their own individuality in order to please others and will present a wide variety of faces, depending on whom they are dealing with. Their self-concept is a poor one, and they have learned to equate love with rejection, so they may enter into, and pursue, relationships that others would find intolerable. Their greatest common denominator, as with alcoholics, is loneliness and a sense of being adrift in a world they don't understand and which feels alien to them. No truer words have ever been spoken about alcoholism than when it was described as "the Lonely Sickness."

What's "Normal?"

It is very common for many of these adult children to feel great confusion emotionally because they are not sure how they should behave, or even how they should feel. By observation, they are able to determine what is appropriate in the way of clothing and social or business behavior, and they are often at great pains to present as "typical" in whatever socio-economic bracket they find themselves. However, this is very likely to represent much effort on their own initiative and to be accompanied by feelings of anxiety until they feel sure of themselves. They did not have a consistent example set for them that they could feel sure of as a model for acceptable behavior and have had to be self-taught in learning how to blend and belong. Therapists dealing with this population, especially while they are still in the alcoholic environment, often find that alcoholics have very little idea of appropriate dress or how to handle a situation on their own, such as going for a job interview.

Some adult children do learn by being observant and becoming good mimics, but others, hampered by a poor self-image, remain unsure of themselves unless they eventually do receive the nurturing and validation that was withheld from them as children. For this latter group, especially in view of the genetic predisposition of adult children to develop alcoholism themselves, the threat of becoming alcoholic is particularly serious. An individual who does not feel good about himself, who feels "different" and undeserving of respect and love as an adult, can all too easily fall prey to the soothing, sedative effects of alcohol to allay his fears, resentments and loneliness. In the same way, they may respond to what is familiar to them by marrying a heavy drinker or an alcoholic. This last assertion may be a difficult one for those unfamiliar with alcoholism to credit, but it is a pattern which those working in the field have seen repeated over and over again. Unsure of themselves and of their ability to fit in to "normal" life, those adult children will fall back on what they know, often seeing in their choice of spouse someone who needs them and to whom they can give the caring they themselves never had. They also tend to act impulsively and without careful consideration of alternatives because they seek immediate gratification, without taking time to think over the long-range implications of what they are doing. To them, the offer of a relationship or a marriage may represent a chance to love and be loved, a status they have long wanted, or simply an escape from their present situation. The child who was repeatedly disappointed when promises didn't materialize feels that he must grab at something while it is available or miss that gratification. He has little idea of what may come next, has not been trained to think things through and see that he could pay a heavy price for that impulse, and he is likely to learn the full meaning of "repent in leisure."

Even for those who have managed successfully to assimilate themselves into society's norms and to achieve acceptance and a comfortable level of material security, there may still be self-doubt and painful introspection as far as his own feelings are concerned. He feels that it is assumed by others that he has answers about himself that aren't there, and he is afraid to ask. His background taught him the dangers of trusting or expressing emotion or talking to others about what is going on, and he is locked into himself, stuffing feelings because he is not sure whether it is all right to have them. The absence of an adult role model who was also a caring guide with whom he could feel safe in talking about his feelings as a child has felt him very unsure in this area, and his most likely protective mechanism will be to deny that the feelings are there at all. Uncomfortable with them, he finds that the safest way is not to show them.

Sam

Sam began coming to an Al-Anon group for Adult Children of Alcoholics with his brother, Al, who was also an A.A. member. Sam was not alcoholic, but he had always been close to Al and had felt great sorrow over his alcoholism. The two had talked at length about it since Al began his recovery, and about the life they had shared at home with their alcoholic father. Both had sworn that it would never happen to them, and they were mystified and troubled that Al had "gone the way Dad did." Sam's reaction to his brother's illness had been to abstain entirely, frightened of alcohol and hating it. His relief at seeing his brother well again was tempered by the emotions he had always towards his father: anger, hurt and a sense of loss at never having felt that he was really loved by him, that he had never really had a father. These were things Sam had never discussed with anyone, and with Al, cautiously, he began to share them. Both were now in their forties, and neither had ever let the other know in any depth how he had felt about the childhood they had shared. Instead they had denied, by their determined silence, that the whole period had ever existed; the subject had been taboo. Sam, moderately successful in his own business and involved with his family and outside activities, considered that he had risen above his earlier situation and that it no longer affected him, since it had all happened years before. A painful memory, and one better left undisturbed.

In reliving it now with his brother, he was surprised at the sharpness of the remembered emotions, recalling how life had been, and he felt strongly inclined to pull back, to change the subject, but Al resisted his efforts to drop it, insisting that he needed to understand why he had "failed" and been "weak" when Sam had not, especially with the example they had both had growing up. Gradually, Sam began to find it easier to go over the common ground that they shared, and to find a measure of release in the discovery that many of his brother's feelings had been the same as his own, particularly that Al, too, had been hurt and bewildered and wished desperately that he had a "real" father, had felt angry and cheated that he did not. Sam, older, had always been the solid, responsible one, the achiever, and Al been in and out of scrapes, clowning around, taking nothing seriously. Sam had tried to cover up for him, to straighten him out, and he had always been fond of him. To discover the commonality of how they had both felt gave Sam a keener sense of the bond between them and made him draw closer to him. After more than twenty years, he found that he was telling his brother more and more about himself and that it made him feel better when he put into words things about their life in their parents' home that he now realized had affected them both in the same way. For Sam, these were real discoveries, and when Al's counselor referred him to the Al-Anon group, Sam agreed to go with him. For both, it proved to be a turning point.

In watching his brother learning to understand and accept his disease by entering into a group process and sharing what he had in common with others, Sam was able to see what had happened to their father and to realize that it had not been anyone's fault. As he did so, he felt a tight knot that had always been in him begin to loosen, and for the first time in his adult life, Sam was able to look squarely at the father he had both loved and hated, and to review unflinchingly episodes that he had resolutely pushed away for years. Meetings were painful for him at first, because they dredged up memories that he had repressed for years. He tried to deny the pain they caused him by remaining forever silent about them. It was a revelation for him to hear those things spoken of openly and to realize that all through those times, he had just been one of a vast number of children who were passing through the same fire. He had never expected to hear bits and pieces of his own story related around a table by men and women he had never seen before, and at first, it was an eerie and disturbing experience, one from which he automatically wanted to pull back. Sam's instinct for self-protection was a strong one, and his initial reaction to any situation in which he felt his emotions being probed was to retreat and to behave as if nothing had touched him. Sam took no risks, ever. His first impulse was always to shield himself, and he remained silent in the group, sliding into the old, familiar role of big brother, there to provide backup, never letting on that anything was churning inside him, too.

It had always been like that for Sam. Even in his marriage, he had had such difficulty in letting feelings out that the words "I love you" had been spoken only once or twice, although he cared deeply for his wife and knew that she did for him. He had never been a demonstrative father, even when his children were small. They had never known hugging or kissing from their father, although they knew that they were important to him and were aware of his protection and concern, and it had bothered Sam that he had kept that distance from them. Yet he felt constrained even in these closest of relationships, even as he strove to provide stability and material security for his family. And it had been important for him, always, to feel that he was in command, that he could handle everything on his own resources. There was in Sam a deep and stubborn resistance to ever relinquishing any of that autonomy; he perceived as threatening any attempt by another human being to influence the set pattern of his life. He and he alone was in charge and in control; he tolerated no interference and asked no advice.

As he continued to accompany his brother to Al-Anon, it became increasingly clear to Sam that the price he was paying for safety was loneliness, and that alcoholism was at the core of it—his father's. He had learned in a hard school to deny feelings and not to trust, and he saw that this had extended even to his own wife and children. It was a completely new thought for Sam that they might be lonely for him, as he had been for his father. One man's alcoholism was now touching a third generation. His father's "lonely sickness" was still there, in his own tidy house, and Sam made up his mind to ask for help. It startled the group when Sam began to talk. Puzzled at first by his silence and by his resistance to their attempts to draw him out, they had come to accept him as his brother's mute but supportive companion who chose to remain apart from them. He was welcome, and they hoped that he was benefiting in some way from the meetings, but they respected his evident wish to be a nonparticipant. A.A. and Al-Anon people are remarkably tolerant and accepting; no one intruded on Sam or tried to coerce him into active involvement, and he was made to feel free to come and sit in whenever he wished. But it made them glad when he began to talk one night, and they listened intently, letting him know by their silent attention that they heard and understood him. It was an entirely new experience for Sam, the first time in his life that he had not only felt impelled to speak about himself, but wanted to. He found himself describing the isolation he had always felt, the urgent need to look after himself and make himself safe and the fear he had always known at the thought of ever needing to rely on other people. He talked of the empathy that he had come to feel for the members of the group, and as he did so, he experienced his first sense of belonging and of sharing freely.

It was the beginning of a new life for Sam and his family. He not only discovered what it was that had kept him locked inside himself since childhood, he was able as well to lay the past to rest. He saw that he had built a thick wall around himself to keep out an enemy that was only imaginary and that in so doing, he had denied himself to the people who meant the most to him. He saw the emptiness he had inflicted on himself by keeping feelings out of his relationships with others, and the sad fact that it had all been needless. The little boy with the drunken father had lived on in the man, and it was painful for Sam to acknowledge that he had been totally unaware of it. It strengthened him, however, in taking a new direction, and it sharpened his enjoyment of his new freedom. He was fortunate in being able to see, through identifying with other Al-Anon members, why and how he had been depriving himself, and in learning through sharing common experiences how to change course and begin to enrich and enjoy the present. It took time to exorcise the ghost of alcoholism in his own house, and it was not easy for Sam to sit down and talk about it, first with his wife and then with his children, but he had the support and the shared wisdom of his group, and he learned that he could rely on that without fail. He felt that they were the first real friends he had ever had. For the first time, Sam felt that he could trust without sensing that he was turning control of his life over to someone else and placing himself in jeopardy, and for the first time, he experienced the give-and-take of normal adult relationships, secure in his own sense of self. Sam remained captain of his ship, knowing that the major decisions of his life remained ultimately his. But he did so as a member of a family and as a friend among friends, open to the mutual process of giving and receiving and learning to trust that the love and validation that he gave would be returned to him. The little boy became satisfied and stopped clamoring and shouting warnings. The man was home safe at last.

Not all children of alcoholics, of course, find Al-Anon and the great majority are not as fortunate as Sam. Most do not find help of any kind, and their lot is to continue to function under the handicaps placed on them during the formative years. Most understandably, they do so with little enjoyment and with a stunted sense of what fun is or of how to have it. For one thing, they have always been hampered by the feeling that they are different from other people, stemming from the fact that as children they knew that other children didn't live as they did and that they felt ashamed of what went on at their house and went to great lengths to keep it a secret. Again, loneliness and apartness. Probably the worst feeling that children can have, given their deep instinctual urge to be just like all the other kids, as far as hindering the development of their social skills. The reaction of those children is to pull away, and they don't get involved in activities and games. They tend to stay on the sidelines, and they don't learn about having fun and enjoying interaction with others.

As adults, one of the outstanding traits of these children is that they take themselves and the business of living very seriously indeed. For one thing, their fear of rejection holds them back from ever doing anything which might make them look foolish. They have a very difficult time relaxing and allowing themselves to play. Play is something they didn't get much practice at, and the caution and wariness that they learned instead has effectively stifled their spontaneity. It is important for them never to attract the kind of attention that would make them feel diminished, never to be the object of ridicule, and so they try very hard to see to it that others recognize how seriously they take what they are doing and who they are.

These people may tend to find an identity in their work and to become too responsible, even perfectionistic, about it. They may arrive early and stay late, worried lest some detail escape them, determined that no one will ever have cause to find fault with them. In the process, they may become very hard taskmasters, not only on themselves but on those working under them. It is never easy to be dealing with a perfectionist or with the sort of individual who is termed a workaholic, and this certainly does increase the distance between people, lessening the chances of the overly responsible one to let down the barriers and enter easily into having fun. Adult children of alcoholics desperately seek approval and will drive themselves to the point of burn-out to avoid criticism, which they interpret as rejection. The irony is that in striving not ever to be found wanting or at fault, they repress the kind of relaxed, spontaneous behavior that would attract others to them as people and enable them to have the warm relationships that have been denied them. And a sad result of being too responsible and dependable is that these people are very apt to be exploited for just those qualities and to be worked to the point where they finally cave in. It is grossly unfair, and yet they may never see, without help, that their behavior has invited it.

The other side of the coin is the adult child who seems never to be responsible or to be able to carry any course of action through to completion. This can be seen as the result of growing up in chaos, and again, there is the absence of a consistent role model. They feel the same pressure to seek approval and validation, but they have never had experience with organization of time and effort, with doing things as a team, or with people who made it a value to finish things that they started. The need for approval may also be so strong that it incapacitates them as far as tackling things, and they will procrastinate or simply abandon a project altogether. In their desire to please and accommodate, they may also have agreed to take on something that they are not really equipped to do in the first place or that is more than they can handle with everything else that they have to do. They are in real need of direction in their lives in order to establish a sense of system and to be steered toward what they show a talent for and will be good at. They are adrift, as they were when they were children, and their apparent irresponsibility and lack of purpose is the result of that confusion. It is important to recognize and deal with the fear that they feel in order to give them that direction and not to add to the feelings of guilt and differentness that have always been with them.

Problems with Being Close

In no area of their lives is the confusion and insecurity common to adult children of alcoholics more apparent than in their intimate involvements with others. They have the same need for love and closeness as anyone else, but here again, the role models available to them as children were certainly not healthy ones, with the message ''I love you'' all too frequently contradicted by ''Leave me alone,'' and being left alone—abandonment—is one of their greatest fears. Growing up with parents whose marriage was a stormy one, or one in which anger and mutual recrimination seemed as much a part of their relationship as a mutual need and love for one another, could not help but instill an impression of the meaning of intimacy that can sometimes be impossible to eradicate. The differentness that children of alcoholics feel makes it difficult for them to see themselves as people others could love, and the very word "love" has a very different meaning in their experience than it does for those who have not had it distorted by alcoholism. They have been told they were loved and then been pushed away by parents who were plainly doing the same thing to each other. After all, they were married, weren't they? Therefore, they must love each other, or why would they stay together? Or at least they *did* love each other once; they must have. So there must be some of that left for them still to be married, mustn't there? The child reasons as best he can, faced with the contradictions between what he is told "love" means and his own experience of it. The "love" that he knows makes him feel insecure, and thus doubtful about his ability to inspire in others the kind of caring that he wants and fearful of incurring anger and rejection. Already secretive and guilty about the situation in his home, his self-esteem is damaged by the ambivalence he perceives in the inconsistent messages he gets from his parents, and above all else, he fears being totally abandoned.

Clearly, this fear makes it extremely difficult for the adult child to enter into a mature relationship with another person, either as a friend or as a marriage partner. He is constantly seeking validation and approval, which can become irritating and exhausting for the other, who keeps feeling called on to provide reassurance. It becomes a trial for a friend, lover or spouse to have to deal with the panic (and often anger) that results from a disagreement or argument, and this often results in the breakup that the adult child had feared, adding to his already heavy burden of low self-worth.

The adult child is often aware of this hang-up, but awareness doesn't make it any easier for him to shake. The feeling is there, and it is intense and difficult to reason away. Lacking the affirmation as a person that he should have received as a child, he has not developed the assertion skills that go with a sense of worth and is unable to enter into the give-and-take required to sustain any relationship between two adults. He lacks the confidence that trust requires. Moreover, he is likely to be extremely self-critical and to feel that if anything goes wrong, he is to blame. He was never good enough as a child, and he lived with the nagging fear that something he did might be the cause of the disruption at home. Certainly, the alcoholic parent(s) put enough blame on him for him to react in this way, and he does. In his fear of disapproval and rejection, he is constantly judging himself negatively, often to the point where he questions every reaction he has, justified or otherwise. And he reacts with panic to situations in which someone with a healthy sense of self-worth would assert himself and stand his ground. The strain that this puts on a friendship, a love affair or a marriage is not difficult to imagine, and it is one of the real tragedies of adult children of alcoholics that they so often give to others the power of determining whether they are going to feel good about themselves or not. By withholding approval or becoming angry, someone who is important in his life can terrify him and bring forth one immediate response: "Don't leave me!"

Again, it must be kept in mind that adult children of alcoholics don't have a clear concept of what other people consider normal or acceptable behavior in relationships. Their personal experience hasn't provided that, and they lack confidence in themselves to the point that they fear the loss of any relationship that they have established. To them, it is a validation that anyone has gotten to know them and still wanted to be their friend, lover or spouse, and they will find any number of reasons to excuse and tolerate actions by that individual that would be totally unacceptable to someone with better feelings about himself. Very often, they will examine the situation and find some way in which they are to blame for what happened. In their eagerness to hold on to a relationship that offers them any kind of security, they will be blind to faults and to abuse of that relationship that would in many cases cause other people to end it, or at least to show that there would have to be changes for it to continue. What is important to them is the security of having a relationship, and since they are in any case used to finding fault with themselves, it is easy for them to continue to do that as the price of holding on to someone.

Molly

Molly came into counseling indirectly, as a result of having her son referred by his school guidance counselor. Alcoholism in the home had been identified as contributing to the boy's acting out at school, and Molly was distraught and tearful at the initial meeting. She hastened to assure the counselor that she was a total abstainer, the result of growing up with both parents alcoholic, and went on to describe the present violence and chaos in which she and her four children were living. It soon became apparent that for the family to survive its present situation, Molly was in greater need of therapy than any of the other nonalcoholic members. Otherwise, there seemed no possibility that there could be an effective intervention on her alcoholic husband or, if that failed, that Molly would be able to take control of the situation and remove herself and the children from it.

She was hesitant at first to talk about herself, insisting that she was "all right" and that it was her son who needed "a little help" because of things "getting out of hand sometimes at home." When they did get out of hand, she admitted, they were pretty bad. Harsh words were shouted, things got broken, and occasionally people got struck. But Frank was basically a good man, she stressed, and there was no reason to believe that he wasn't; what Molly needed to understand was that he was a sick man and that he was only going to get worse unless he was confronted with his illness and persuaded to go for help. This was something that she was willing to learn about and accept, and the first order of business was for her and the children to grasp the disease concept of what had happened to Frank. Once this was accomplished, and they were able to react differently to the situation at home, the focus of therapy shifted to Molly as the one in the family who would have to take positive action.

What began to emerge from the counseling sessions was a picture of a woman who was hanging on desperately to an impossible situation because it provided her with the only identity she had ever known. A timid, sensitive person, Molly had grown up in considerably better circumstances than those in which she now found herself. The daughter of a professional man, she had been given "advantages" growing up, but these had not compensated for living in an atmosphere of discord and confusion in which her first instinct was to make herself as inconspicuous as possible. Molly avoided making friends because she felt different from other children and ill at ease with them, knowing that she could never ask them to her house. She read a lot, she said, and found escape in fantasy. "I knew I wasn't like other kids, and it was easier not to try. Mother had to make me go to birthday parties and things like that, but I was relieved when I got older and wasn't invited out much. It was just easier, and I had my books and records. I would have died if I'd ever had to have a party at my house in my teens, because it was really bad by then; they were really out of control when they were home."

Molly went to college and did well, but her good grades didn't earn her more than absent-minded praise at home. She was used to that, used to not feeling important or particularly noticed, unless there was some sort of problem or inconvenience associated with her. No one seemed to notice that she knew very few people and seldom went anywhere. "Oh, that little grind," was her mother's comment when Molly once tried to talk to her about her "best" friend; Molly did not repeat the attempt. But she did try, consistently, to earn validation by doing everything as perfectly as she could and taking great care never to irritate or anger anyone.

The only proposal she ever had came to her when she was in college, and she accepted it immediately, afraid that if she didn't, Frank might change his mind. She knew he drank a lot and that other girls he tried to date turned him down, but she was flattered by any attention and was able to create very pleasant little fantasies about him. And she was used to drinking. One of her favorite fantasies was that she, unlike her mother, could nurture and care for her husband, help him so that the drinking would disappear and they would live happily ever after. He reminded her of her father, whose attention and approval she had always dreamed of having one day (when he, too, of course was well), and she impulsively eloped in her senior year.

The realities of her own marriage to an alcoholic were quick to take form, but Molly refused ever to admit that she had made a mistake in choosing a husband. She also refused to hear any criticism of him, even when he lost jobs and they moved further and further down the scale. Even in the face of verbal or physical violence, she determinedly played out a genteel charade for herself and the children that everything was normal, everything was going to be all right. She blamed herself for many of his outbursts, finding in things she had done or had omitted to do the causes of the disruption and steadfastly maintaining that one day Frank would "find himself" and everything would "work out."

Molly was adept at avoiding reality. Like many children of alcoholics, she was a survivor, but she had learned to survive by retreating into herself and a never-never land that she created. Unlike Sam, she was not an achiever who derived satisfaction from facing the world on his own resources and winning. Molly was never going to win unless she could be made to see her fear of separation, even from Frank, and the self-delusion that was the basis for her life, both as the direct result of growing up with her parents' alcoholism. Molly had always been pitifully isolated and fearful. Understanding, and coming to grips with, her real feelings was a slow and painful process for her, and she needed a great deal of support to see her through the realization of who and where she actually was. A counseling team helped, and so did Al-Anon. She was strongly motivated as well by coming to understand that unless she gained strength enough to break the syndrome in which they were living, her children were threatened by lasting emotional damage, and this was certainly the crucial factor in her decision to intervene in Frank's drinking and to hold her ground.

Fortunately, her husband was receptive to the idea of counseling and, finally, in-patient detoxification and rehabilitation. Not all cases end on a hopeful note, and it might have been necessary for Molly to take steps to separate the family. Nonetheless, she has continued in therapy for herself, recognizing that she has been a passive victim of other people's alcoholism and that she strongly needs an identity of her own in order to know the fulfillment of functioning as a whole, healthy individual.

There are tens of millions of adult children of alcoholics in the United States, most of them functioning under heavy emotional handicaps and most of them not understanding why they feel and react the way they do. Unhappily, most also do not know that they are not unique or "different" and that help and ongoing support are readily available in most communities. The reality of what is really wrong is readily accessible to them, along with a process of growth and self-realization that will enable them to cancel out the past by understanding it.

7. Friends of A Friend: The Other Drugs

It has become an accepted fact of life today among those working in the alcoholism field that the "pure alcoholic"—the individual whose drug involvement is confined solely to alcohol—is becoming the exception rather than the rule among those presenting themselves for treatment, and this appears to provide a sound indicator of present-day patterns in drug use.

For many, this reality is bewildering and cause for much greater alarm than is the ancient and familiar syndrome of alcohol addiction. Mention of alcohol has been made ever since Man began keeping written records, and its place in human society has been a constant one. So, too, has the accompanying fact been taken for granted that many in any alcohol-drinking culture will fall victim to the addictive process. As has been noted previously, this has in no way interfered with the widespread custom of drinking alcohol, which is clearly too deeply entrenched for even a constitutional amendment to be anything more than a hindrance to be gotten around and laughed at. The bootlegger was a popular figure during Prohibition, and the Volstead Act was a joke. People developed alcoholism then, too, but they always had; that was something that had always been with us, just as it is today. And just as it has always been, no one who takes his first drink has any idea that he might be the one out of ten drinkers who will become alcoholic. The odds are against it, certainly. In fact, they are far worse than they are for the one who is lighting his first cigarette, and much more concern is voiced about the risk of smoking than has even been heard about the risk of drinking. Alcoholism remains a cloudy area for most, something that happens to other people, somewhere else, and the prototype alcoholic is the skid row derelict. The great majority of adults in our society drink, and 90 percent of them will be perfectly safe in doing so. With this kind of ratio, it appears to be an indisputable fact that drinking has always been and always will be, and that there will always be those for whom it becomes a nightmarish prison.

The "drug culture," on the other hand, is a very recent phenomenon, and this is evidenced by the fact that most "pure" alcoholics tend to fall into the forty and over category. There are many younger alcoholics, but even when their drug of choice has been alcohol, it is very likely to have been combined with some other substance; at the very least, they have probably smoked marijuana as well, and there are millions of drinkers who have never even seen another drug. Great numbers of people can remember a time when drug use and drug addiction were something they read about in novels or saw at the movies, something far removed that went on in opium dens in Shanghai, not in the local junior high. Drug use has remained alien to most of us. It is illegal and justifiably frightening from a variety of aspects. To the general public, "street-drug" terms are as unintelligible as Swahili and the world of the "junkie" is murky and full of menace. They are aware that it is controlled by organized crime, not the U.S. Bureau of Alcohol, Tobacco & Firearms. The girl in the old-time novel who was drugged and forced into a life of shame by white slavers has been transformed into someone they read about in their hometown paper who has become "involved in drugs," and they fear for their own children. The escalating fear of muggings and housebreaks has become another fact of life, and people have long since ceased to feel safe on city streets, although there is dispute as to whether the blame should be laid solely at the feet of the drug trade or incorporated as well into the growing criticism of our judicial and penal systems.

There can be no question, in any case, that drug use is no longer a curiosity hidden away in the slums of New York or Chicago, and that it has become deeply-rooted in Hometown, USA. To describe it as an epidemic is not an exaggeration or a scare tactic; it is everywhere, it is reaching down to school children as young as six and seven, and it gives every indication of being here to stay, at least for the foreseeable future. Even given the increasing interest in, and understanding of, alcoholism, the specter of drug use looms larger and infinitely more threatening in the popular mind than the legally and socially acceptable use of alcohol. Certainly, there is a marked contrast between someone stopping in at the package store on the way home and the furtive, illegal procedure of buying a gram of cocaine from a pusher in a men's room or a seedy apartment.

Again, people are familiar with alcohol, and alcohol addiction is a commonplace and an old, old story. Whether rightly or not, people also think that they understand it; and they discount the possibility of it ever happening to them. A tray of cocktails is a welcome and festive sight; it is not hard to imagine the reaction in most circles were the host to bring out a tray of syringes. The use of other drugs is new and the drugs themselves are mysterious, the means of obtaining them shadowy, and the results of use a source of confusion. Drugs are uniformly considered bad in a way that alcohol will never know, and the sinister mystery surrounding them makes them feared as alcohol will never be. To the alcoholism worker, there is a bitter irony in hearing someone say of a young person whose drinking is causing concern, "Well, at least he isn't on drugs," when in fact he is, and on the drug that causes more suffering and tragedy than all the others combined. Nonetheless, the substances that have proliferated over the last twenty-five years constitute a truly ubiquitous and horrifying problem to society, and one that has enormously magnified for it an evil with which it has lived for thousands of years. What adds to the magnitude, of course, is the fact that it has remained so overwhelmingly the domain of the young, making the sense of fear and calamity associated with it even more acute.

Categories

To begin to unravel the aura of mystery with which these hitherto relatively unknown chemicals have been surrounded, it seems logical to begin by separating them into distinguishable categories. The oldest and thus the most familiar group are the *narcotics*, the only source of which is the opium poppy. The word is of Greek origin and reflects the benign use of opium derivatives, which is to eliminate pain by deadening the senses. Pure opium is a gummy liquid which yields only two natural derivatives, morphine and codeine. In 1874, a semi-synthetic morphine derivative, heroin, was produced, and this has been added to by a variety of other semisynthetics, most notably Numorphan and Dilaudid. Purely synthetic narcotics have also been produced, of which the two best-known are Demerol and Methadone, and which produce effects remarkably similar to those of morphine, most notably euphoria—the addict's "high."

Generalized Central Nervous System (CNS) Depressants form a group that gathers together alcohol, barbiturates and the "minor" tranquilizers. All of them can be addictive, but unlike narcotics, they are not effective in reducing or eliminating pain. Pharmacologically, they vary significantly, but they do have a number of properties in common: they are addicting; withdrawal can be traumatic enough to cause death; a consistently high tolerance to them cannot be developed; in Western cultures, they are the most abused and figure most often in drug-related deaths; their users are the most easily detected because of deterioration in physical appearance, abnormal behavior, and impaired motor functions (speech, balance, coordination). Barbiturates are classified as "sedative-hypnotic" drugs, which means that they initially have a calming effect and then induce sleep. Because of the distinctive colorings of the capsules, these "downers" are identified on the street as "reds," "yellows," "blues," etc., and the most commonly abused are Nembutal, Tuinal, Amytal, and Seconal. There is also enormous use of nonbarbiturate drugs in this classification, such as Doriden, Placidyl, and Quaalude ("ludes"). Another branch of this sedative-hypnotic group includes the antianxiety compounds known as Librium and Valium, which are also capable of producing addiction and withdrawal patterns.

CNS Stimulants have millions of users in this country who are involved to widely varying degress with amphetamines ("speed") and cocaine, as well as with the legion of amphetamine derivatives, among which the most notable is possibly Methedrine ("crystal" or "crystal Meth"). These are the "uppers" and are taken for the opposite effect of the relaxing, sedating "downers." Their attraction lies in the euphoric "high" produced for those who are looking for kicks, and while they are not physically addicting (questions have been raised recently about cocaine in this regard), the "speed freak" has been known to develop such an obsession with intensifying and prolonging the effect that going on a "run" of a week or longer during which speed is continuously injected is not uncommon. Speed overdoses can kill, and heavy use can result in a paranoid psychosis that can last as long as a week.

Finally, the *Hallucinogens* fall into two primary categories: those produced from plants and those manufactured synthetically. The cannabis sativa plant is the source of more than twenty compounds categorized as cannabinoids, two of which are psychoactive. In marijuana and hashish, the psychoactive compound is tetrahydrocannabinol, known as THC. It is THC which gives marijuana and hashish their mood- and perception-altering properties. The peyote cactus has been used for centuries to produce vivid hallucinatory effects, first among Mexican and then among Great Plains Indians. Mescaline was isolated from it in 1968 and has the advantage of producing the hallucinogenic experience without the preliminary hour or two of nausea that is the price of a peyote "trip."

However, the two do share other unpleasant initial effects, and for this reason, demand for them is relatively low. Psilocybin is the hallucinogenic compound in the Mexican "magic mushrooms" sold in either liquid or powdered form and usually taken orally, as are peyote and mescaline. The most widely used synthetic compounds are lysergic acid diethylamide (LSD), phencylidine (PCP, angel dust) and dimethyltryptamine (DMT). As is true of the other hallucinogenics, these are not known to produce physical addiction, but they are certainly subject to abuse; LSD and PCP can produce prolonged toxic psychoses, and LSD threatens its users with involuntary recurrence of the experience for up to a year, chronic changes in thought and behavior patterns, and chronic anxiety reactions accompanied by depression, imaginary physical symptoms, and greatly decreased functioning.

Some Confusion in Terms

Perhaps because of the tremendously increased activity in combatting drug abuse, which is certainly a reflection not only of the epidemic that is currently confronting Western society, but of the rising concern among the general public, terminology has shown a bewildering tendency to overlap as far as defining the degree of involvement that a particular substance is capable of generating. Terms such as *addiction, habituation, abuse* and *dependency* seem to be tossed around more or less interchangeably, and yet to the average citizen (and, for that matter, to those working directly in the field), they carry with them very definite gradations of meaning. Most people will hear two entirely different things when they are told that a man is *addicted* to a specific drug or that he is *dependent* on it. *Addiction* generally carries with it a far more serious meaning, and implies a far deeper and more sinister relationship, rather like describing someone as a "dope fiend." It is a far older word than *dependency* and tends to conjure up visions of lost souls or of a murky twilight world. It is parallel to the word *alcoholic* having the connotation of dereliction, and there is just enough reality in it to sustain the image. Most people would far rather have it suggested to them that they are dependent on alcohol (or that they have an "alcohol problem") than to be told baldly that they are alcoholic, and *dependency,* a term which began to come into general use in the 1960s, seems to many to have come into use as a way of sugar-coating an unpalatable fact.

As mentioned, the word *addiction* is an old one. Sherlock Holmes was a morphine addict. For many years, the term was in general use to describe habitual use of drugs, and after opium and its derivatives were no longer available across the counter (laudanum seems to have been the most widely used) and became illicit, the term took on the meaning of something outside the law and even criminal. Thus was born the popular image of the drug-crazed dope fiend. Yet the term, properly used, is based on pharmacology and refers to a process of physical dependence, as is the case with alcohol. An individual becomes addicted *physiologically* and will experience physical withdrawal if the drug is cut down or stopped. Narcotics and generalized CNS depressants are *addictive*, if this classification is used; CNS stimulants and hallucinogens are not.

In the early 1930s, a distinction was made by separating drugs into two classifications: addictive and habituating. Habituating drugs were those which might be used excessively and produce a variety of emotional difficulties, but there was not a physiological aspect to their use, and if they became unavailable, there would not be any physical distress. Despite what seems to be very clear-cut differentiation, it was often not adhered to, and the distinction became blurred. In the opinion of many, the emotional involvement connected with the use of habituating drugs was deep enough, and troubling enough, to justify describing the victim's state as addiction. Habituation, it was felt, did not adequately (or frighteningly enough) describe the condition to which the user had been reduced. It is common today to hear cocaine described as "mentally" or "emotionally," but not "physically," addictive. That this is often heard among professionals is a good indication of the present-day departure from the earlier definition of the term.

The word *dependence* came into use originally in the hope of resolving the confusion and was intended to be a blanket term for both addiction and habituation. The particular substance involved was to be added for clarification, giving us morphine dependence, amphetamine dependence, etc. This did little or nothing to make it any clearer to people in general just where the definition of *addiction* began and ended, and there was (and is) considerable uncertainty as to whether or not it is synonymous with *dependence*.

In the meantime, *habituation,* except possibly in medical circles, seems to be falling more or less into disuse. To compound this new cloudiness, the term *abuse* came into being, again as a more or less blanket term. Obviously, almost any drug can be "abused." The labels on over-the-counter cough syrups give specific dosages, and the implication is that this will prevent excessive amounts being taken. Getting drunk at any time could be described as alcohol abuse. The National Institute on Alcoholism and Alcohol Abuse implies by its very name that there is a distinction between the two, and yet "alcohol abuse" is very often used in the sense of alcohol addiction. The tendency today seems to be very much in the direction of using *abuse* in an all-purpose sense, and a "drug abuser" can run the gamut from someone who smokes marijuana once or twice a week to a chronic alcoholic who is regularly drinking a quart of whiskey a day.

Nonetheless, the classic definition of *addiction* as indicating physiological dependency which will cause physical withdrawal symptoms if the drug is cut back or removed seems to define and limit the term satisfactorily, and it is the most widely accepted. Withdrawal from addictive drugs can cause death, in the case of CNS depressants, and extremely harsh physical suffering for narcotics addicts. Real emotional duress may very well be felt by the long-term, heavy user of CNS stimulants and hallucinogens, but withdrawing from his "friend(s)" presents no physical threat whatever. He is dependent, habituated, an abuser or what you will, but he is not, within the limitations of the term, an addict, no matter how strong his psychological dependence has become.

A Common Bond

In present-day treatment facilities, as stated above, the polydrug user is becoming far more in evidence than is the "pure alcoholic," and this is unquestionably a statement about the times we live in. A certain prejudice sometimes exists towards him, and this is based on several factors. First of all, the alcoholic is often more likely to be looked upon as a victim. He began drinking because it is a most acceptable social custom; in fact, considerable pressure is often felt to begin drinking. People will be "insulted" if you don't join them, or suspicious of you; you will be considered a goody-goody or a wet blanket; if you're a man, you may feel your masculinity is called into question; in brief, you're an outsider. It is also a rite of passage, an admission into the world of adults, an eagerly sought mark of sophistication. Advertising is a strong influence. Depending on the brand, it means you're suave, or you're a success, or you're sexy, or you're fun, or you're part of an attractive crowd, or you're discriminating and a cut above the ordinary. And of course, alcohol is legal, obtainable anywhere, and a considerable source of revenue for the U.S. Government. Why, then, would you not drink? The thought that *you* could ever become an alcoholic is so remote that it is easily brushed aside, and that is most understandable, given the odds that 90 percent of drinkers will never develop it. In fact, alcoholics in treatment are encouraged to focus the guilt away from themselves and onto the drug, and quite rightly so. What has happened to them was a subtle, insidious process of which others were aware long before they were, and the nature of alcohol addiction is that the victim will not look at reality and will continue to struggle to control his illness, rather than recognize his defeat.

The polydrug user may well be addicted to alcohol as well, but a heavy load of guilt is placed on him by society for his involvement with other drugs. How could he not know what would happen to him? How could he not know what he was getting into? To moral indignation is added a strong element of mixed fear and resentment. Drugs are seen as a frightening cancer on our society and are blamed, with ample justification, for the street crime and the corruption of the young that have assumed such grim proportions over the last quarter-century.

What is often not taken into account is how the drug use began. To begin with, young people are a notoriously, and often sadly, susceptible population. One of the worst things that can happen to them is to be different from the other kids, to be set apart from their peers. And they are very likely to be notably lacking in judgment. It is not difficult to imagine how easily they can be persuaded and/or coerced into trying amphetamines or barbiturates or alcohol, how easily persuaded that "it won't hurt you, you're not going to get hooked, it's just for kicks." But some do get hooked, and the experiment develops into dependence. There also exists a medical phenomenon known as cross-dependence, which is pharmacological in nature. Simply stated, it means that once dependence, whether physical or upon other effects, has been established with one in a group of drugs, the dependence will extend to all drugs in that group. Thus, barbiturate use could easily extend out into alcohol, or amphetamines make one a sitting target for cocaine.

Even without actual physical addiction, emotional dependence can become very powerful for anyone who becomes involved with drug-taking on any sort of regular basis. What people are doing, basically, is altering how they feel, and this is true, certainly, of social drinkers as well. Whether they are at home, unwinding after a long day, or in a convivial setting with others, people drink to change how they feel, and while they know that the change will be transitory, they fully expect it to be pleasant. That is why people serve alcohol at social gatherings, rather than fruit juice or ginger ale. It relaxes their guests, gives them a little euphoria, and makes for more conviviality. Simple. Everybody knows that.

The same principle applies for using other drugs, and many young people begin using them in a social setting. It's part of "the scene," and part of being accepted, just as alcohol has always been, and they have no idea of becoming hooked on them. But it does happen. It happens physically with alcohol and with the CNS depressants, and it happens emotionally, or "psychologically," with all of them for some who become victims, just as the "pure alcoholic" is a victim. There are those, of course, who jump much more wholeheartedly into drug use, once they have discovered how it can make them feel. These are most likely to be people with problems: kids who are shy, or who have unhappy home lives, or who are having a difficult time with the turmoil of adolescence, with restlessness and rebellious feelings. Or they may be the ones who feel inadequate at school and with their peers. Certainly, a prime target are the poor, who feel trapped in their slums and see little prospect of ever getting away from the daily ugliness surrounding them. Drugs will take all these people out of their everyday lives and take away the feelings that trouble them. They will experience instead the lovely ease of the depressants, the excitement of amphetamine, the colors and fantasies of the hallucinogens. They enter a wondrous place, and they want to go back to it again and again. It is escape.

That is the hook that gets some people. They become dependent on chemicals that take them to another plane of being and awareness, that change how they feel, and they become less and less acclimated to reality, less and less willing to live in it and face it. As dependence deepens, they feel more and more that they have to be "high," because the real world is increasingly unacceptable to them, and they don't develop the skills that they need to live in it. They begin to experience growing difficulties with interpersonal relationships, particularly at home and with authority figures whom they see as "square" and as the embodiment of all that they want to get away from. Moreover, these are the people who wouldn't understand what these friendly, wonder-working substances mean to them and would try to take them away, forcing the users to live without relief in a reality that they reject.

Disputes at home and at school will become increasingly acrimonious as dependency grows, and the user will tend to withdraw, seeking solitude if he cannot be with others who share his understanding of how things can and should be. The most fundamental human relationships are put in second place. Parents, brothers, sisters, spouses, children—all are pushed to one side in the determination to have the drugs. There is lessening interest in family activities, or none at all. The job will suffer, and the employer will join the family on the list of secondary figures in the user's life. The drug-dependent person will gravitate for understanding and empathy to other users, and these will become the important people in his life because they are on the same wavelength. Tragically, the truly significant people will become the enemy. They are the ones who must be deceived and lied to; they are the ones who get angry and make threats; they are the ones who cry.

The parallel with the alcohol addict is self-evident. Only the substances being used are different. Both victims wear the same set of blinders and have the same tunnel vision that focuses only on gratification of an increasingly demanding need. Both are involved in the same headlong flight from reality and responsibility, and both endure the same moments of truth, when realization of what is happening to their lives falls in on them and they are swamped with guilt and remorse. The answer at those times is the same, too: Run! To anyone who has witnessed the struggles of an alcoholic or drug-dependent, the scenario is all too familiar. The moments when truth insists on recognition are very terrible ones, and the only logical answer to the kind of anxiety they produce is to have more of whichever drug it is.

Those who have watched a representative cross-section of this growing population presenting themselves for treatment have become well aware of the commonality of experience shared. All are fearful, unsure not only of what is going to be done to them, but of how well, or if, they are going to be able to adapt to "the real world" without their drug or drugs. They feel suddenly exposed, stripped of the facade they have developed and afraid of being seen at last as they really are. Self-esteem is in short supply, as is self-confidence. There is suddenly no escape from the sense of guilt and self-blame.

Many feel an active dislike, or even loathing, for themselves and feel panic at the thought of confronting what they have done in their sickness. To compound this, there is the fear that others will share those feelings when the truth is known, and that they will never recover the esteem and love of those they have injured. Or perhaps they have already lost those things. Their instinct is to run from all of this emotional ferment, and in the case of the physically addicted, there is the withdrawal from narcotics and/or alcohol. This can vary in severity, depending on the individual and on the degree of physical dependence he has developed. The tremors, sweats, dizziness, nausea, etc. that constitute physical withdrawal unless a more gradual, medicated process is set in motion have been witnessed (and experienced) by many who are presently working professionally in the drug field. They can attest to the fact that the emotional suffering is very often far more agonizing; certainly it is more long-lasting and complex. Detoxification is a fairly brief process, over with, on the average, within seventy-two hours. The usual stay on the medically supervised unit of a rehabilitation facility is not longer than that, and can be as short as twenty-four hours in the absence of physical dependency. The process that follows, which is that of making a solid beginning at restoring the emotional health of the patient, is a far longer and more involved one.

Alcoholics and those who have developed dependency or physical addiction through the use of the other substances that seem to be getting almost as commonplace today share a great mutual affliction, and through that, a great common bond. Physical dependency can be broken and will not recur unless the narcotic or CNS depressant is reintroduced into the body chemistry. There is no great trick to that, and it can be a relatively comfortable procedure if done medically. What all of these newly recovering people face is, first of all, beginning to face reality—the world as it really is—without the escape offered by their erstwhile friend or friends, their chemicals. A part of that reality is the aftermath of their illness, all of the wreckage that is waiting for them when they leave treatment. All of it will be very real, whether it is human or financial, and it all has to be met and dealt with. These individuals will come from a wide variety of backgrounds and circumstances, but they will share a common anxiety, not only about what the final resolution of those issues will be, but about their own ability to cope with them and about the prognosis for their sustained sobriety. Every person who arrives at the point of seeking help for his drug use does so by a path that is uniquely his own. There is only one of him on this earth; he is the only one in his particular life situation, with all the factors that make it up. In recovery, however, he will lose some of his uniqueness, in that everyone who is also newly on the road to recovery shares with him a great common experience, beginning at the faraway day when they had their first encounter with whatever it was that was ultimately to defeat them and leave their lives in chaos. They have a great deal to share. The A.A. preamble speaks of sharing "experience, strength and hope" in order to recover from alcoholism and "to help others achieve sobriety." The preamble—indeed, the whole program of Alcoholics Anonymous—has been adopted by Narcotics Anonymous, an offshoot whose membership is made up of people recovering from the abuse of "other drugs," for the principles are the same. There are many who, poly-addicted/dependent, attend both groups and are completely comfortable in doing so. There is no reason why they should not be. The commonality of what happened to them is such that it cannot logically make very much difference whether the agent of their pain was alcohol or heroin or cocaine or barbiturates or any combination of any description. The pain was the same. Calamity is calamity, whatever form it takes. And so is the message of hope.

On Sharing

One of the saddest aspects of drug addiction and dependency is the isolation that it inflicts on its victim. Anyone who has survived this syndrome will speak of the terrible aloneness that he or she felt, even when surrounded by other people. They all remember vividly the sense of apartness, of living a desperate interior life in which no one else could enter, and they remember as well the defenses that they put up so that no one would try to. To begin to share what they have experienced in common is often very difficult for them, for it involves letting down those defenses and making themselves vulnerable emotionally, something that they instinctively never dared to do, particularly with anyone who might use it to take their drug away from them.

Almost universally wary at first, they come to realize that it is by sharing, by allowing others to know who they really are, that they will find common ground for support from others who have "been there" too, and this is the secret of success of A.A. and of the other "Anonymouses" that have sprung from it, groups for drug users, gamblers, overeaters, men who have abused wives and parents who have abused children. Sharing is the cornerstone of recovery from these compulsive afflictions, and it is born of the despair and desperation that the group members have felt and which they have recognized they are powerless to deal with alone. Losing their terrible sense of uniqueness, and the relief that that brings, is a strong force in bringing them together, and so is the fear of relapse if they try to go it alone. Once an individual becomes aware of the strength of the hold that his illness has on him, and of how easily he might never have been able to break it, he becomes eager to bond closely with others who are also finding solid ground beneath their feet and to share that "experience, strength and hope."

The experience of the drug user, as opposed to the alcoholic, is a widely different one. In an overall view of the syndrome of addiction and dependency, we must take as a basic premise that each person has been in an obsessive relationship with a mind-altering substance or substances and that this life has been controlled by a compulsion to obtain and use that substance. In addition, if he is addicted, he will be driven by the fear of physical withdrawal. Moreover, whether he be a "garbagehead" poly-drug user or a "pure" alcoholic who has never even sampled marijuana, he has become conditioned to coping with the world in a drug-altered state and has great difficulty in adjusting to dealing with life on his own resources, particularly in early recovery, when he is so lacking in confidence that those resources will be enough to sustain him. Sharing hopes and fears is important in gaining that confidence, and this is done on a foundation of mutual experience, a significant number of which the alcoholic does not share with the user of other drugs.

As noted previously, alcohol addicts buy their drug legally in a liquor store that is state-licensed. They pay a tax on their purchase to the Federal Government, and they are assured by that government that what they are buying is exactly what it says it is. Unless they are under age, they are not committing any offense, and if what they have bought is 100-proof bourbon whiskey, they can carry it openly out the door and home with complete confidence that it is 50 percent alcohol,

no more and no less. They are free to drink it and to offer
it to a friend without fear that government agents could catch
them at it and arrest them. An alcoholic could even sell a bottle
of liquor to a friend or acquaintance with the thought never
crossing his mind that the other man might be a federal agent.

None of this is true for the drug user. His compulsion for
a drug experience takes him outside the law, even if he is buying it in his school, and it may very well take him into some
murky and often dangerous places. In negotiating with a
pusher, especially if he is buying narcotics or cocaine, he can
be dealing with a very unknown quantity, but with the certainty that his "connection" has been with organized crime.
If he is buying on credit, as is often the case, it is not like
running up a tab at the bar or having Joe at the package store
wait until Friday. Again, if he is buying narcotics or cocaine,
he is committing a serious offense; he is also risking very
serious reprisal if he does not pay his debt, and that will often
go up into the thousands of dollars. He will buy anyway.

In no way can he be sure of what he is buying. Not only
are drug deals illegal, the drugs themselves are always diluted,
and the buyer has no way of knowing to what extent or with
what adulterant. Nor, in most cases, does he have any practical redress if he finds that the "bag" of heroin he has bought
contains no heroin at all. At the most, it will contain somewhere between 3 and 5 percent on the average. Conversely,
the buyer might by chance obtain a far higher concentration
of the drug, and it could even be so high that he will overdose
and die from it. An additional hazard is that the adulterant
could kill him when injected.

Buying marijuana is a similarly uncertain business, although
there is not the risk of overdose, of injecting a lethal substance
or of contracting hepatitis or tetanus from using a needle.
What the smoker has to contend with is not knowing whether
he is buying "good" or "bad" marijuana from the standpoint
of how much it has been cut with inert substances.

The purchaser of LSD or amphetamines can be running a
uniquely terrible risk, in that he has no way of knowing what is

actually in the pills he is being sold. Amphetamines are made legally; LSD is not. Nonetheless, the user has no way of knowing what he is actually holding in his hand. It may be that what he has just paid for is no more than aspirin or some other innocuous substance that has been pulverized and colored and formed into tablets. However, with the proliferation of self-taught chemists that the drug market has spawned, he might take a mixture of chemicals that could send him on a "trip" that is a psychotic episode lasting several days. What might happen to himself or to others in that time is impossible to foretell and could have a lasting effect on a number of lives.

There is very lively speculation at present with regard to the question of drug-induced psychosis. Claims have been made in medical circles that the toxic psychosis resembling schizophrenia that has occurred in amphetamine users can last for a number of years. It is an accepted fact that years of heavy alcohol consumption can produce the "brain damage" characterized by disorientation, confusion, apathy and impaired memory and learning ability known as the Wernicke-Korsakoff syndrome, or more popularly as the "wet brain." Many feel, however, that there is insufficient evidence to substantiate a claim that a lasting paranoid schizophrenic psychosis can be induced solely by amphetamines in what would otherwise have been a completely normal individual. There is no way of accurately checking, in many cases, whether that person was prepsychotic before using the drugs and would in all likelihood have developed the illness without them. There may have been as well a pre-existing, but unidentified, psychiatric illness that was brought out more fully by the drug experience. Similarly, it is hard to determine whether drug use arrested psychosocial development in a given individual who would otherwise have matured normally, or whether the person was already maladjusted in that area before beginning drug use. It is probably advisable to wait until a conclusive body of evidence can be collected before accepting claims of this sort.

Alcoholics and Cross-Tolerance

The dangers of mixing alcohol with other CNS depressants are very real and are brought dramatically to the public's attention when a celebrity comes to grief as a result. Tolerance refers to the amount of a drug required to produce the desired effect. Someone taking barbiturates in order to sleep may find that they need to increase their dose because the original dosage no longer does what they want it to. Increasing doses of morphine to kill pain may be required as a patient develops tolerance to it. People will also become cross-*dependent* on drugs in one group, such as the CNS depressants, so that they can ward off withdrawal from one by using the other. Thus, an alcoholic who has run out of liquor might take barbiturates as withdrawal from alcohol becomes increasingly uncomfortable.

An alcoholic who is also taking sleeping pills and tranquilizers, let us say Seconal and Valium, is taking three drugs in the CNS depressant group and is in a potentially hazardous, or even fatal, situation. What happens when they are taken simultaneously is that the liver, which metabolizes drugs, deals first with the alcohol, so that the other substances remain active instead of being processed through the bloodstream. Just as the alcoholic is finding he needs larger and larger doses of alcohol because his tolerance to it is increasing, so he finds he needs more Valium to steady him through his daily routine and more Seconal to give him a reasonably good night's sleep. In using the three drugs, all in the same group, the alcoholic has set up a process of cross-addiction that is intensified by his alcoholism.

His withdrawal symptoms are also intensified, and in the late-stage alcoholic, the tolerance as the body weakens will drop. He will need increased doses of his alcohol, Seconal, and Valium in order to relieve his increasingly severe symptoms and to try to feel "normal." Moreover, he is very likely to become increasingly muddled as to how much he has had to drink and how many pills he has taken. It goes without saying that he has no conception of cross-tolerance or cross-addiction. He only knows that he is feeling worse and worse, and he is buttressed in his use of prescription drugs by the fact that they were prescribed by his doctor. What he chooses to ignore is that his doctor warned him about mixing them with alcohol and that he lied to the doctor about how much he drinks.

As he is always conscious of the possibility of withdrawal, he will substitute the Valium at those times when getting a drink is difficult or impossible, totally ignoring the prescribed dosage. The same is true with his Seconal dosage when he desperately wants to sleep, and he will swallow more of them if he wakens in the night. At the same time, he is now experiencing a three-sided withdrawal syndrome and self-medicating against it with all three substances. Clearly, it is a blueprint for disaster, especially as his tolerance drops in the later stage and his confusion and emotional distress grow. Death from overdose, whether unintentional or not, is a frequent end to this dilemma, and those of Elvis Presley and Judy Garland only mirrored on the front page what has happened to countless others. Alcohol, the great crippler and killer, has close friends, all equally seductive and almost as readily available. To know them for what they are and can be is excellent insurance against them. There is safety only in awareness, and it is a mistaken concept that other lethal drugs come only to those who seek out the pusher. Theirs is a very mixed ambiance, and it includes the prescription pad as well as the friendly package store.

In looking at the phenomenon of addictive illness from any point of view, whether it be that of the afflicted individual, a concerned friend or family member, or just a member of the general public, it is almost invariably the case that there is very little real, practical knowledge on anybody's part about the problem at hand. At best, the understanding will be very hazy as to the specific properties of the substance, or substances, that are causing the dysfunction. To compound this difficulty, there may be as well a hampering mixture of misinformation and folklore that gets in the way of bringing the addicted or dependent person to effective help.

Certainly, this has been the case for centuries with alcoholism. Not until very recently, beginning really with Jellinek's work in the early 1950s, has there been a realization of the physiological basis of alcohol addiction, and with it, a different perspective on the alcoholic as the victim that he or she is. And even in 1986, that perception is shared by a sadly limited number of people. The alcoholic continues to be viewed by most with repugnance. In the popular view, he or she is someone who has ''let this happen'' because of a lack of character and willpower, who is utterly self-centered and indifferent to responsibilities and to the pain inflicted on others. It is realized by a relative few that the alcoholic, especially as the syndrome inexorably progresses, is living with depression, fear and self-condemnation that can be fully appreciated only by others who have themselves experienced it.

The majority view is the one that is almost invariably shared by the alcoholic, as well. The first order of business in alcoholism treatment is (or should be) to give the patient sound understanding of exactly what has happened to him, pharmacologically and psychologically, and insight into the complete helplessness he has been experiencing in his struggle to gain control of the situation. This teaching aspect of treatment is vital to its success, and optimally, it will be possible to extend this understanding to those who are close to the alcoholic. For those who work with alcoholics, it is commonplace that the men or women they are trying to help will have absolutely no knowledge of the exact nature of the affliction that has overtaken them and turned their world inside out. Nor will their family, friends or employers, in the vast majority of cases. Clearly, this is one reason why addictive illness goes untreated for as long as it usually does, and why it will almost always take some kind of real crisis to force an individual into treatment.

This is a very sad reality of dependency and addiction. It is unquestionably true that much human pain could be prevented if there were a more universal understanding of the symptoms, which are quite standard, of the true nature of what is happening to that person, and of what he is threatened with if steps are not taken to head off the all-too-predictable outcome. It also needs to be universally understood that any person beginning to use any mind-altering substance could very possibly become involved in a pattern of abuse, and that there is no way of foretelling whether or not that will eventually happen. Use of these substances is just about always entered into lightly, usually for fun and/or kicks, and if there is some initial hesitancy, it is quickly overcome by the gratifying fulfillment of promises made. There are few among us today who cannot attest to that, and yet how many of us the first time we had a drink or took a tranquilizer or a sleeping pill, had even the remotest understanding of the pharmacology of what we were introducing into our systems? Somewhere in the back of our minds, there was the common knowledge that "people get hooked on this stuff," but in one's own case, this is a far-fetched possibility that is quickly and easily dismissed.

Perhaps it is the odds that influence us. There is no certainty of getting hurt, as there is with touching something that is red-hot or sticking one's finger into an electrical outlet. We are governed by many healthy fears in our daily lives and have developed many automatic cautions, such as looking before we move out into traffic and walking carefully over ice. We are certainly influenced by odds as to whether or not we go swimming when there is heavy surf or enter a yard in which there is a strange dog. These healthy, self-protective fears are founded on known factors. What makes anyone vulnerable when beginning drug use is ignorance of the exact nature of the substance being used. Even in the case of narcotics, the beginning, experimental use is influenced by a misunderstanding of the drug which leads the novice to believe that he or she can control it and will never be reduced to the pitiable state of the street junkie. He or she is confident of being able to restrict use of the drug and keep it within bounds, just as the frazzled executive who begins using Valium or Seconal has no plan to use either harmfully when he has his first prescription filled. Through overconfidence and a great dearth of practical knowledge, our society today plays with a great deal of fire and views with dismay the often tragic results.

Probably no specific group is more likely to fall victim to the fallacy that "it could never happen to me" than is the young, whose naivete, overconfidence, and trust make them by far the most willing to experiment. As pointed out earlier, they are also far more likely to be influenced by peer pressure than is any other group. These are the factors that account most for the horrifying fact of drug use moving down from one age group to another until it has been detected in children as young as seven or eight, the most pathetic drug-using population of all. The legacy of the pot-smoking, LSD-tripping Flower Children of the tumultuous '60s seems to be a "drug scene' that has spread like an evil fungus into every community and against which not even stable homes and a loving family can offer protection. It seems logical that to combat an enemy, it must first be understood, so that its presence can be detected and not mistaken for something else, and so that it can be warned against with factual knowledge, and not merely on "moral" grounds.

Trouble Right at Home—Volatile Solvents and Aerosols
Inhaling intoxicating fumes is not a practice unique to the twentieth century. Elizabeth Barrett Browning was one of many in the last century to become addicted to periods of brief intoxication from sniffing an ether-soaked handkerchief after ether and nitrous oxide made their appearance as anesthetics. Since the early 1950s, many have had their first experience with a "high" by trying what is commonly referred to as "glue-sniffing," but which actually encompasses the inhalation of a variety of everyday solvents. Gasoline, lighter fluid, nail polish

remover, plastic cement used in making model airplanes ("airplane glue") and cleaning fluids are among the easily obtainable sources of a quick jag, and the best high of all is attributed to toluene (toluol), which is found in thinners for paints and lacquer and paint brush cleaners. Users will follow Mrs. Browning's example and inhale from saturated rags, with the intensifying effect not available to her of placing the cloth in a plastic or paper bag and inhaling with the bag held tightly over the mouth and nose.

Legislation has been enacted to put the two most toxic solvents, benzene and carbon tetrachloride, out of reach of the sniffers, but there remains a wide spectrum of other intoxicants: toluene, naphtha, acetone, a host of hydrocarbons. Hydrocarbons in aerosol propellents are another common source of intoxication, but there has been no effort whatever made to control abuse through legislation.

For the most part, the psychoactive substances are CNS depressants and will produce effects similar to alcohol intoxication: slurred speech, loss of equilibrium, dizziness, euphoria, altered judgment and often a feeling of abandon or of being able to lick the world. The experience is brief, lasting usually fifteen to forty-five minutes after the inhalation, and followed by an hour or two of sleepiness and lethargy. A price may be paid during and after intoxication in the form of eye irritation, nausea, sneezing, coughing, diarrhea and chest pains. Some, but by no means all, users will experience visual and auditory hallucinations that may or may not be pleasant. The effects of sniffing are felt almost at once and can be speeded up by warming the bag containing the solvent.

Sniffers will become subject to habituation, but there is no reliable evidence that they are susceptible to physical addiction. What does take place is a psychological dependency with some users, and this is seen as the result of a psychic predisposition, rather than a generally predictable result of sniffing. Tolerance is also developed when the practice is continued regularly over a period of months, and larger quantities are needed to produce the desired effects. All of the substances have a potential, very rarely documented in sniffers, of causing damage to lungs, heart, liver and kidneys, but these effects have been noted for the most part only in industrial settings where workers have been exposed to constant and excessive amounts of fumes over an extended period of time. The danger of dying as as result of sniffing appears to be mainly that of suffocation after losing consciousness while using a plastic bag, although there are a very small number of documented deaths due to accidents while intoxicated or to very stressful activity following intoxication in which still-present anesthetic agents caused heart failure.

For the most part, solvent and aerosol use is undesirable in that it is mind-altering and can cause aberrant behavior which can have unpleasant consequences. Even more than that, it introduces young people to the realm of altered consciousness, to the whole deadly spectrum of substances that will make them high as an alternative to living in reality and learning the coping skills that will enable them to function normally in the adult world. As a springboard into involvement with drugs that cause physical addiction and a crippling psychological dependency, it has a truly terrifying potential for destructiveness. There are many sad sights to be seen as a result of chemical use, but certainly one of the saddest is the young person who has been robbed of the experience of normal emotional growth, who has gone from adolescence into young adulthood without knowing what it is to live and learn from the mixture of trials and pleasures of which life is composed, and who is thus unequipped to deal with life on a level that matches his chronological age. He has been cheated out of a time of life than can be very painful, but also filled with joys not found in later years—his youth. The newly recovering young person is always faced with a tremendously uncomfortable dilemma: he has been left far behind in maturity that comes from living in the world as it really is. He becomes very much aware of his emotional inadequacies and of the lack of experience in functioning as a "straight" person that will cause him great apprehension when he is no longer able to reach for his mood-altering friends. Like all false and fair weather friends, they will leave him disillusioned and embittered, but his will also be the sad awareness of having lost a time that can never be recaptured.

Probably the most likely step in the progression of drug use, after the apprenticeship of sniffing, is smoking marijuana. Of all the high-producing substances, this is far and away the most common to be found in schools and other public places, both because of its availability and because it is so easily carried about. From the point of view of convenience, it has a clear advantage over alcohol, and unlike alcohol, it is the center of a wide controversy concerning whether or not it is even harmful, with many supporters of the premise that it is an innocuous and much-maligned recreational item that should be legalized and made freely available to the general public. The rebuttal to this will be presented here, but first it seems appropriate to explore its history and what it actually is and does.

A Long and Varied Past

Marijuana is a derivative of *cannabis sativa,* the hemp plant. Its name comes from Mexico and means "Mary Jane," a slang term that was originally used for cheap, inferior tobacco and that accompanied it across the border into Texas and Louisiana around the turn of the the century. Its use was a fairly localized custom, confined largely to the lower socio-economic level and to jazz musicians until Prohibition made it a sought-after substitute for alcohol and its use began to spread. As that occurred, uninformed public outcry depicted its users as in the "dope fiend" category, and it was eventually outlawed by Congress in the Marijuana Tax Act of 1937. Nonetheless, marijuana is, after alcohol, the most-used drug in the United States today, and it is estimated that somewhere between a quarter and a third of the population has tried it.

Its use goes back to thousands of years before the Christian era, and in one guise or another, cannabis has been known throughout the world. The Chinese and Egyptians cultivated hemp three thousand years ago, or longer, to use in making rope and fabrics, and their writings reflect as well a knowledge of its drug effects. A mixture of hemp resin (hashish) and wine was used in China three thousand years ago as an anesthetic. The Scythians, who originated in central Asia and later migrated through much of southeastern Europe, made much of the known world aware of the mind-altering qualities of hemp. Their practice of putting the seeds on hot rocks and inhaling the smoke was recorded by Herodotus. The Greeks and Romans were using hemp for rope and sails before the birth of Christ, and the Romans introduced the plant into Gaul and Britain. It was widely cultivated in Europe during the Dark and Middle Ages for its fiber, and later on provided the rope and sails for the great navies of Henry VIII and his daughter, Elizabeth I, with the result that it was brought to North America at the beginning of the seventeenth century. It was an important cash crop, especially in Kentucky, until the latter part of the nineteenth century.

Most striking is its history in the Orient, and particularly in India, where it was valued as a medicine, far and above its incidental euphoric and hallucinogenic powers. The array of ills for which it was considered a remedy is astounding: it was considered an antiphlegmatic, a sedative, a mind-quickener, a digestive and a stimulant for the appetite, as well as a specific for catarrh, leprosy, whooping cough, fever, headache, both constipation and diarrhea, mental illness, insomnia, earache, beriberi, malaria, rheumatism and female complaints, to give a partial list. In India, it was a sacred plant as well, drunk to purify and to ward off evil. Medicinal use in this country and in Europe did not develop until the nineteenth century, when it was used for relief of pain, insomnia, and nervous conditions. Once an important item pharmaceutically, its use was discontinued because of difficulty in standardizing it and regulating dosage, and it has not been used medicinally in the West since the 1930s.

As seen previously, the drug effects of cannabis depend on the action of the psychoactive compound tetrahydrocannabinol (THC) in marijuana and hashish. Smoking marijuana produces an intoxication much like that of alcohol, with a euphoric sensation of calm and well-being, as well as a feeling of heightened awareness of surroundings, deeper insight into relationships and an ability to get to the heart of complicated issues. What is funny seems funnier, what is sad, sadder. There may be a feeling of depersonalization, of leaving the self and becoming an observer of the world below, with wisdom to solve its riddles. With the eyes closed, images may come and go, although one is aware that this is the result of the drug. The passage of time is frequently distorted and confused, and there may be a loss of immediate memory, so that the user will have difficulty in completing a thought he is trying to express, and become confused in trying to separate the past, present and future. Oddly, and in marked contrast to alcohol intoxication, people in a mild to moderate state of intoxication will often find it relatively easy to suppress voluntarily. THC will induce drowsiness, and a heavy dosage will put the user to sleep. Physical dependency is not involved in cannabis use, and there appears to be no increased-tolerance effect with prolonged use, in the sense that with regular use over an extended period, it is not observed that there is an increase in the amount of THC sought by the user in order to achieve a consistent effect. What has been very interesting, on the contrary, is evidence that smaller amounts may be sufficient after long-tern use to produce the desired intoxication in heavy users, which would constitute a reverse tolerance; this phenomenon, however, is still under investigation.

The ultimate in marijuana intoxication will go beyond a mere sense of euphoric well-being and will open the way to another world of visual and auditory sensation. Colors will become vivid and shimmering; vision will become three-dimensional, and colors something that can be "touched" as well as seen; sounds will also become more vivid and varied, heard with a greater clarity; the senses of taste, touch and smell will become intensified and sensual; the body will feel more alive, and filled with a glorious energy and vibrancy, capable of beautiful coordination. A concomitant of this euphoria is a feeling of closeness to others, of heightened empathy and a desire to be closer to people.

Very naturally, the possible adverse effects of cannabis use are not stressed by those seeking legalization of it, but they are very real. Antisocial behavior can also result from cannabis use, coupled with a loss of inhibitions in acting out. Instead of the euphoric closeness, alienation from loved ones can occur. People who were on the borderline of mental illness can be pushed over the edge into delusions and schizophrenic or paranoid psychosis; this is also a possibility in otherwise normal people as a result of heavy usage over an extended period. A behavioral disorder known as the "cannabis syndrome" is characterized by apathy, diminished drive, lowering of motivation and a marked lack of interest in the future. Detachment from reality can take place, accompanied by bizarre behavior and personality deterioration. While it is true that such extreme reactions are relatively rare, and that they will disappear gradually with discontinued use of the drug (accompanied in some instances by therapy), just the fact that they are possible results of its use would seem to be a strong argument for not having it available across the counter in drug stores and supermarkets.

Physical effects on the brain are now seen as possibly permanent. Brain atrophy in young men who have been heavy users over a long period has been found to be comparable to that found in men of ninety, and because of the accumulation of cannabinoids in the brain the atrophy will progress, with resultant shrinkage and replacement of fluid in the inner cavity of the brain with air. This progressive brain damage will be manifested in long-term learning deficits, memory loss, loss of motor control and "marijuana thinking:" impairment in abstract thinking and an inability to distinguish between the concrete and the abstract.

Chromosome breakage, which occurs in the aging process, can cause premature aging in users and has led to investigation of the extent of birth defects as the result of chromosome transmission. It has certainly been established that use by a pregnant woman has sharply increased fetal death and fetal abnormality. It has also been definitively shown that it alters hormone levels to bring on early menopause at a rate six times higher in users than in nonusers, even if the use is as low as two cigarettes a day.

In the male, there is significant lowering of the level of testosterone, the reproductive hormone. Users have, in 44 percent of those in one study, a lower testosterone level than nonusers, and in 35 percent, the sperm count was low enough to classify them as sterile.

Heavy smoking of cannabis over a prolonged period will produce a much greater accumulation of tar in the lungs than will cigarette smoking. Precancerous bronchial lesions have been found in twenty year-old marijuana smokers that would not be normally found in a cigarette smoker under forty, and this is due in large part to the deep inhaling of marijuana smoke and the holding of it in the lungs for thirty seconds or more. Cannabis produces about 50 percent more tar than does tobacco, and given the way in which a "joint" is smoked, as contrasted with a tobacco cigarette, a couple of joints will be as harmful to the lungs as a pack of twenty tobacco cigarettes. Smoking marijuana also causes bloodshot eyes and an increased heart rate, but in smokers with normal hearts, these effects are apparently temporary and not significant.

Study results indicate that the vast majority of pot smokers do so in combination with other drugs, particularly alcohol, and this is probably due in large part to the social aspect of much smoking. It seems clear also that those who find marijuana enjoyable are very likely to experiment with other substances, either to experience variety or in an attempt to intensify their drug experience. They are also very suggestible when in a state of marijuana intoxication and much more likely not to exercise caution that would otherwise deter them from trying many of the more unpredictable substances. Alcoholics leaving treatment are warned strongly about the danger of substituting pot for alcohol, a thought many who are experiencing the uncertainty and apprehension of early sobriety admit to having entertained. They are seen as particularly vulnerable to the euphoric, what-the-hell thinking of pot intoxication and in real jeopardy of reactivating their alcohol addiction in that altered state. Their struggle to remain abstinent can be difficult enough as they face the real world without the support of their friend; the defenses that they have worked so hard to build might very well give way when their sober judgment is placed in an unequal contest with euphoria.

The wrangle over the decriminalization (imposition only of fines as a penalty for possession) and/or legalization of marijuana seems to have abated somewhat. A year after the "Oregon Experience" of decriminalization began in 1973, survey results seemed to show no significant increase in pot use, and the police noted not only a marked improvement in their relations with young people, but cited as well the freedom that they had to attend to more vital concerns. One very real worry for the police, however, remains the hazards presented by marijuana-affected drivers. They are on the road with distorted perceptions of time, distance and speed that constitute a real menace to others.

Opponents to the lifting of sanctions against marijuana possession and use cite the multitude of problems resulting from the relegalization of alcohol and question the wisdom of allowing a second mind-altering drug to circulate legally. It remains for them a Pandora's box with someone at least trying to sit on the lid, and there is certainly justification for their fears that the number of daily users will increase, that significant numbers of children will become involved at an earlier age, and that the strength of the drug will increase. This also opens up the question of the availability of hashish if marijuana is legalized and thousands of acres are put under cultivation. The argument that consumption of alcohol and tobacco would decrease is valueless, and the medical hazards of moderate and heavy smoking of marijuana—respiratory problems, "marijuana thinking," and the very real possibilities, still under investigation but with an ominous likelihood of being validated, that smoking pot causes chromosomal damage, affects the reproductive system, and injures fetuses—are strong arguments against lifting restrictions. Well-founded suspicions, coupled with indisputable facts, make the wisdom of such a step very dubious indeed.

Other Friendly Travel Agents

The best-known of the hallucinogens, after marijuana, and certainly the most widely distributed of the street drugs, is LSD. Its emergence twenty years ago was accompanied by much fanfare from Dr. Timothy Leary that extolled the sublime, mystical properties of the "trips" that could be taken by swallowing (it is rarely injected) lysergic acid diethylamide. "Acid trips" are often experienced by street buyers who have thought that they were purchasing THC, PCP or some other substance, and it is a frequent, and dangerous, diluent in what are ostensibly amphetamines, barbiturates or narcotics.

Qualitatively, the LSD experience is very similar to that of marijuana, but the effects are far more intense and will last from eight to twelve hours. As with pot, the user will usually be aware that he is in the midst of a drug experience. He will have the same sensation of leaving the self and being an observer, while he experiences the "psychedelic" effects: colors become more intense, and may be "smelled" or "felt," as may sounds; fantastic shapes and designs will come and go, and his sense of time will become distorted. Typically, he will feel he has crossed the threshold into new and profound philosophical realms, with dazzling insights into himself and the world around him. He may feel omnipotent and that his soul alone has been selected to live forever.

An acid trip is not predictable, however, and may be hideous and terrifying. The user may experience acute panic and feel certain that he is about to go insane. He may be seized with sudden suicidal or homicidal impulses, and the danger inherent for users with pre-existing psychiatric problems is a very real one. Conceivably convinced that nothing can kill him, he could jump off a building. A severe paranoid state may be induced. Schizophrenic and paranoid schizophrenic reactions may endure over prolonged periods ranging from weeks to years. Sometimes they will disappear for a time, only to re-emerge later, and they are often resistant to treatment. The common explanation offered has been that this has been an outcome of LSD use in people who had a psychotic condition before use, but documentation exists that indicates that psychosis has developed after an LSD experience in people who were experiencing no previous personality disorder.

As with marijuana, the user is also often subjected to "flashbacks," a disturbing phenomenon in which the acid trip is re-experienced without taking the drug. The flashback may be welcome if it is pleasant, but it can be a panic-inducing experience for others that may fill them with a fear that they are going mad. As with marijuana, lasting states of apathy that can lead to dropping out of the mainstream of life have been observed as a result of LSD use. So has a remarkable passivity, a tendency to avoid violence and confrontations of all kinds, and an absorption with love and gentleness. This "psychedelic syndrome" is seen by some as severely limiting its possessor's chances of succeeding in a competitive world, but the question is rightfully raised as to whether this state is solely LSD-induced or whether it is a reflection of what would have been the individual's basic inclination in any case.

Questions also have arisen as to the effects of sustained use of LSD with regard to chromosome breakage, spontaneous abortions and genetic birth defects. In this area, definitive conclusions have not been arrived at, and the general tendency seems to be to suspend judgment until indisputable evidence one way or another appears. LSD is not physically addicting. A high tolerance to it can be developed, but it will subside if use is discontinued. There is no factual evidence of death having been caused directly by an overdose, and the lethal dose for a human has not been determined. One very strong caution, however, bears repeating. The enormous production of street drugs by chemists working in the cellar or out in the garage has brought with it what should be a very intimidating uncertainty as to what the purchaser is actually getting. There appears to be very little in the way of scruples in the street trade, and pushers are notorious for misrepresenting their wares. A mixture of LSD and amphetamines, for example, could produce an effect so deeply disturbing that it has been given the name of "death trip." Since LSD is only manufactured illegally, there is no way of knowing what may actually be in a "bag" of LSD, and unless users are very sure of their source, they are running a very grave risk in embarking on a trip whose passage and destination are unknown.

Of Peace and Angels—PCP—

Also appearing on the illicit drug scene in the mid-1960s, but overshadowed by the enormous interest in LSD, was Phencyclidine, commonly called "angel dust" or "peace pills." Originally developed by Parke-Davis and marketed briefly in the 1950s as Sernylan, it was intended for use as a painkiller and anesthetic but was discontinued because of extremely unpleasant postoperative agitation and delirium.

On the street, it appears in both powdered or tablet/capsule form and can be swallowed, inhaled, injected or sprinkled on tobacco and smoked. In small amounts, it will induce euphoria, a loss of inhibitions, and a feeling of social ease and well-being. However, intoxication will be typically accompanied by a sensation of numbness, but no other problems occur at low dosages. Dosage is all-important in avoiding very bad experiences with PCP, and again, the uncertainty of just what is being purchased illegally enters (or should enter) into consideration of using it. It can cause, if the dosage is not carefully monitored, acute panic that is worsened by a terrible feeling of isolation or of having ceased to be. The sense of touch is greatly interfered with, and sensory blocking is truly terrifying. A very common manifestation is hostile and troublesome behavior, and PCP trippers often find themselves in jail as a result of outbursts when intoxicated. On ten milligrams or more, toxic psychosis can occur that has caused users to be hospitalized as schizophrenics, with accompanying agitation and aggression which can be physical and violent. The user may be in such a state of emotional chaos, accompanied by an inability to distinguish between reality and fantasy, that he will withdraw into a catatonic stupor in order to hide. The psychosis can last for as long as several weeks and is optimally gone through in seclusion in a hospital.

Incredibly, doses of as high as 1000 milligrams have been recorded, and this high an overdose can bring coma or death, both of which have also been documented in PCP users. Also startling is the fact that following an episode leading to coma, there will be total amnesia regarding the entire experience. Lasting, chronic effects can result from sustained PCP use, among them depression, confusion, anxiety and recurrent psychotic episodes. Unpredictable tantrums and physically belligerent behavior are characteristic, or there may be a complete withdrawal from all social contact. A very dangerous substance, but one that has, in the opinion of many, overtaken LSD in prevalence and use. It is ironic that one of the reasons for LSD's decline in popularity is the perceived hazard of having a "death trip," and frightening to realize the extent and the casualness of PCP's use as an adulterant in mixtures purporting to be LSD or THC on the street.

A Quieter Companion—Methaqualone
Another product of the 1950s that became prevalent in this

country in the 1960s, Methaqualone is a nonbarbiturate "downer" and is manufactured legally by a number of pharmaceutical houses, most notably Rorer, which puts it out under its most commonly-known name of Quaalude (shortened on the street to "lude"). If falls into the sedative-hypnotic category, and one of the most enduring misconceptions about it is that because it is not a barbiturate, it is therefore not physically addictive. It does produce physical as well as psychological dependency; tolerance can be developed to it, and physical symptoms (tremors, weakness, delirium and possibly convulsions) occur in withdrawal. Like barbiturates, it produces a state of intoxication that is very similar to that of alcohol, which is the same group of CNS depressants. Rather than the excitation and vivid, psychedelic effects sought by the hallucinogen users, Quaaludes are taken for their soothing, sedative effect. They are frequently taken by alcoholics to sustain their state of alcoholic intoxication and by narcotic addicts to supplement the diminished concentration of heroin or morphine in the "bags" sold on the street today.

Unquestionably, the explanation for its enormous popularity rests in the enduring myth that it is nonaddictive and can be used safely in combination with alcohol because it is not a barbiturate. Discouragingly, a number of physicians have been known to share this delusion and to prescribe it as such. It is every bit as lethal in combination with other CNS depressants as the barbiturates are, and overdose, either alone or in combination, has killed. Running a close second in explaining the demand for it is the persistent claim that it is a highly-effective aphrodisiac, an assertion that is difficult or impossible to verify, particularly in view of the very active level of sexuality present in any case in the adolescents and young adults who make up most of the drug's following. Again like alcohol, Quaaludes have a disinhibiting effect, but in large enough doses, they may make sexual activity impossible, a serious disappointment to the man who thought he was loading up on a sure-fire aphrodisiac.

Other products in the nonbarbiturate sedative-hypnotic classification are numerous, and there are devotees of Valmid, Placidyl and Doriden. Methaqualone is also marketed by other houses as Sopor, Somnafac and Dimethacol, among other names. All are subject to abuse in the same manner and to the same degree as are the barbiturates. All of them can addict and kill people.

A Faster Crowd—The Amphetamines

This is the exhilarating group, the CNS stimulants. First developed in the 1930s, they enjoyed a more or less contained use for thirty years as occasional sources of stimulation for exceptional needs: students cramming for exams, athletes in need of an extra burst of energy, or cross-country truck drivers who had to make a run nonstop. They were also used in the Benzedrine inhaler as a decongestant and were prescribed as a diet aid. As "pep pills," they had a fairly innocuous history until the drug revolution of the 1960s, when they began to be used as a substitute for heroin and to intensify and prolong narcotic and hallucinogenic episodes. At the same period, severe abuse began to appear in the form of injecting "speed" at regular intervals to get and sustain the maximum effect, sometimes for days at a time, which is known as a "run." The intake of a "speed freak" may be as high as 30,000 milligrams a day. Methedrine is a derivative, one of many, and slightly less powerful. It is known on the streets as "Meth" or "crystal" and often has the over-all term of "speed" applied, in view of the very small difference.

For the most part, speed is taken orally, just for kicks. It is not physically addictive, and there is no withdrawal syndrome. Heavy users cite a feeling of lethargy and depression upon discontinuing use. The speed freak is in a different category. His primary craving is for the euphoric "flash" that follows injection. During the run, he is enjoying a sensation of hyperalertness and omnipotence, and will repeat injections whenever he feels the drug effects lessening. During this period, he becomes hyperactive, talkative, impulsive and lacking in judgment. He will also commonly become paranoid and hallucinate in an amphetamine psychosis. He is difficult to be around, and may be actually dangerous.

The paranoia will become standard in repeated runs, appearing progressively earlier until it is manifested finally at the beginning of the run. The heart is damaged as a result of this practice, and the case for liver and brain damage appears to be a sound one. An additional danger for speed freaks is combining their drug with heroin or using heroin to de-escalate from a speed run. In time, heroin may replace the speed and a narcotic addiction will result.

The Queen—Cocaine

The use of coca leaves among the Incas dates back thousands of years. They were chewed, and at the altitude at which the Indians lived, the effect bore no resemblance to the high experienced when cocaine powder is inhaled through the nose ("snorted") in this country. For the Indians, coca fought tiredness and hunger and made their work in the mines bearable. A CNS stimulant, its effects are very similar to those of the amphetamines, but its price is monumentally higher, and its reputation is that of giving a high without equal. This writer recalls a physician who related that when he was using cocaine, the anticipation the night before was such that he was unable to sleep.

It seems very likely that a great part of cocaine's reputation is based on a certain amount of "hype" and buttressed by its very high cost, which has given it millionaire status. Actually, injection of a large dose of amphetamine can produce much the same effect, and the cocaine experience is a much shorter-lived one. Moreover, it is rarely found on the market in a pure state, and the street purchaser may buy such a diluted product that he may actually be receiving a powder that is only 3-5 percent cocaine. Amphetamines are one of the frequent diluants. Because of dilution, a method known as "free-basing" has evolved, in which the adulterated mix is boiled in ether to free the pure drug, which is then inhaled or injected. The "flash" which follows is extolled as pure ecstasy but is actually very similar to the amphetamine flash. As with amphetamines, users become hyperstimulated and experience feelings of euphoria and omnipotence; they are also prey to the same paranoid toxic psychosis, which, like that brought on by amphetamines, will subside when use is discontinued. To ward off excess stimulation, users sometimes combine the drug with heroin, making what is known as a "speedball." This is analogous to mixed amphetamine use in which heroin and speed are injected simultaneously.

As with speed, withdrawal from cocaine can produce listlessness and depression, known as "crashing," and use will be maintained to avoid the "crash." Argument is being increasingly put forward to classify cocaine as addictive, inasmuch as tolerance—needing larger doses to achieve the same effects —is thought to be established, and the psychological effects of discontinued use—depression and inactivity—are considered by some to constitute physical withdrawal effects. This is considered insufficient in other quarters for cocaine to be classified as addictive in the classic sense, and we will leave the controversy there.

Whatever its classification, the power of cocaine to recruit followers who will go to any lengths to obtain it is truly astounding, especially at $2,000 an ounce or more (for the highest, unadulterated quality) to experience a sensation which doesn't last longer than twenty minutes. Its status as the Rolls Royce of drugs appears unassailable. For those, however, whose daily task it is to view the wreckage and attempt to restore order and balance into lives distorted into nightmares by chemical use, all drugs fall into just one category. They are, singly or lumped together in one unholy mass, the enemy.

8. Getting The Alcoholic to Treatment

Alcoholism stands unique among primary physiological diseases in that even when it has been positively identified and there is no question that if its course continues unchecked the victim will die, it is only with the greatest difficulty that he or she can be convinced of that fact, and that even then, considerable effort is needed to bring that individual to help. Certainly, many diagnoses will produce shock, and even trauma, in the recipient. Being told that one has multiple sclerosis or an inoperable malignancy is devastating, but the reality of it will register on the individual, and some sort of adjustment to it will begin, however stunned the patient may feel when leaving the doctor's office.

This is not the case with alcoholism. For one thing, most diagnoses of it are not made in a doctor's office. Alcoholics lie to doctors when questioned about their drinking, just as they lie to everyone else. They do everything they can to keep their alcohol consumption a secret, and they certainly don't want their physician to be aware of it, because they know what he would say to them. Also, it is sadly but undeniably true that most physicians are as much in the dark about alcoholism as the rest of the population and share many of the same misconceptions. Not until the alcoholic's condition has reached a point where his appearance betrays it when he enters the office will it be as apparent without an examination as it is to the people who pass the patient on the street. Until that point, the symptoms presented by a normal-appearing alcoholics could very well have another cause. In the early and middle stages of the illness, and often well into the chronic phase, problems with heart, pancreas and liver could be misdiagnosed as to origin. Insomnia and "nerves" are all too often handled by prescribing barbiturates and tranquilizers which compound the problem and can be lethal in combination with alcohol. Not until the patient gets honest with his doctor, unlikely in most cases, does the situation become clear. The doctor will be puzzled, and the alcoholic will hope that some remedy will be found that will leave his drinking safe and secret.

When the patient's alcoholism has reached a point where it can no longer be concealed and where the physical damage has become so severe that it requires hospitalization, and even surgery, the alcoholic will in all likelihood be in such bondage to his drug that while he may listen to explanations of the danger presented by continued drinking, and even assure the physician that he understands and will become totally abstinent, it is very doubtful that he will keep any such promise. Once the immediate crisis is past, a chronic alcoholic will almost invariably resume drinking. It is very possible that he may try to reduce his intake initially, but the nature of his addiction is such that unless he abstains entirely, he will quickly lose control over his drinking again and the disease will resume its briefly interrupted course. What is needed, after a medical crisis, is for the alcoholic to be gotten as quickly as possible to treatment for his alcoholism, and unless there is skilled maneuvering on the part of concerned people, this seldom happens. The crisis is over, and the alcoholic feels relieved. He had to accept the necessity of going to the hospital and submitting himself to his physician's judgment and possibly to that of a surgeon as well. In this area, his logic was working for him, and he recognized the need for what had to be done. His addiction, however, he keeps as his own very personal domain, and because his emotional involvement with the drug is so intense, he will discount and rationalize away the warnings he has received. To worsen his situation, he may also still have his supply of antidepressants, tranquilizers or sedatives to further his delusion that he can somehow drink and get away with it. The relationship with alcohol is too personal and too binding to be affected by warnings. They might frighten him at the time, but his addiction will alter that. The alcoholic will focus on the drink he wants and "needs" right now and make vague plans for a healthier regime sometime in the future dur- ing the solemn confrontation with his doctor.

The doctor, of course, will consider that he has done his duty. Certainly, he has done all that was possible about the patient's pancreatitis or his hepatitis or his neurological dysfunction, and he has warned him that the problem will return and get worse if alcohol use continues. Whether or not the patient heeds the warning is, he feels, not his domain. He may very well feel compassion for his patient, but he may also share a very common reaction to alcoholism and feel some disdain for it and that "it's his funeral." However, it seems very likely that that would not be the case if he had a fuller understanding of what is afflicting his patient, physiological- ly and psychologically, and if he had at his disposal a plan of action that offered the possibility of bringing him to a total recovery.

It is encouraging to see that a number of medical schools are now offering intensive course-work in alcoholism, instead of what was often just one class in a four-year program. Among younger physicians, there is growing sophistication in this crucial area, an awareness that millions of people have alcoholism and do not present as such in an office visit. There is more careful probing of telltale symptoms, more alertness to other indications that might otherwise be overlooked, and more willingness to involve other family members in seeking a fully accurate diagnosis. Armed with this knowledge, a physi- cian can do a great deal for an alcoholic patient. He can iden- tify the syndrome at a stage in which the patient might other- wise have been successful in concealing it. He can explain to the patient more explicitly just what is taking place and go into further detail about the implications of continued drinking. Even if the patient refuses to believe him or denies, possibly angrily, that he has any significant alcohol involvement, at least a seed will be planted in the patient's mind that could influence him later in making a decision to go for help.

The doctor can also have some resources to which he can direct the patient and be able to explain to him just what they are and what they offer; needless to say, this is far more likely to be effective than making a generalized suggestion that the patient "get some help," or go to A.A. The latter, at this point, could certainly backfire and have the reverse effect from the one intended. The doctor's knowledge of treatment resources, whether in- or out-patient, can be enormously helpful to troubled family members who have no concrete idea of how to address the problem and who will give far more weight to a recommendation coming from a medical professional than to the same idea when it is voiced by a friend or relation. Involving the family in a consultation about the patient's drinking and its medical implications can be the beginning of the end for the grip the addictive process has on the threatened family member. If the issue remains a private one between the alcoholic and the physician, leaving the decision to seek help entirely in the hands of the alcoholic, the time at which that decision may be made is moved forward considerably, for it is certain that the alcoholic will never go home and repeat what has been said to the family.

Finally, this newer, alerted segment of the medical profession is more attuned to the emotional tip-offs that alcoholism may be present. He will look more carefully at complaints of depression, jitteriness, anxiety, mood swings, irritability and insomnia. Perhaps some (or all) of them are presenting in a middle-aged woman. She is pleasant, nicely dressed, middle-class. She is certainly sober and gives rational descriptions of symptoms and answers to questions. There is nothing about her to suggest skid row or any other popular stereotype of an alcoholic; there is no odor of alcohol on her breath, and her eyes are clear. The doctor may question her about problems connected with menopause, or stress at home or at work.

She may very possibly say that she has no idea why she is having the symptoms, and the simplest and most obvious solution may be for him to give her a prescription for a sedative or a tranquilizer and hope that she will respond satisfactorily and not keep calling for appointments. He takes at face value her statement that she has a cocktail before dinner when he asks about her alcohol intake, and nods when she adds that if she and her husband are out socially, she may have a little more. There may seem to be nothing more to discuss, and yet if her husband were asked, a very different picture might be presented, and concern over her drinking might be voiced. Questions in the physician's office might also yield indications that she is not being truthful about her drinking, and the doctor could be alerted to further indications on subsequent visits until he felt he had enough information to investigate more openly and possibly involve family members. Awareness of the possible basis for complaints of an emotional/psychological nature can lead to more careful monitoring and eventually disclose alcoholism which has not yet become apparent to the casual observer. Most alcoholics are not yet in that stage, are not visible on the street, and are still able to present themselves as average and "normal," except to those who are more closely involved with them. There is still that measure of control left, and there is still massive denial of a problem, as well as conscious minimizing and covering up of symptoms.

The Denial Syndrome

The most commonly cited symptom of alcoholism is loss of control over one's drinking, and accompanying it, invariably, is the alcoholic's firm denial, to himself and to others, that this has taken place. It does not matter how often he has stopped off on the way home, determined to have just two beers, and stayed in the bar until closing time. It does not matter how often he has sworn he would pace himself at a party or a quiet evening at home and ended up getting drunk. It does not matter how often he has bought a bottle of whiskey on Monday to last until Friday and had it all gone on Tuesday morning. The alcoholic will find a logical reason to alibi himself with and persist against all logic in his belief that he is in control of his drinking and feel confident that the next time, that control will prevail. With his stereotypical skid row bum in mind, he will angrily and incredulously reject the suggestion that he could be alcoholic. It is one of the most baffling, and yet most common, manisfestations of the addiction that the victim will refuse to recognize irrefutable facts that are staring him in the face and to see that they form a sequence of incidents that can only have one possible explanation: he is powerless over alcohol once he has introduced it into his system, and he is in the grip of a physical and emotional compulsion that makes it impossible for him not to do so.

He will push these facts aside and delude himself into believing the excuses he finds, however flimsy and illogical, to justify his drinking. It is his wife, his boss, his job, his children. It is being tired, overworked, frustrated, bored, misunderstood, unappreciated. It is anything and everything except what it really is. That, he will steadfastly refuse even to consider. He will lie about how much he drank and end up believing it himself; how often does one hear the euphemism "a couple of/a few drinks?" Sometimes an effort at control will be made. He will decide to abstain and succeed in doing so for a brief time, usually with some fanfare. How could he "have a problem" (never *alcoholism*) when everyone saw he didn't have a drop for two weeks, or all week, or whatever it was? Or he may, by a great effort of will, limit himself to a set amount. He may cheat on this, but if the family is convinced, he will disregard the drinks taken in secret and point proudly to the limit he has kept in front of them. He may switch to something that is lower-proof. The outcome will always be the same. He will take pride and comfort in having proved his control over alcohol, and he will revert to his former pattern buttressed by that totally false evidence.

If it occurs to him at all, he will dismiss the fact as well of the effort that his abstention or reduced consumption or change in beverage cost him, and the evidence therein of the hold alcohol has on him. He will continue to see his drug as his friend, his source of solace and peace, and never entertain the thought of giving it up. His lack of logic will be sustained even when the progression of his condition leads him to morning drinking; he just needs something to straighten him out so he can get to work, and that is something he understands, but other people wouldn't, so he does it secretly. He knows there's nothing really wrong. He's getting to work, isn't he? Or if he's not, why shouldn't he take a day off once in a while? Everybody else does. Above all, there's no problem. This is just his little relationship with his friend, and it's nobody else's business.

What is curious about this intense, internal life of the alcoholic is that if he were watching the same thing going on in a movie or on television, he would recognize at once what was being portrayed. However, he is living it himself, and by himself, and his illness is blinding him to the reality of what is happening to him, because it couldn't happen to *him*. Alcoholism is always something that happens to the other guy, is something that has happened to the skid row bum or to that guy in the plant who got fired. It doesn't happen to you.

The syndrome that has overtaken the alcoholic can often be extended to members of the family. Motivated by fear or shame, or both, they may also refuse to recognize what has happened to the alcoholic. Despite the evidence before them, they will insist that he isn't "that bad," and this is a mixture of denial and of hope that it all may someday just go away. It won't. The only thing that it will do is get worse, and the family will become increasingly dysfunctional.

The family reacts without understanding what is taking place in front of them and probably with no informed source to spell it out for them. Instead, they will listen to people who are as misinformed as they are; they may try a series of ploys to bring the alcoholic's drinking under control or to stop it altogether. They may try to ignore it; they may try to placate and pamper him; they may close ranks against him and shut him out. None of them will work. But they may consistently refuse to acknowledge that what they are dealing with is alcoholism. The very word terrifies and shames them, and it may also fill them with guilt, especially when it is parents who are watching an afflicted son or daughter.

The outcome of this denial is that the family will often tend to put the cart before the horse and see the drinking as the outward manifestation of deep-rooted emotional problems. They do not see that the emotional disruption has come about as the result of an illness that is physiological in origin. Instead, they feel that the solution to the mystery lies in finding out what is troubling the alcoholic, and they will often be sure that the key lies in his childhood or in some other remote area in which there are still unresolved conflicts that have tortured him, perhaps subconsciously, until he has been driven to find relief in alcohol. Parents will feel that they have failed in their role, and spouses will feel that they have failed in theirs. Hope is extended to them by the idea that the underlying cause or causes can be uncovered by a psychiatrist or psychologist. It may even be possible that the fault is not theirs, after all.

This is infinitely preferable to the idea that they are dealing with an alcoholic, and this is because they do not understand what alcoholism is. With the confusion of misinformation and folklore that they have accumulated over the years, they have not the slightest comprehension that the cause of the alcoholism is alcohol and the addictive-allergic reaction to it in the alcoholic's system. They have no idea that it is a progressive syndrome, like Parkinson's disease, and that what they have been watching and agonizing over is that progression. They desperately need that information in order to deal with the illness and bring the alcoholic to an understanding of it that will enable him to arrest it permanently, just as a diabetic needs understanding of his illness in order to bring it under control.

Instead, the scenario that ensues when the family finally decides that something had got to be done is one in which the alcoholic embarks on what may be a lengthy and costly exploration of the conscious or subconscious emotional basis for his drinking. Until comparatively recently this was the accepted explanation for alcoholism in many quarters, and it was considered a far more enlightened view of the problem than the time-honored one of considering the alcoholic simply as morally unfit and a weakling. In any case, "problem drinking" is for many a far more acceptable term than alcoholism, because the Puritan Ethic has by no means disappeared, and it remains a strong, if often unexpressed, reaction to alcoholism and to alcoholics.

There is also popular support for the theory that alcoholism is no more than a bad habit, and that like other bad habits, it can be broken by behavior modification once the source of the habit is determined and dealt with. The alcoholic will often welcome the idea that his drinking is an emotional disorder. It gives it a more respectable explanation and absolves him of guilt. What is more, it puts the responsibility for "curing" it squarely on someone else—the therapist— and excuses his drinking as long as he keeps his appointments until the cure is found. He may also feel that he has at least found a sympathetic ear after years of being misunderstood and will be able to further manipulate his family by citing, or fabricating, what the doctor has said to him about them. For an alcoholic, going into therapy can be a godsend as far as removing immediate pressure from him, and we have known a substantial number who have thus managed to extend their drinking, some for a period of years, both as in- and as outpatients. In every such case, what has happened is that the true nature of the illness has not been identified and that the symptoms have been dealt with, rather than the cause.

It is undeniable that emotional problems are engendered by alcoholism and must be addressed. It is also true that there are emotional "triggers" in every alcoholic that must be identified and with which the patient must learn to cope to forestall a relapse into drinking. Anger, frustration, feelings of inadequacy and shyness—the list is a long one and embraces most human problem areas. Once alcoholism develops, these emotions will feed into it and keep its active phase going. After attaining sobriety, the alcoholic must learn coping skills to deal with them so that he won't seek relief in alcohol.

First of all, however, denial of the existence of alcoholism must be eliminated, both in the alcoholic and in the family, and this will come when what it is has been carefully explained and all concerned are able to place the blame on the alcohol, where it belongs. Only then will the guilt and stigma be removed, as though they were shown a bacillus under a microscope and were told: "There it is. That's what's caused it." With this knowledge, the family will see what has been going on with the alcoholic in an entirely different light, and they will become able to deal with it in a far more effective fashion. They will be freed from their feelings of anger and guilt and inadequacy, and it will be possible to show them how to intervene effectively to arrest the progression that the alcoholic is powerless to deal with.

The Intervention

Up until this point, as has been noted, the family has been floundering in their efforts to bring the alcoholic's drinking under control, largely because they have had no informed guidance. Instead, frightened and uncertain, they have also been inconsistent and ineffective. Once they have a sound grasp of what they are dealing with and are able to look at it more objectively, they can be introduced to a concept known as "tough love" that will enable them to break down the alcoholic's denial and defenses without compromising their relationship with him.

What they must be shown how to do is to set up a "surround" on the alcoholic in the course of which they will present to him, calmly and factually, exactly what has been happening. They must be rehearsed in this procedure, and they must have precise facts to present, with concrete examples, in order not to fall into the trap of generalizations and vagueness which will give the alcoholic an opportunity to quibble over details and destroy the effectiveness of what they are presenting to him. Again, this must be done calmly. It must also be done with caring and concern, so that there is no element of accusation or of being judgmental. It is essential for the alcoholic to sense that caring, in order to avoid as much as possible the alcoholic becoming hostile and trying to break up the process by starting a fight. Provocations must be ignored, and the family must carefully sidestep getting into an argument with him. Instead, they must persevere in presenting to him their enumeration of the incidents and behavior that it has been decided to present to him as the basis for their feeling that he must go for help. The ploys that he will use to try to defend his drinking and to make them feel that they are exaggerating and blowing things out of proportion will be obvious, as will his protestations that they are misconstruing his behavior or that incidents they are citing didn't happen as described. By remaining calm and by showing their concern for him as the motive for what they are doing, they will make it clear to him that they are not attacking him and that they are doing what they are doing out of caring. There is no more effective weapon against addiction than love. It can motivate an alcoholic to look at his drinking and what people close to him are saying in a far more positive way than can any amount of threats and recriminations.

What has happened first, of course, is that those staging the intervention have come to realize that they are trying to rescue a gravely ill individual from a sickness that has distorted his perceptions to the point that he is denying that there is a valid base for concern. It is often difficult for people to realize that this is truly what they are looking at and to try to put themselves into that person's head. Probably it is true that only another alcoholic, recalling his own mental state at the time when the syndrome was active in him, can approach actual empathy with the cornered object of a surround. Nonetheless, the rescuers can have enough awareness of the confusion, panic and desperate defense measures that their maneuver is causing to make them gentle in their approach and calmly rational in countering the alcoholic's frightened reaction. They *have* cornered him, and their strategy must be one that will calm and reassure him.

It will be some time before the alcoholic realizes what has actually happened to him and can see the extent of his denial. Those intent on saving him will have to understand them before he does, and they will have to be prepared to confront that denial and to stand firm in the face of the various tactics he will employ in order not to be separated from his drug. They will have to pursue, gently but firmly, their objective of having him enter treatment, and he will try to avoid this by any means that comes to hand.

What has just been described is certainly "tough love," in that it involves an unflinching confrontation with an alcoholic about his alcoholism. This is a final showdown from which a great many people will pull back, hoping against hope that a resolution to the dilemma will somehow materialize from some other source and save them from having to deal with it themselves. Barring something like a fatal car accident, it is highly unlikely that this is going to happen, and the best course of action is for them to put themselves in the hands of a trained person who can bring them together as a unit with a common goal and coach them in the technique that they need to use. Such persons are readily available at alcoholism treatment centers and at outpatient counseling facilities.

What they will learn from that person is that they must use a caring approach, that they must be united in the single purpose of getting the alcoholic to the help that is available, and that they must gently but relentlessly pursue that goal and not allow themselves to be diverted from it by being drawn into arguments by the alcoholic or taken in by his insistence that he can do it on his own. They must not be deterred from their objective by tears or promises or blame for his condition that he may well attempt to put on them. They must not allow him to make them so angry that they will abandon the project and leave him to stew in his own juice, which is exactly what he wants. They must not be moved by pity, or by guilt at his accusations of plotting behind his back, to soften and give him "one more chance." They must realize that his promises are valueless and that to give in now would make it inevitable that even if there should be a brief respite during which he will try to abstain, the drinking will inevitably resume, and they will all be back where they started. They must also be aware that they are the ones who know the realities of the situation and that the alcoholic may well be very sincere in what he is promising to do, may truly believe that he can do it on his own and thus be spared the indignity of having to be admitted to an "institution." This, he does honestly view with fear and humiliation, and he sees it as well as a sudden and traumatic separation from his friend. It is over this point that he may dig in his heels and refuse to listen. In the back of his mind, what he is desperately looking for is a means to buy a little more time, and he is trying to flimflam those about him in order to put off that separation for just a little longer. Thus, the point to make by those doing the intervention is that time has run out and that none of this twistings and turnings are going to extricate him this time, that "this is it." The alcoholic, in his panic and desperation, is capable at this point of taking only the short-term view, which is that of not being denied his alcohol in the very immediate future and of somehow not having to get into a car and be driven to what he views as a lockup. Those intent on getting him to help are taking a much longer-range view of his situation and must be aware that he is unable, at this juncture, to look rationally that far ahead. Again, they must be patient, but firm.

It is now that the toughest part of tough love must make its appearance. The alcoholic has had presented to him all of the carefully prepared documentation intended to bring home to him the gravity of his condition and to leave him with as little space as possible in which to argue that these are isolated instances that "could happen to anyone" and that are being blown out of proportion. Once this consistent sequence of events is laid out to him in such a way that a clear and distinct pattern can be identified, treatment is proposed to him as a logical course of action. The diagnosis of alcoholism is made to him, although it may be tactfully referred to as something like "your drinking problem." Even in the fact of the solidly established evidence that treatment is indicated, however, he may refuse to consider any method of addressing the problem but his own and state positively that he will not go to "one of those places," that it is absolutely unnecessary, and that he can "take care of it myself."

He must be told now that it *is* absolutely necessary, and it must be clearly stated to him what the results of refusal will be. This is when the coaching received really meets its test, because this is when all the cards are put on the table, and there can be no holding back in order to avoid the unpleasantness of having to say some very difficult things. What is going to be said must also be very carefully determined beforehand. The rescuers cannot afford to make empty threats; they must be certain that they can back up their words with actions, and they must fully intend to do so, if it becomes necessary. Thus, a wife must be very sure of herself and of her ground when she says to her husband, "Jack, if you are going to refuse to say, right now, that you will go today to get some help with your drinking, then I am going to leave, and I'm going to take the children with me." Even more strongly, she may be in a position to say, "If you don't go today and get help with this, then you're going to have to leave this house, and if I have to, I'll start legal action to keep you from coming back." Parents may have to say, "If you are determined not to do as we ask, then you're going to have to leave, and there will be nothing further forthcoming from us. You will be on your own, and you will have to take care of yourself as best you can. There is nothing further we can do if you won't let us get you the help you need." Again, these can't be empty threats. The core of the intervention is that the alcoholic must be made to understand two things: 1) that those confronting him care about him, and 2) that they can no longer endure living with his active alcoholism, and that they realize that to do so is only prolonging it. It must be clear to him that there is no way in which he can alter their decision or make them reverse their stand, and they, in turn, must be prepared either for an explosion or for a flood of self-pity and "How can you do this to me?" In either case, they must hold absolutely firm and make the alcoholic see that this time, nothing is going to work and that he must make a decision *now* to do one or the other.

It is hard to imagine anything that could be more difficult to do to an individual one loves, and it is very easy to understand the reluctance that most feel in considering taking such measures, as well as the forlorn hope that somehow, something is going to happen that will lift the necessity of doing it from them. Yet it is a desperate measure that is born of love and that is taken only because there is no alternative except to go on living in the same house with that individual and helplessly watching him destroy himself. There is tremendous fear in laying down such alternatives to someone who is not fully rational, and there is anguish in imagining what could happen to that person if one is forced to follow through. It is encouraging, then, to know that this has been proven to be the most successful method devised to get an alcoholic to help, that once he is backed up against the wall and made to realize that the game is up, he will himself see that the choice has been made for him. It is, of course, a gamble. There are people who do leave the house rather than go to treatment, but again, what is the alternative for the family? Moreover, one must never discount the strong likelihood that the alcoholic will recognize, and respond to, the love that lies behind what is being done. Certainly, the words "I love you" should be spoken and repeated during the confrontation. And if worse comes to worse, finding himself out on his own may bring the reality of his situation home to the alcoholic in a way that will never happen if he is allowed to remain where he is, with his alcoholism untreated.

Kenny

With that in mind, let us consider a factual case involving

a man of thirty-four whose mother came to a counseling agency seeking help. Her son, Kenny, was a chronic alcoholic. At one time, he had been married and had been a very successful salesman for a large car dealership. His wife also had a well-paid job, and they had no children. Kenny and his wife had enjoyed a comfortable, and even fast-lane, style of living for which they had plenty of cash and credit cards. The mortgage on their house in the suburbs presented no problem to them, and there seemed to be no obstacle to Kenny's continued rise in his company. He was intelligent and personable, and the customers liked him. Kenny spent a lot on his clothes and presented the kind of image that his boss liked, a blend of style and confidence that was an asset on the sales floor. He liked a good time and could be relied upon to entertain important people successfully; the maitre d's around town all knew him, and he was smooth at ordering the right food and wines on the credit card the company gave him.

By the time Mrs. Oakes was talking to a counselor about him, Kenny had a job on an assembly line in a small tool and dye plant and was punching a time clock. The wife, the house and the bank account were all long gone, and he was a nonpaying guest in her home. Mrs. Oakes had a long litany of complaints. Kenny was drunk more or less daily. He seemed to have no appreciation of what she was doing for him and made no effort to make her work load lighter. She went on in great detail about her arthritis and the fact that Kenny was often not around even to drive her to the market. He was careless about his clothes, and she was continually having to pick up after him, as well as doing his laundry. He did no household chores, and made excuses when she asked him to help out. On several occasions, she had paid bills for which he was being dunned, and he had made no effort to reimburse her and became irritable if reminded of it. Moreover, he was continually borrowing money from her which he seldom, if ever, repaid. She complained about his friends and about his language, and stated that as a result of being disturbed late at night by Kenny and his friends, her tenants upstairs had threatened to move.

Mrs. Oakes was a classic enabler. The counselor tried to point out to her that all of the things that she was doing so that Kenny wouldn't get "upset" were making it possible for him to go on drinking because she was making it unnecessary for him to take responsibility of any kind. Mrs. Oakes didn't like the word "alcoholic" and protested that her son certainly had a problem, but that he wasn't "that bad"; after all, he worked every day. She was not receptive to the idea of going to Al-Anon, and throughout the time the agency had the case, she could not be convinced that it would benefit both her and her son.

Efforts to persuade her to stage an intervention with Kenny were also unsuccessful. He did come several times to see the counselor, and it was clear that he was very unhappy with his situation and that there was some motivation to address his drinking. He even went to A.A. sporadically, but made no firm commitment to it and neither joined a group nor got a sponsor. He talked a good deal about what he recognized was his alcoholism, but preferred to dwell on what it had cost him and what it had reduced him to, rather than to give any serious thought to taking any concrete steps to free himself from it. On several occasions, he called the counselor late at night in a tearful and maudlin state, declaring he was "through with it," but this was never followed up by any concrete action, and it was clear that if the impasse was ever to be overcome, Mrs. Oakes was going to have to take some positive steps.

To this end, several of the counseling staff staged a sort of intervention on her. A concentrated effort was made to persuade her that to help both Kenny and herself, she was going to have to give him an ultimatum, and that the agency staff would be glad to provide her with back-up and both moral and legal support. It was suggested that she tell Kenny that he would either have to get help and overcome his alcoholism or live elsewhere. Treatment alternatives were spelled out for her. While she was thinking about it, it was also strongly suggested that she require him to contribute to the support of the household and do household chores for which he was better suited than she. In addition, she was advised to leave his clothes where he threw them and to stop doing his laundry. In short, to put any and every kind of pressure she could on him to try to break the pattern he was in. And the staff continued to urge her to take the only decisive step she could to get him into treatment. None of this worked. Mrs. Oakes continued to allow things to go on exactly as they had and used the agency only as a sounding-board for her continuous complaints, until it became necessary to tell her that unless she made a decision to follow the suggestions made to her, the staff could no longer afford the time simply to listen to her.

The staff had no leverage to use on Kenny because his mother refused to provide it, and about a year after the case was closed, Kenny died as a direct result of his untreated alcoholism. The sadness and sense of waste felt at the agency was coupled with frustration and anger when his mother complained to the director that the staff had done nothing constructive to help her with her son. The response to that was obvious, but it seemed pointless to make it.

The Employer

It is considered by many that the employer has the most decisive impact of all on an alcoholic. A great number of people working with alcoholics have noted that this often works where family pressure has failed, particularly in instances in which either the alcoholic is already living outside the home, or it would be difficult or impossible to force him to do so. Many interventions are staged with the employer present, and a large number are held in the workplace itself. Many companies now have Employee Assistance Programs which take on the responsibility of the intervention and may or may not involve family members. The Employee Assistance Person (EAP) has come to be a presence in a rapidly-increasing number of organizations which have recognized the wisdom of making an effort to save a valuable employee, and while there is certainly a significant element of altruism in this policy, with concern for both the alcoholic and his family, it has also been found to make a good deal of sound business sense. The company has put time and money into the employee, and they are reluctant to have to find and train a replacement who is an unknown quantity, when they know what kind of work the employee is capable of when he is well. That such a policy pays is evidenced by the fact that it has been adopted and expanded by such organizations as General Electric, Raytheon and AT&T.

Essentially, the intervention approach is the same. The alcoholic is made aware of the concern felt about him as a person, and not just as an employee; it is made clear that this is not an attack on him, and that what is being said is not a moral judgment. The reasons for the conclusion reached have been carefully documented and are spelled out in an organized way: "George, it can't be any surprise to you that we've been concerned about what's been happening for some time. Your work hasn't been getting done, and there have been mistakes that we know you wouldn't have made if you had been yourself. Over the past six months, you've taken nearly forty sick days, many of them on Mondays. There has been friction with your co-workers, and we've had a lot of people tell us they've smelled liquor on you in the morning. We've heard a lot, too, about your drinking at lunch and after work, and about your behavior, and just last Friday, you told your supervisor to go to hell and correct your report himself if he thought he could do as good a job as you do." And so on.

The employer has a very significant kind of leverage on the alcoholic. He can take from him not only his income, including his drinking money, but also an essential element of what remains of his self-esteem. Having to make the choice between getting treatment and getting fired will often achieve results, and with a minimum of protest or argument on the part of the alcoholic, that the family's pleas can not. The alcoholic knows that he can't say the things to the personnel director and the EAP that he can say to the family at home, and it is likely that his resistance will be considerably less when he finds himself in this either-or situation.

Intervention works. There are various scenarios that can be put into motion, using the same basic plan, and it is vital for those concerned about the alcoholic to decide to confront the situation head-on and make a concerted and well-thought-out effort to utilize the resources they have to bring him to the help he needs. Counseling and guidance are available. With recognition that the illness will only get worse if drastic measures are not taken, people who are in a position to take them can provide the initial impetus for the alcoholic to find the road to recovery.

9. The Treatment Process

Not until the twentieth century, and particularly in the past two decades, has hope begun to emerge that the centuries-long nightmare of the untreated alcoholic is ending. Only the plight of the insane, viewed historically, seems to match that of alcoholic men and women living alone in the lengthening shadows of a progressive illness. Like the insane, they were viewed with a mixture of contempt and repugnance, as well as providing a certain horrid fascination. Paradoxically, they have also been a rich source of humor. Just as Shakespeare's drunks provided comedy for the Elizabethans, so have the mad Brewsters convulsed countless audiences of *Arsenic and Old Lace.*

The victims of madness and alcoholism have also endured roughly parallel treatment through the ages. Both were shunned because both inspired fear and disgust. Both were hidden away by their families and treated as shameful secrets. Eventually, when their condition became such that they could no longer be controlled, or lived with in safety, both were put into confinement in asylums, and everyone tried to forget about them. This, of course, restored sobriety to the alcoholic, and being locked up was an intermittent thing for him, at least until such time as he suffered irreversible brain damage and had to be placed in custodial care because he was no longer competent to take care of himself. When that time came, he would join the "incurably" insane and spend the rest of his life in the asylum. Two alternatives might intervene to prevent them living out their days there. As still occurs frequently, an accident might end their lives. Alcoholics have falls, and they die in fires, and they die in automobile accidents. Or they might, while intoxicated, commit some act that would put them in prison, sometimes for the rest of their lives. Unquestionably, under the harsher laws of earlier times an alcoholic's crime might well be one that was punishable by death; even in relatively recent times, theft was dealt with by hanging.

There is, however, one very striking variable between the view taken of the alcoholic and the way in which the mentally ill were perceived. Almost without exception, the alcoholic was seen as someone who was inflicting his condition on himself, a moral degenerate who drank because he or she liked to and was indifferent both to responsibilities and to public opinion. Sympathy went to the family, and the alcoholic was universally viewed with opprobrium as an outcast. Even in ancient times, the madman was considered a victim; at no time was he seen as being insane because that was what he liked to be, and there was pity mingled with the instinct to pull away from him. Not so with the alcoholic. The Puritan Ethic is by no means limited to the American culture in this regard; alcoholism has always been the object of moral judgment and censure, and this remains overwhelmingly the attitude today, even of the alcoholic himself, who comes to treatment with a shattered self-esteem and a fear that he will never be "any good."

In past centuries, and even at the beginning of this one, anyone putting forth the suggestion that alcoholics were in fact sick people and needed help with their sickness was either laughed at or shouted down. Righteous indignation greeted suggestions that drunkards should be placed in humane environments where they would be treated as patients, rather than as the self-obsessed and spineless specimens they were popularly taken to be. The idea angered many, and they reacted strongly to the idea of spending good money coddling people who were "no good, and never will be." There was no conception of the terrible isolation and anguish of the alcoholic, nor of his own confusion at his powerlessness over the drug. Instead, people shook their heads over the lack of character that would keep him from ever pulling himself together. It needs to be stressed that this is often the view shared by alcoholics themselves. Their sense of hopelessness until very recent years can well be imagined, as can their despair when out-patient psychotherapy and in-patient treatment in mental hospitals were unsuccessful in relieving their addiction.

This last school of thought has attempted to treat alcoholism as the result of emotional stress or trauma, and a host of alcoholics have endured, often over a period of years if their financial resources were equal to it, a fruitless probing of their psyches to try to identify the experiences and feelings that have driven them to drink. That the real culprit is alcohol and their physiological reaction to it is either not known by the practitioner or is dismissed by him. Childhood traumas or unresolved conflicts do not cause alcoholism, any more than weakness of character does. Alcohol causes alcoholism. An approximate one out of ten drinkers will develop alcoholism because of the reaction of their body chemistry to the drug, and extensive statistical studies have unquestionably established a genetic/hereditary factor in the syndrome. There remains the elusive "X" factor which triggers it in millions of others in whom there is no known alcoholic forebear, and this category embraces an overpowering array of people of every description: they are "good" people and "bad," from every stratum of society, their lives otherwise blessed or cursed by fortune, and of every imaginable psychological make-up. Alcoholism hits as indiscriminately as did plague or tuberculosis in past eras, and it can be as readily identified by its very consistent symptoms. The great question today is: How does it start? What causes it? What sets off the physiological reaction, sometimes almost instantaneously and other times after years of nonaddictive drinking? To this, there is as yet no answer, but the issue is totally ignored (or unfamiliar to) those who treat alcoholism by putting the cart before the horse. No one who has observed the active illness could question the fact that the victim is experiencing profound psychological and emotional disturbance as a result of his or her drinking. The error lies in seeing the *result* of the drinking as the *cause* of it. Alcoholism makes people depressed, anxious, isolated, hostile and frequently suicidal. Yet the view taken by many who are attempting to treat it is that the patient is alcoholic *because* he or she is depressed, anxious, isolated and so forth, and they try to find in that individual's life history the causes of those emotions, acting on the premise that once those issues are identified and dealt with, the alcohol problem will disappear.

Yet another approach is to view alcoholism as a bad habit that can be conquered. Addiction is often not taken into account, and the objective of some of these behaviorists is actually to enable the alcoholic to control his drinking, not to stop it. Various techniques have been tried, and in some quite reputable institutions. One is to have a bar available to the patient who is "troubled" by alcohol (the word "addicted" is not used). There he or she is free to drink, as long as the drinking is not excessive or too rapid. Should that occur, the patient is given an electric shock to indicate that the boundaries of acceptable drinking are being exceeded, in the expectation that by thus duplicating experiments done on laboratory rats, the patient's "behavior" will be "modified." What is being dealt with, however, is drug addiction, not a rat who gets an electric shock instead of food when he responds to a signal. It is also a fact that after the alcoholic leaves this kind of treatment, he will not get electric shocks when he exceeds acceptable limits in bars or at home. What the behaviorists do not seem to be aware of is that one of the primary symptoms of alcohol addiction is that the alcoholic is unable to establish control over his consumption on a permanent basis. By the very basic definition of the term, an "alcoholic" who is capable of doing so was not an alcoholic to begin with. One might as well try, by behavior modification, to induce a diabetic to achieve control over what sugar will do if introduced into his system. The "results" an alcoholic can show while in a controlled and protected setting will be completely negated by what will happen to him if he continues to try controlled drinking when he returns to his everyday environment. Certainly the test of whether or not he is actually alcoholic will be made, for if he is, his drinking will very quickly be out of his control again once he is on his own.

The efforts of the psychotherapists and behaviorists are well-intentioned, and they usually feel that they have the wherewithal to solve their patient's problem, but they are stalemated by not recognizing the physiological basis of the illness they are dealing with, so that the sufferer does not receive a practical explanation of it, such as a physician gives when informing a patient of the nature of what he has. Instead, emotions are dealt with, many of them caused by the illness, and existing in an individual who is unable to deal with them effectively. The latter is true most emphatically in the case of the out-patient who is drinking between his appointments, as was the case with Sally, a chronic-phase alcoholic who had been seeing a psychiatrist for three years in an effort to bring her drinking under control. Acute physical complications of her disease finally brought her to hospitalization, and it was during this period that she discovered the true nature of her alcoholism from a recovered alcoholic who was on the hospital staff. Coupled with the realization that her drinking had given her cirrhosis, her continued investigation and subsequent A.A. involvement enabled Sally not to control her drinking, but to stop it, especially when she began to realize that her emotional problems were the result of her alcoholism and not the cause of it. Her attitude was completely reversed when she was able to see that alcoholism was her primary disease, rather than a symptom. She later encountered her therapist socially and was unable not to say to him, "Why didn't you *do* something? I nearly died. Why didn't you do something when I told you I'd had two gin-and-tonics before I was even dressed in the morning?'' The doctor's answer startled and dismayed her: "Sally, I just didn't know *what* to do."

Sally's experience has been echoed many times in A.A. meetings and in conversations between recovered alcoholics. What she did not encounter, but what has been a reality for many, is indifference or hostility within the medical profession and in hospitals. Despite the frequently-heard, "Oh, of course, I know it's a disease," there is still a very long way to go before that statement is backed up with fact and it ceases to be just "the thing to say." All too often, alcoholics run up against the old Puritan Ethic, rather than a sound understanding of the disease and a recognition that they are as much victims of an illness they did not knowingly bring upon themselves as is any other patient, that they are people to whom something calamitous has happened and who need care and understanding from the helping professions to which they have turned. There are still many occasions on which they are denied that recognition and are instead subjected to impatient, and even rude, attention, treated for their other complaints, and dismissed. While it is true that many medical professionals honestly do not know what to do when confronted with alcoholism, other than make a vague suggestion that the patient "ought to cut down" or "ought to see somebody about your drinking," the reaction can just as well be a very negative one which makes itself felt even though the issue is passed over in silence. What is disturbing is that medical people can look at a life-threatening illness (and even state that they believe it is an illness), one that could be affecting as many as twenty million people in the United States, presenting itself in an individual who is right in front of them, and say and do nothing about it. Indeed, that afflicted individual may instead get the "bum's rush" once his other needs are attended to, and the physician or nurse or emergency room staff will be relieved that he is gone. To be fair, note must be taken of the indisputable fact that what is all too often lacking is not simply understanding and compassion, but an efficient system of referral (aside from that of the drunk being taken to the state alcoholic ward by the police), and this is joined with an awareness of the alcoholic's resistance to accepting help for his alcoholism. It is certainly true that many people do not attempt to deal with alcoholism not just out of ignorance or indifference, but because they feel that they are helpless in the face of it and that whatever efforts they made would be futile. In many instances, this is sadly true, but the fact remains that the alcoholic tends very consistently to be lost in the everyday rush and to be met with rebuffs and attitudes which indicate that society's perception of him has not changed all that much. In his case, the Puritan Ethic is alive and strong, and the progress being made in bringing him to help does not even begin to meet the need.

Light at the End of the Tunnel

For there is a need. The gap presented by the inaccessibility of effective alcoholism treatment to the general public can be more accurately described as a yawning hole in the fabric of health care services in the United States today—and in most other countries as well. Yet there have been dramatic changes in the last twenty years, and although the changing trend in treatment is a new one, and its effects to date have been limited to a relatively small percentage of the alcoholic population, it is treatment that works as no other method ever has. The result, of course, is that facilities based on this model are beginning to proliferate across the country. It is quite evident to those working in the field that alcoholism, once the stepchild of the medical care industry and relegated for the most part to being an adjunct to psychiatric facilities, is coming into its own in that industry, and that would never have begun to happen if effective treatment methods were not available. It is true that just about all of these facilities are private and have involved a large capital outlay. For this reason, patients must either have insurance coverage or private means, for the average treatment is twenty-eight days, and the costs are high. Nonetheless, much of this newly emerging methodology is being adopted by the public sector, in programs funded by state and federal grants and in the Veterans Administration, with very discernible results. Many of these programs are out-patient and lack the intensity of the twenty-eight day in-patient treatment received in private facilities, but what is encouraging is that there are more of them, and that more people are getting what they need and are getting well.

Fifteen years ago, the prototype of "treatment" was the drying-out place where alcoholics did little more than get detoxification, a rest and a balanced diet for two weeks in an alcohol-free setting. Most left with very little practical understanding of their illness, or none at all, and the relapse rate was very high unless they were returning to a set of supportive factors that would give them high motivation to stay sober. Alcoholics Anonymous was available, and nothing has ever equaled its astounding success, but the number of people sober in A.A. is perhaps one out of thirty-five alcoholics in America today: half a million or more out of twenty million. The remaining alternatives were the psychiatric hospitals and the state facilities, many of which were revolving doors for the chronic and destitute. To look at the very bottom of the heap in 1970, the state of Rhode Island was ranked fiftieth in available treatment and facilities, and there was controversy as to whether it was second or third in per capita incidence of alcoholism (Nevada ranked first). There was no general hospital in the state, including the V.A. Hospital, that admitted with a primary diagnosis of alcoholism. The only treatment available was at the state's one psychiatric hospital or at the state facility. Alcoholism counseling was limited to undermanned and underfunded programs of the storefront variety sparsely scattered across the state, and most of the general public was unaware of their existence. There was one halfway house struggling for survival in Providence's worst slum. And that was it, except for the always valiant efforts of A.A. The state facility was a mockery, an ancient firetrap in which "patients" were locked up for a few days in appalling conditions before being dumped back onto the street, often with no resources and nowhere to go but back downtown. For those who could pay, but who did not want to go to a psychiatric hospital, the only alternative was to go out-of-state to a variety of establishments set up to receive them.

Today, there is a close network of alcoholism agencies in Rhode Island, and an Association of Alcoholism Counselors that has established criteria for counselor certification. The state hospital recently dedicated a new building to house its alcohol unit, and a number of general hospitals, including the V.A., have in-patient programs. Within the past five years, two private treatment facilities have opened, one of them with 160 beds. The Family Court has an alcoholism counseling unit, and there is an alcoholism course in the Brown University Medical School, as well as at the University of Rhode Island. These are enormous strides in a state community which only a short time ago was almost totally bereft of services for its large alcoholic population and in which many of those who were able to afford treatment felt impelled to seek it elsewhere. Rhode Island will still have to go a long way to catch up with the treatment networks of states such as California and Minnesota, but it has unquestionably responded to the new and heartening currents that are dramatically altering the prospects of recovery for the nation's alcoholics.

It has been a long struggle to bring the alcoholic out of the age-old darkness of bias and misinformation, and much of the credit is attributed to the late Dr. Jellinek, whose work in establishing a disease concept was the opening gun in what gives every promise of being a winning battle. The perception of alcoholism as an illness also received a great push forward in the 1940s from Marty Mann, one of the early female members of A.A. and founder of the National Council on

Alcoholism. She was involved as well with the very significant beginnings of the *Quarterly Journal of Studies on
Alcohol,* published by the Laboratory of Applied Physiology
at Yale University, which also became the home of a School
of Alcohol Studies (both of these operations have since
moved to Rutgers University). The influence of these pioneer
efforts to bring the physiological basis of alcohol addiction
into focus and to change the popular view of the alcoholic
has been profound. It is the cornerstone upon which the most
successful approach to treatment has been built, despite the
persistent miasma of scorn and distaste that still surrounds
the syndrome and its victims. It has stimulated what is today
a lively research effort, particularly in the hunt for the "X"
factor, the trigger that sets off the biological abnormalities
which are the start of the illness. The hope extended today
owes much to the courage of a handful of determined individuals who were willing to do battle against odds which
has been piling up since antiquity and which must often have
seemed an insuperable barrier to ever leading the victims of
alcoholism out into the light.

The foundation for beginning to successfully arrest a chronic
condition such as alcoholism is twofold. First, of all, the
patient must acquire a sound understanding of the nature of
his malady, stripped of all the myth and folklore that surrounds it and reduced to its simplest terms. Just as a physician needs to explain carefully to a patient just what his
diabetes or high blood pressure is all about in order to give
him a factual basis for following a prescribed regime and to
eliminate any misconceptions he may have, so an effective
treatment program must begin their patient's recovery process by spelling out for him exactly what he has, stressing to
him always that the condition can be arrested but never cured
("There is no such thing as an ex-alcoholic.") and that the
ultimate responsibility for his continued well-being rests in his
hands alone *("You are the only one who takes the top off
the bottle").* The analogy is often used of the diabetic who,

equipped with a practical comprehension of the malfunction in his chemistry, must take the responsibility for following the diet and insulin dosage prescribed in order to keep his disease under control.

The other purpose in stressing the disease concept to an alcoholic is to begin the process of removing from him the stigma and guilt he feels by bringing him to the realization that he has been in every sense of the word a victim of a subtle and insidious process over which he had no control and which he did nothing consciously to activate or extend. This is enormously significant in the very early phase of treatment in stimulating the response in the patient that comes with restored self-esteem. If he can allow himself to set down the burden of guilt that he is carrying, he will free himself to enter into the process of planning a healthy life for himself with an optimism that will steadily increase. Even the word from which he recoils—"alcoholic"—can be made to carry no more onus for him than the other medical "-ics": rheumatic, arthritic, diabetic, paraplegic, paralytic, etc. The relief of this discovery is indescribable for the shamed and frightened newcomer. It is the first of the tools with which a good treatment program will supply him in order to start rebuilding his life, and it gives him something solid to hold in his hand. It is a far cry from being told to "get a grip on yourself" or "clean up your act" at a time when he was powerless to do so and could only try, grimly and unsuccessfully, to exercise enough willpower to abstain, to limit his consumption or to switch from whiskey to light wine. It is a great improvement as well from vague suggestions that he pray, or talk to a clergyman, or, vaguest of all, "talk to somebody."

The disease concept is the foundation of the treatment that is finally coming into use today, and which has proven itself again and again to be the most effective ever devised on which to build a program of recovery. With this in mind, we can begin to follow one of these treatment models.

The Process Begins

Whether the patient is intoxicated upon admission or not, it is essential that he be placed in a medical setting for close observation until it is determined absolutely that he is no longer toxic and is physically well enough to be moved into the rehabilitation program. He must be carefully checked for any medical, orthopedic, or neurological condition that might require transfer to a general hospital and readmission at the facility when that condition has been addressed. Detoxification requires monitoring of blood pressure, heart rate and pulse, and bed rails are most advisable.

If it is clear that the patient is experiencing withdrawal, or is about to, it is essential to evaluate the severity of it, since this will vary greatly among patients. The rule of thumb in detoxification is that within seventy-two hours a patient will be through it, although it is often accomplished within twenty-four hours, depending on the progression of the patient's addiction and the quantity of alcohol he has been consuming over an extended period of time. Symptoms of shaking, agitation, sweating and insomnia can be alleviated by medication, Librium being the most frequent choice. Barbiturates are contraindicated, since they are addictive and belong to the same group as alcohol (CNS depressants). In very severe withdrawal, Valium and Dilantin are often used to ward off the danger of convulsions, and for extreme agitation, chloral hydrate or Dalmane may be prescribed for sleep, to be discontinued as soon as possible. Valium has also been found effective in relieving severe tremors, although again, it is a CNS depressant and use should not be prolonged. Delirium Tremens (DTs), which commonly caused death in the patient strapped down in the old-time asylum, can be anticipated and prevented by prudent medication in the management of withdrawal, as can panicky or hyperactive symptoms, or episodes in which a patient may become belligerent.

Finally, dehydration and nutritional deficiencies must be addressed. The typical patient has been eating poorly or not at all, and he should be started on a regime of B-complex vitamins as soon as he has been made comfortable. Reintroducing him to wholesome food and well-balanced meals at regular intervals is a vital part of restoring his physical well-being, and there should be a nourishment area where juices, fruit, and high-protein snacks are always available. The patient's appetite may return with a rush, and renewing their acquaintance with food may result in putting on twenty pounds in a month's time. He may also develop a craving for sugar to replace that in the alcohol. Alcoholics are very prone to sugar disorders and should be checked for both diabetes and hypoglycemia, for low blood sugar can bring on "alcoholic" complaints such as fatigue, irritability, insomnia and depression. Eating ice cream and cookies will relieve the symptoms, but the alcoholic is then subject to mood fluctuations and "sugar hangovers" which can make the urge to drink reassert itself. The importance of a low carbohydrate intake should be thoroughly explained to him as a lifetime proposition in order to avoid recurring hypoglycemic symptoms, as well as to maintain a figure that will add to his sense of well-being. The five hour glucose tolerance while in treatment is an excellent idea.

Rehabilitation Phase I

Entering the rehab unit is usually an unnerving experience for the newly sober patient. He is apprehensive about what will be done to him and expected of him, and even in two or three days on the medical unit, he has established empathetic bonds with fellow-sufferers from whom he may now be separated, if the facility follows the model of having a number of very self-contained rehab units. It is foresighted, therefore, to have orientation for him into the rehab process beforehand. Groups for this purpose can be held before transfer, and patients can be asked to come from rehab to talk to the new patients, answer questions and attempt to reassure them.

Once on the rehab unit, the patient is expected to participate fully in all activities. He will have individual meetings with his focal counselor, but he will also do assigned readings and written exercises, be involved twice a day in group therapy, attend lectures and films designed to teach him about his disease, go to exercise in the gym and to all meals, and be present at all A.A. meetings and introductory sessions held in the facility. He will be given his own copies of *Alcoholics Anonymous* (the A.A. "Bible," known usually as "the Big Book"), *Twelve Steps and Twelve Traditions,* which explains A.A.'s twelve steps to recovery, and *Twenty-four Hours a Day,* a small book with a meditation for each day based on A.A. philosophy. He will be expected to acquaint himself with the initial steps, possibly to do some writing on them as applied to himself, and to go over them with his counselor and discuss them with fellow-patients.

A.A. almost invariably is an integral part of a recovery program, and for one very strong and basic reason: nothing has ever matched A.A.'s success in reaching and helping alcoholics. It is stressed in the rehabilitation process because it will be an essential support to the patient after treatment, and because its teachings and philosophy strike a common chord among patients and help to make it possible for them to reach out to one another. The lecture program and the counselor and the readings and the recreational program all have their vital place in the patient's recovery, but the great strength of the program lies in what takes place between the patient and his peers. It is through one another, through sharing their mutual pain and their mutual hope, that they begin to lose their sense of isolation and uniqueness and come to accept their illness, for it is the common bond that has brought them all together to live in such a close and feelings-oriented environment. A.A. will be for them an extension of that sharing process when they leave, and thus a crucial factor in sustaining sobriety in the world outside. Within "the Program," they will continue to develop a sense of security born of the understanding and camaraderie that a shared experience with affliction brings. They will be able to be more candid and outspoken about themselves than is often possible in their daily routine, to vent feelings that they would otherwise keep to themselves, and to know that they are in a place where they will be heard and understood. Equally vital is A.A.'s role in "keeping the memory green." for while the alcoholic is able in sobriety to transcend the pain of the past, it will be fatal for him if he forgets that he experienced it, and what caused it. This is the great danger for him, and those who are guiding him in treatment know it. Pain fades, but the memory of pleasure remains. Time is the great healer. But this works against the alcoholic, for it is the nature of addiction that it overrules logic, common sense and past experience. We only have to be burned once, very early in life, to be very careful of fire and to avoid that pain automatically. It is a lesson that needs to be learned only once, and it lasts a lifetime. This is not so with addiction. The addict must have the nature of his condition consistently reinforced, reminded that it is chronic and will never leave him. He must never allow the memory of the suffering it caused him to recede, soften and fade away. However lengthy his sobriety, however fulfilling his life becomes, he must be constantly aware of the siren song of his addiction, and this A.A. will do for him. On his own, he will be on risky ground, as summed up in the A.A. saying, "The farther away you are from your last drink, the closer you are to your next one." It is a program of constant vigilance, necessary for survival, and no one knows this better than the rehab personnel. They have watched patients return who did nothing about their aftercare programs and who either never went to A.A. at all, or dropped out of it after a while. Some staff have had the same experience themselves, or have watched it happen to others in A.A. It is knowledge based on personal experience and usually accrued over a long period of time, and they will keep repeating it to their patients: "Stay with A.A., and stay with the winners." Above all, the patient must never feel so well, so far away from the pain and dysfunction of his active alcoholism, that he forgets how much it hurt him and begins to think, "I bet I could handle it now. I wonder what would happen if I just had one . . ." And he must never again let himself become isolated emotionally, with his feelings stuffed down deep inside him, to the point where his need for relief from them becomes unendurable and he reaches for alcohol's quick release. No therapeutic regime has ever equaled A.A.'s ability to maintain equilibrium and perspective in alcoholics. It is a magic that must be experienced to be fully appreciated and understood.

Patients usually arrive to begin their rehabilitation very well-defended. They have had to be, to protect their drinking. To protect themselves, and because of the increasing depression and anxiety they have been experiencing, many have become withdrawn and isolated, preoccupied with feelings of resentment and self-pity. One and all, they are frightened; that is the great common denominator. First of all, they are threatened by the loss of their "friend," and they cannot imagine coping without it. Following close behind is their remorse and shame over things they now remember all too clearly having said and done, mixed with anxiety over what is awaiting them as a result, once treatment is over. Treatment itself, an unknown quantity, scares them: What is it all about? What is going to be done to them? Are they going to be accepted here if people find out who they really are? Are they going to be held up to scorn or ridicule?

The impulse for many, when they are newly sober and realize fully what they have let themselves in for, is flight. Many do leave during their first days in the facility, often from the medical unit, and the urge to run may be strong during the early days on rehab. At this point, it is very important that the treatment process be explained to him and that he be reassured that his fears are groundless. He must be able to believe that the program's only purpose is to teach him about what has happened to him, so that he can stop blaming himself, and to help him to feel good again. If the counselor is also alcoholic, telling something about himself with which the patient can identify is helpful in allaying feelings of being alone and abandoned. The other patients, remembering clearly how they felt, will extend themselves as well to bring the newcomer into the group and lessen his anxiety.

Somewhat reassured, but still wary, the new patient will begin to learn about his disease. He will attend lectures and be given reading material that will cover not only the very consistent physiological aspects of it, but the emotional and behavioral ones as well. The latter will often startle him, and give him an eerie feeling that someone has been observing, and writing about, *him.* Casual conversation on the unit after the treatment day is over will continue this process of identification and help him to realize that he is not unique, that what he has felt and his reactions to those feelings have followed a pattern that those around him have also experienced. At this juncture, he will probably be for the most part a listener, for he is aware that he is in a treatment place for *alcoholics,* and there may be a painful internal struggle going on in applying the word to himself. His defenses leap to the rescue, and he begins to compare.

"It may be true for this one or that one, but not for *me.* I've never done this or that. I haven't sunk that low." The alibi system of rationalization which he used to explain his drinking to himself and to others comes into play, and he will invent excuses for himself: job pressure, his wife's nagging and lack of understanding, frustration with his situation in general, all the old, soothing bromides that he has used to soothe himself and to transfer the blame to people, places and things. He may even dismiss what he is being taught about the disease concept and tune out the lectures and readings. He may himself be a subscriber to the Puritan Ethic and have firmly in mind all of the old attitudes about alcoholics, stereotyping them and listing all of the factors in his life that lift him far above skid row. *He* is certainly not an undesirable.

And yet, his past actions will keep coming back to haunt him, and he will continue however unwillingly, to identify with things he is hearing. While it is certainly true that the alcoholic may be the last one to accept alcoholism as a disease, it is rare indeed that this realization does not come in twenty-eight days of intensive treatment. His guilt may be so enormous and so powerful that he will refuse for a time to set it down, but the overwhelming evidence being presented to him, didactically and in getting to know his peers on a sharing level, is just that: overwhelming. With growing familiarity, the term "alcoholic" loses its old horror, and he becomes comfortable with it. Whether it is his alibi system or his guilt that is hindering his acceptance of what he has, it is seldom that the realization does not come and that the patient does get a sense of relief that could come from no other source. Moreover, by relegating his old fears and uncertainties to their proper place, and by recognizing that his enemy is an identifiable medical syndrome, he can begin to recover his sense of self and to plan his strategy for keeping his condition in remission.

The Group Experience

More than any other, one aspect of treatment may be more threatening and more difficult, or impossible, to tune out than any other. This is group therapy, in which the patients will be divided into small groups to discuss their reactions to treatment and the emotions they are presently experiencing. In its best form, it is a free-flowing discussion which confines itself to the Here and Now, and a counselor will be present only to act as a facilitator, not to lead the group. It is a workshop in which the patients process what they are feeling and give one another feedback, and it is an invaluable device for breaking down the defenses that present the greatest barrier to recovery.

The alcoholic will tend to cling stubbornly to what is familiar and to resist change. Change to him is unsettling and often, in early sobriety, causes an unreasoning anxiety. Moreover, he may have done a pretty good job of rationalizing his drinking to himself, even if those around him have long since seen it for what it is, and he has become adept at side-stepping issues that hit too close to home. If he continues in this self-delusion, he will certainly drink again, and Group is designed to make him see what he is doing and to acknowledge the true state of affairs. Obviously, this can be a painful, and therefore angry, process if the other patients don't let him off the hook about why he is presently in a treatment center for alcoholism. Certainly, being confronted will provide him with food for thought after the meeting, when he is back in his room.

Eliminating his denial is often the first of a number of changes the alcoholic needs to make if he is to deal successfully with his illness. Once he has begun to accept the illness he sees around him in himself, he will recognize the need to begin coping with the world with a new set of tools. He learns that he has not been handling feelings and situations with an elixir that made it easier for him, but with a depressant that made him anxious and distorted his view of reality. He learns, too, that it made his first impulse in any difficult situation that of running away, and that his way of handling things had been to stick his head in the sand via alcohol. His defenses when forced to deal with reality may be so ingrained that he may not realize they are there. One may be defensive anger, and when it is his response to probing in the Group situation, it may be called to his attention that he is using it. Others may be self-justification, or wandering from the point to distract others from a line of questions or comment that is getting uncomfortable for him. He has to learn that the alcoholic haze he has been trying to function in is not reality, and that reality is not going to go away, but must be faced and dealt with.

This includes reality about himself and who he really is. Only when he has restored his lost identity will he be able to come to grips with the world around him, and stripping away layers of self-delusion can be an agonizing process. Yet, if he cannot learn to accept and deal with reality, his return to drink-

ing is almost certain. To protect himself from this catastrophe,
he must identify the realities and the feelings which threaten
him with relapse and learn new coping methods in order to
deal with them.

Many alcoholics have had their emotional growth stunted
by long-term drinking, and they can be made to see their im-
maturity and the fact that they need to begin growing as adult
individuals able to take responsibility for themselves, rather
than living in a never-never land of drug-induced illusion. It
becomes time, as many have said, to put away the toys and
start using the tools. Group, whether in a structured setting
or as an informal meeting in someone's room at night (known
as the minigroup) can be the catalyst that forces an individual
to take a long, hard look at himself and to recognize the triggers that could propel him back into active alcoholism. Many
things will emerge that he has built up a wall to conceal: anger,
frustration, loneliness, a sense of inadequacy or failure, old
hurts carefully kept alive, sexual problems, long-standing guilt
and remorse, fear, low self-esteem . . . the list of the things
people try to keep out of sight can be endless. The alcoholic
needs to identify and deal with these emotions in himself to
keep himself sober, and he must come to grips with the realities
of his life situation, seeing realistically what he can or can't
do about them. To help him, there is the Serenity Prayer that
alcoholics have made their own and this is very likely to be
repeated after meetings:

> God, grant me the serenity
> To accept the things I cannot change,
> Courage to change the things I can,
> And wisdom to know the difference.

We have seen that the first order of business for the alcoholic
patient entering the rehabilitation unit is to gain a clear
understanding of the nature of the illness that has overtaken
him. Grasping and accepting the disease concept will put the

horse back in front of the cart for him. He will begin to see that alcoholism is his primary disease, and that it has caused the emotional problems from which he has been suffering. It is a great relief to realize that he has not become an alcoholic because he is emotionally unbalanced, and many will speak of the growing fear while they were drinking that they might be losing their sanity. This is a very real fear in a great many alcoholics, and, of course, drives many of them further into destructive drinking, because they now instinctively use alcohol to run from things that frighten them.

This seems a good point at which to bring up an issue that causes confusion and apprehension in some alcoholics, and in their families as well, when they are admitted. In today's culture, a very large percentage of the patients in any facility have been using, in addition to alcohol, a variety of other substances. This is particularly true of adolescents and of those in their twenties and thirties, and it is, quite simply, the nature of our culture today. One can deplore it, but it is a fact of life. Many alcoholics would be denied treatment if admission standards dictated that only those who are involved *solely* with alcohol are to be allowed in, and this would be a great injustice, as well as denying a present-day reality. There just aren't that many alcoholics anymore who have limited themselves strictly to alcohol.

A Mixing of Friends

A large percentage of those in treatment today have been relying on at least one other substance to induce a sense of well-being and to keep from having to look at the world as it really is. They are all mind-altering substances, just as alcohol is. Whether they were sedating themselves with alcohol and Valium and barbiturates, or getting high on cocaine and marijuana, or taking fantasy trips with LSD, changing how they felt had gotten to a point where it was pulling their lives apart and causing them unendurable emotional pain. That pain is their great common denominator. It makes no difference what paths they took to reach the point where they have all met. The feelings are the same.

Each has had his friend, or friends, on which he depended to keep him feeling good, which was later modified to feeling all right. Finally, he was reaching desperately for it, or them, just to try to feel "normal" and be able to cope with his everyday life. Each has finally had his world cave in on him. Each has experienced the same anguish. The catalysts that got them into treatment repeat themselves again and again. They have all felt they were going to lose things that were precious to them: spouse, children, job or just simply themselves. Or a combination. There may have been an intervention, or there may have been an increasing sense of dread, or a confrontation at home or in the personnel office, or a moment of truth one day in which that person said to himself, "I can't take this anymore." There is not much variety. And the sameness of the pain and of the problems presented in treatment has led to the emergence of the term "addictive disease" to encompass the common suffering of all.

It is not, strictly speaking, accurate. Only those whose problem has been with CNS depressants and/or narcotics are physically addicted and thus addicts in the purist's sense of the word. Only they have undergone physiological addiction. Almost every patient, however, *is* physically addicted to alcohol. What he has in addition is the complication of a massive dependency on something else, as well. Marijuana seems to be almost as ubiquitous as alcohol, and today's surge in cocaine use is amounting to an epidemic, while narcotic use appears to be significantly declining and the street drugs to be more and more the province of the young and the poor. In all classes, however, snorting coke and smoking pot are common practices, and quite logically, this is reflected in patients coming into treatment. The "pure" alcoholic who is not involved with any other drug is increasingly rare and tends to be older, forty and above. Again, this is a reflection of our times, and a sad one, but it must be dealt with.

The reason that the poly-drug user tends to arouse alarm and distaste in the pure alcoholic is a parallel to the source of the same reaction toward the alcoholic by the nonaddicted person. Just as "alcoholic" calls up the stereotype of the skid row derelict, so "drug addict" brings forth the mugger and the degenerate. Violent criminality is popularly attached to him, and this frightens the newly arrived alcoholic patient and summons up all that is judgmental and punishing in him. The alcoholic makes the polyaddicted alcoholic the victim of the same kind of stereotyping and moral preconceptions that have for centuries condemned him. While no reasonable person can argue with the idea that the proliferation of other drugs has been a major factor in our skyrocketing crime rate, it is simply not true that every poly-drug user has had a criminal career. Many have been purchasers, and nothing more. Others, in order to obtain cocaine and pot themselves, have gotten involved with selling it, but this has been the extent of their illegal activity, and they have often been terrified of the suppliers they have been obliged to negotiate with. The memory of what their drug-dealing involved is often a powerful element in their motivation to stay drug-free.

Still, the fact remains that the histories of the pure and of the polyaddicted alcoholic will vary widely. Many of the latter group have been led by their sickness down paths that the former have never known, and there are experiences that they cannot share back and forth. As treatment progresses, however, the differences become far outweighed by the commonality of the pain that they have all felt, and are feeling, and the variations in their stories matter less and less. They come to feel that they are, basically, all being treated for the same thing, and the gulf between them narrows and disappears. Treatment for all is the same, and this reinforces the concept that all share a common affliction. And they do; it is enough for our purposes here to use only the term "alcoholic."

Admitting vs. Accepting

It would be difficult for anyone who finds himself in a facility for the treatment of alcoholism not to admit that he has a problem with alcohol, even if it is his view that he has been coerced into being there because significant people in his life perceive his drinking as such. Although he feels that they are blowing it up out of all proportion, it is still clear that they do not view his drinking as they view their own or that of other people. Therefore, there is unquestionably a problem.

The majority of people coming into treatment are aware that there is something wrong with their drinking. Many will state that they believe they have alcoholism, even though they are filled with misconceptions as to what that means. As the teaching part of their treatment moves along, and they identify with that, as well as what they are hearing from their peers, they will learn that alcoholism is a primary, readily identifiable, medical illness. Those who were sure to begin with that they had it, will have it confirmed. Others, who were not sure, will be brought to see that they do. Finally, even those who are loud and angry in their denials, insisting that they have been railroaded, will be obliged to acknowledge (even if only to themselves, at first) that at least part of what they are hearing applies to them. It is usually the case that by the end of their stay, the rest of the pieces have fallen into place. Denial would have to be very strong indeed to resist the combined influences of clinical evidence being presented in teaching materials (lectures, films and readings) and the shared experiences of those around them.

The disease concept makes it a great deal easier to accept the hitherto unpalatable truth: "It has happened to *me*. I have alcoholism. I am an alcoholic." The patient might never have reached even this point if he had only been going to A.A. meetings, with all of his instinctive defenses working hard to keep him from relating to the people around him. Or if he had been seeing a therapist privately once a week and then returning to his usual surroundings. It would have been easy for him to keep those defenses, the denial and the untruths and rationalizations that he has come to believe himself, intact. Doing so when his alcohol has been taken from him, so that his mind clears, and he is in a protected environment, surrounded by people who are in the early stages of struggling with the same affliction, is quite another story. Unless there is something very wrong with his reasoning and deductive powers, he will have to become honest with himself, and for many, this is a very painful process. He will be greatly helped in it, however, simply by the fact that he is feeling so much better physically under his present regime. Even if his secondary withdrawal continues to cause him some insomnia, aggravated by anxiety, he will still exclaim over his returning sense of well-being and be pleased at comments from his visitors about how much better he looks. Even the most hardened case of denial will know that this is because he is chemically-free, even if he qualifies it by adding that he is also free of business pressures and stress at home. The realization will still be there that he is not having hangovers and blackouts and that he gets up in the morning healthier, and with a clearer head, than he has for a long time.

For some patients, the admission for having alcoholism will come very easily, particularly when they come to see it as an illness which they have developed through no fault of their own. Even though they are gravely troubled by the memory of things they have done while drug-affected, they are beginning to shift the burden of guilt from themselves to the alcohol, and the Puritan Ethic that has made them hate themselves is starting to loosen its grip. So, too, is the relentless physical addiction and/or psychological dependency that drove them. They may occasionally feel the urge for a drink or a line of cocaine, but they are vastly encouraged that it is no longer the irresistible force that had turned their lives upside-down. The relief in that realization is enormous. They are aware as well of their physical recovery, and that it is due to the absence of alcohol (and/or its friends), as is the return of their reason and the ability to put things in a clear and logical perspective. The protected and benevolent environment helps by giving them a place of retreat where they can put other issues in abeyance and focus on gaining insight into the illness that has brought them there, absorbing what is being presented to them, sharing their experiences with others, and asking others for help they need to restore balance in their lives.

As we have said, it takes some longer than others to involve themselves in this process, but all of the tools are there for them to work with, if they are willing, finally to become honest with themselves. Their peers will put considerable pressure on them to do so, in most cases, and this can be very effective. Coupled with a growing sense of identification with those same peers, closed minds begin to open, and these "hard cases" will also discover the relief that comes with seeing what the syndrome is, admitting that they have it, and realizing that they can be free of it forever if they truly want to be.

The step that will achieve this for them is acceptance, and by this is meant the decision that comes to do something about it and to begin to plan out how they are going to live their lives around it. The analogy with the diabetic patient is useful in spelling out to the alcoholic what acceptance involves. The diabetic, too, may react with dismay to the diagnosis the doctor gives him. Unlike the alcoholic, however, admitting that the condition is present in him will present fewer difficulties. He doesn't attempt to argue with the laboratory results, which are very concrete, and of course he *has* had the symptoms. They are what brought him to the doctor's office in the first place, just as the alcoholic has come to the treatment facility.

Unlike the alcoholic, the diabetic is not addicted to a mind-altering substance. However, he and the alcoholic each have a life-threatening illness, and each is going to have to both admit that fact and accept it. Both are going to have to abstain from a substance or suffer and die as a result. The diabetic is going to have to follow a rigorous diet and may have to begin taking insulin. He has a clear choice in the matter. It is up to him to accept the fact of his illness and to follow the doctor's instructions. If he does so, he will arrest his disease and will be able to live a normal and productive life. He has to learn to go around sugar, because it is always going to be there; *but not for him*. People are going to sit at the same table with him and eat desserts. He is going to pass by ice cream parlors and candy stores. He is going to push his cart past the cookie shelves in supermarkets, and he's going to see pastry ads on television. It's going to be tough, and he is always going to have to keep in the front of his mind that he is diabetic. If he does accept his disease, he will persevere, even when he craves sugar, and as time goes by, he will become more and more accepting of his disease, and more comfortable with it. It will become simply a fact of life, along with his diet and his insulin. This is acceptance, and it will get easier with time.

It can be argued that this is a whole lot easier for the diabetic. He can use sugar substitutes, for one thing, and there certainly are not alcohol substitutes. He doesn't have an emotional involvement with it. He's not going to feel conspicuous by refusing dessert, or be pressured to have it, so it's not a big thing for him socially. All true, but a matter of degree. There are going to be many times when he is very sorely tempted. Ask any diabetic if that is any picnic and if he doesn't often feel sorry for himself, and deprived, and ask, "Why me?" Ask him, too, if he enjoys his rigid adherence to his diet and his dialy injections. For him, it is a very big thing indeed, and a matter of daily acceptance. Every day.

So must it be for the alcoholic. If he introduces his drug into his body chemistry again, he will reactivate all of those millions of addicted cells, and the compulsive drinking will start. The addiction is there, always. Even if it has been thirty years since he has had a drink, putting alcohol back into his system will trigger the process anew, and with a very horrifying discovery: his active addiction does not return at the point where he left off, thirty years before. Instead, it has been progressing despite his abstinence, and he will find, upon reactivating it, that it will hit him with far greater force than he anticipated, far greater than he remembers, because it *is* far greater. It is as though the genie he had succeeded in getting back into the bottle had continued to grow during its imprisonment, so that when he once again removed the top, it rushed out at him many times its remembered size. The relapsed alcoholic will find himself overwhelmed by a demon that has grown far more ferocious during the time of abstinence.

Like the diabetic, the alcoholic must take care of himself on a daily basis, never allowing himself to forget what he has. He can never forget that his disease is only arrested, not cured. Just as there is no such thing as an ex-diabetic, so there is no one who becomes an ex-alcoholic. Acceptance of that fact involves a different kind of regime for the alcoholic, based on the fact that he has an addictive syndrome with an emotional factor in it that will keep telling him that relief from feelings that trouble him is always available. He does not have to follow a strict diet or take medication, but he must be aware of what those emotions are that could trigger him into relapse.

To keep the reality of his illness always before him, A.A. offers him a built-in support group and reminder. Identifying with others in the group as they talk of feelings, past and present, will keep that reality alive and well for him. The pain is gone, but he must never forget that it was once there, and he shares as well the gratitude for having been spared from alcohol's final catastrophe as he talks about his life today. Part of his acceptance is his realization that he needs this reminder and this understanding from his peers. That is the alcoholic's insulin. He knows that he must never be alone with his disease, just as he knows that he must cope with feelings and situations without having recourse again to alcohol. The alcoholic does not pick up a drink again after experiencing sobriety because he is looking for a good time. He has long since put that aspect of drinking behind him and knows that the fun times are long gone, never to return. It has gone far deeper than that. What drives him back to his drug is an over-powering need for relief that he has not learned to achieve by other means.

This may be relief from loneliness, boredom, frustration, anger, insecurity, a poor self-image, anxiety or a host of other emotions, all part of the human condition of the alcoholic, however, is that, like a Pavlov's dog, he has acquired an automatic response to certain stimuli — in his case, to equate surcease with drinking. Another factor in his acceptance is that from now on, he must have different coping skills, because that door is forever closed to him. Again like the diabetic, he must live with alcohol constantly around him; ours is a drinking society. And he must learn to walk around it, because it is never going to be otherwise, even if he bans it from his own house. It will always be there for others, and they can have it (most of them) in perfect safety, but it is not for him. He will need help in distinguishing what these "triggers" are that could impel him to pick up another drink, and help in learning what he can do instead to deal with them. Old habits and reactions are going to have to be put aside, and this is no easy task.

In accepting his disease, he is also accepting the need to explore himself and to discover what changes are going to have to be made to insure his equilibrium and sustain his sobriety. He can never afford the luxury of complacency, of assuming that he has his illness licked for keeps and that he need not be constantly aware of what is going on within him emotionally. The physical craving will subside and fade away, but his feelings will always be a potential threat to him, and he must always be aware of the danger that one impulsive, unguarded moment could present to him. It is stress that could make him return to drinking, and therefore he must do all that he can to continually keep himself well emotionally. It is a tall order, for some taller than others, and it begins for the alcoholic in the treatment process, when his sobriety is very new.

Who Am I, Really?

Once the presence of his disease has been admitted, and
finally accepted, it may appear to the patient that there isn't
much else left to do as far as remaining permanently sober.
After all, his head is clear now, and he's a mature adult. He
knows that if he were told by a physician that he was diabetic
that *of course* he would do exactly as he was told. It would
be stupid not to. "And I know," he will say, "that if I start
to drink again, it will kill me, just as eating sugar would kill
the diabetic. And I'm not crazy." What he is, at this point,
is feeling relieved that his new knowledge and understanding
have shown him what he has and taken the guilt away. And
he's feeling optimistic; now it all looks so cut-and-dried, as
if there were nothing further to discuss. He's feeling better
than he has for years; he has the camaraderie of his new
friends; the treatment staff has been approving of the gains
he's made in trying to understand his illness and in working
to accept it. Perhaps for the first time in years, too, he's feeling good about himself, and this will be added to im-
measurably if he has been getting support and respect from
the people who mean the most to him. Being away from the
everyday, workday world will have contributed a lot to his
sense of well-being; he has been free of the daily stresses that
can be so draining, and he's been eating a healthy diet and
getting regular exercise. The fear that he can't control himself,
or that he may actually be losing his mind, has been lifted
from him. All these factors have combined to make him feel
that he can handle anything that comes along. Of course, he
can, just as other people do, but the problem of which the
staff will be aware is that of complacency as far as his
alcoholism is concerned. They know only too well that one
of the pitfalls awaiting the recovering alcoholic is the
underestimating of his addiction as his sobriety lengthens and
the pieces of his life fall back into place. They know that he
will have to be constantly in touch with the reality of having
it, and that it is an infinitely subtle and powerful adversary,

that it will lie in wait the rest of his life for that one unguarded moment when he feels that now he can "just have a little one" of for the crisis in which he throws caution to the winds and turns again to the drug that will give him the relief—or oblivion—that he feels he cannot live without. Alcohol's patience is endless. It can wait forever.

The recovering alcoholic needs to know that he has not gotten bigger and tougher than his opponent. On the contrary, he is a human being, with all the feelings and frailties common to his species. In his treatment for the illness, he has acquired insight into it that he never had before, and he has learned that he has been a victim of it, along with millions of others. He is certainly not unique. Nor is he unique in his relationship with alcohol now that he is sober. Unappetizing as it is, he must digest the fact that one of the hallmarks of what he has is relapse, perhaps not in the immediate future, but someday.

This is usually the last thing he wants to hear, particularly now, when he is feeling so terrific after all he's been through and everyone has been so encouraging about his prospects for living a full and contented life. Yet this is just the point at which he needs to hear it. This is when he is most sharply aware of how good he feels and how bad he felt, of all the things he has lost, or could have lost, of the pain he caused the people who love him, of the pain he caused himself, of all the things he wants, and of how promising life looks to him in sobriety. It is a very delicate moment in that human being's recovery and growth up and out of pain, and as such, it must be used to put the strongest case possible to him for taking every means to make sure that he never loses the gift he has given himself.

What every patient in treatment must do is to learn as much as he can about himself, so that he can accurately assess what his particular relationship with the drug has been. In stressing to the patients the commonality of the cause and effects of their illness, the staff has never lost sight of the fact that they are dealing with individuals, and that each of those people is uniquely himself. As if it were a TB ward, the rehab unit holds an assortment of people from a variety of socio-economic strata who have all come there because they share a common disease. In some, it has progressed further than in others, but all are equally threatened if the course of it is not checked. All must learn the nature of that threat and how to take care of themselves. The difference with the alcoholic, of course, is that his disease cannot be cured. He must continue to take care of himself for the rest of his life, and he must be convinced of the need to do this. The key lies in learning about who he really is and what it is that alcohol has been doing for him.

To answer this question "Who am I?" the patient may have to peel away layers of defenses that he has made for himself and possibly come to believe wholeheatedly. To rationalize and excuse his drinking to himself, he will have constructed a system of blame that can run the gamut from what was done to him in his childhood to being singled out by God as someone who is never to be given a break. He will be tireless in putting forth reasons why he drank, and he will very often be awash with self-pity, seeing himself as the misunderstood and unappreciated victim of people and situations and trying to explain away his own shortcomings. These are areas that he must begin to explore and to face honestly, for they are elements of himself that fed into his disease and kept it going, although they didn't cause it. He must be told that repeatedly. The blame for his alcoholism lies in his physical being, in that "X" factor that gave rise to the addictive-allergic reaction that he has to alcohol, but the danger of relapse lies in whatever there is in his emotional make-up that could trigger it, and he must become aware of what that is, so that he can learn to cope with it by some means other than sedating himself with alcohol (or using any other of his mind-altering friends). Each patient is an individual and has his own set of troubling feelings. They are all common human emotions, such as anger, jealousy, loneliness or loss, and they are emotions that everyone has had to deal with. They are part of the human condition, and this must also be reiterated to the patient. It is just that in this case, one or some of them provided the fuel thrown on the fire of his alcoholism, and his conditioned response to them has become that of reaching for a drink. Over the years of his drinking, he sought less and less to find some other way of dealing with them, and finally, he stopped trying.

It is while he is in the protected atmosphere of the treatment facility that these aspects of himself have to be identified and addressed. Some of them he may find very unattractive and be unwilling to own up to, especially if they break up the image and facade that he has carefully built for himself and tried to foist on others. Efforts to crack this shell can become quite strenuous and may provide a set-back for his new-found sense of good health and confidence, but they must be pursued. For they are the emotions that could tip him over unless he learns to deal with them in an adult and rational manner. Some patients present few difficulties in this phase of recovery and are very willing to acknowledge that this or that has been a problem for them and that it needs to be looked at and talked about. Some are eager to do so, finding for the first time an atmosphere in which they can do so honestly and without shame or anxiety. It becomes for them a part of the process of shedding guilt and of being purged of feelings that have long troubled them. They recognize that alcohol had tricked them and that they had been caught on a merry-go-round of drinking to rid themselves of emotions that drinking was intensifying. "I didn't know," they will say, "that what I was taking to make it go away was making it worse." For all, depression and anxiety were primary symptoms of their alcoholism, and in many cases, this was the cause of the "Jekyll and Hyde" mood swings with which those who have lived with an alcoholic are for the most part very familiar. This is the swift change from a pleasant and agreeable frame of mind to a sudden and often violent outburst of anger, very frequently over a trivial and unintentional cause. In retrospect, the alcoholic himself may feel bewildered at his own reaction, and those who got the brunt of it will be angry, fearful and hurt. "Being around him when he was drinking," they will often relate, "you felt like you were walking on eggs. You just never knew when some little thing was going to set him off." The alcoholic deals with painful emotions by drinking, unaware that it is alcohol itself that is either causing them in the first place, or else distorting and magnifying them. In either case, as his addiction deepens, other options for handling them occur to him less and less, and it finally leaves him not knowing what else to do but drink.

Abstinence and treatment have now freed him from that physical compulsion and given him time to take stock of the situation in which his illness has left him. He is beginning to see that his flaws and failings have not caused his alcoholism, but that they are the factors in his psychological make-up that could cause a relapse by triggering the impulse to drink in order to escape from situations that upset him and emotions that he doesn't want to deal with. It may be pointed out to him, for example, that his short temper or resentments or impatience or tendency to alibi himself have repeatedly tripped him up and caused him unhappiness, and that rather than deal with the root cause or causes of that discomfort, he has sought relief in the bottle. He must see that changes, not just in behavior but in attitude, are going to have to come if he is going to be comfortable enough with himself not to feel the impulse to drink.

It must be stressed constantly to the patient that he is not going to succeed in remaining sober through an application of willpower or moral strength and determination. That would be very much like making up his mind to stay on the Scarsdale Diet for the rest of his life (and feeling certain that he could do it through a sheer effort of will). What will keep him well is having his life so greatly changed for the better that he won't *want* to pick up a drink again, and this he will achieve only by consistently doing what he can to be as much at peace with himself as possible. Change is all-important. Old attitudes and patterns that are now recognized as having brought tension and discord into his relationship with himself and others are going to have to be weeded out and discarded. At the same time, he is going to have to see that no one is asking perfection of him, and that no one wants to turn him into a plaster saint. What is being suggested to him is that he work on recognizing the emotions and impulses in himself that have brought on thinking and behavior that have interfered with the quality of his life, for it is by improving that quality that he will lessen his chances of returning to alcohol. Certainly, this is pretty much a lifetime proposition, and it must be coupled with an ever-present awareness that he has alcoholism and that the best protection he can give himself is to be as secure and content as it is possible for him to be. It is a radical change from the old alcoholic thought processes and behavior, and one about which he is going to have to think a great deal, not just theoretically while in the protected environment of treatment, but practically, in the world to which he returns. Alcoholics tend to be rather good at theorizing, and to get enthusiastic about it, much as a child enjoys building castles in the air. Where they tend to fall down, all too often, is in the practical application of their plans and ideas. Procrastination is a very common trait among them, and the tendency to duck things that require consistent effort or that they just don't want to do seems to be a spin-off of the ducking or reality that they were doing while they were drinking. Alcoholism teaches its victims to be afraid. It also teaches them to cut and run when they are faced with things that they would prefer to avoid, or not do. Unhappily, this frequently carries over into their recovery, and they may start to slide away from the bright plans and goals they set for themselves in treatment. Overconfident, they may not follow up on the counseling and/or the support group (usually A.A.) that they felt so positive about when they were talking with their counselors, or they may go for a while and then drop out: "I'm tired at the end of the day. I need my rest, and I've got a million other things to do. I'm not all that worried about drinking again; I've got the picture, and there's no way I want to feel like that again." And so on.

An alcoholic who is alone with his disease is on dangerous ground. Without a steady reminder, the memories of pain will fade. Without a well-thought-out aftercare plan that meets his individual needs, old habits and thought patterns will come back, buttressed by his complacent certainty that his demon will never again look to him like an old friend, and one that he has missed a lot. He must be made to see, while still in treatment, the urgent necessity of staying in close touch with others who have been through the same fire and who are walking the same road with him now. He must have a workable plan for changes that he wants to make in himself and in his relationships with others. He must continue to be aware of who he really is, to share that awareness with others, and to strive to make himself as comfortable with himself and with the world around him as he can. The aftercare that he sets up should be a concrete and simple game plan, a blueprint for sustaining the well-being he felt the day he left treatment. Marked on it should be the emotional pitfalls that threaten him with feeling like having a drink again. Beside them, there should be notes to himself on the decisions he made about how he's going to handle them.

The effectiveness of an aftercare plan will depend, of course, on the individual's commitment to sobriety—the intensity of his desire to stay well and his willingness to do what he feels is necessary for *him*. The degree of that intensity and willingness will determine how successful he is, for it is easy enough to sit with one's counselor at the end of treatment and say all the right things, to comply with what is expected and paint a rosy picture that will earn everyone's approval, including one's own. The final proof of how well treatment has worked for any alcoholic is whether he or she stays sober. That alone will indicate how well the disease has been understood and accepted, how much insight into the self has been gained, and how willing that man or woman has been to try new approaches to living in the world as it is and to follow through on them. Again, a question of acquiring the serenity to accept what cannot be changed, the courage to change the things one can, and the wisdom to know the difference.

Tom Revisited

Let us pick up with our alcoholic, Tom, at the point where he is getting ready to go home, and review his treatment. When we left him, he had just lost his job. His marital, family and social life had become dysfunctional, and he was still unaware that he was in the chronic phase of alcohol addiction. Devastated, he was standing alone in the hall of his office building, trying to digest the fact that he had not only lost his and his family's livelihood, but a career that he had followed since college and his status as an executive. Instinctively, he did what an active alcoholic does do; he went downstairs to Charlie's and got drunk.

Very late that night, he woke Sue and told her. Then he got into bed and slid into the oblivion he had known his drug would give him. When he woke, Sue had already been on the telephone to his boss, and Tom, shaky and with his head pounding, was astounded and dismayed to learn that his boss would be at the house that afternoon. Characteristically, he blew up. Sue, however, stood solidly in the eye of the storm and delivered an ultimatum: either Tom would listen to what she and his boss had to say, or she would take steps to have him leave the house. Tom, terrified, angry and dazed, did listen, and he ended by accepting a twenty-eight day treatment program as a condition of reinstatement in his company. The arrangements had already been made. He was unable to see the concern and effort on his behalf, only that they had ganged up on him, pushed him against the wall, and that his protests were useless and his choice was clear. Furious, he sat and defiantly drank while Sue packed his bag, and he pushed her away when his boss left them to put the suitcase in the car and wait for him. The two-hour drive was a silent one. Neither man could think of much to say.

Tom spent three days on the medical unit, trembling badly for the first thirty-six hours. He was resentful, frightened and deeply shamed by all that had taken place. He contemplated leaving, but knew that if he did, his marriage and his job were finished. Resisting all efforts to get him to respond to friendly overtures, he stayed, emerging from his room only when he had to. He tuned out the informal orientation talks and hated the patients who asked questions. Locked away in his misery, he shunned everyone while his racing mind went over and over the events that had brought him there.

His first week of rehabilitation was not a happy one. He answered his counselor's questions briefly and remained silent in Group unless he was asked a direct question. To, "How are you feeling today, Tom?" he answered gruffly, "Fine." "What do you mean by 'fine,' Tom?" "I mean I'm O.K. What are you trying to get me to say?" "I'm trying to get an honest answer out of you. That isn't one." Only when his counselor called him in and told him, calmly but plainly, that if he continued to resist the efforts being made to help him start to put his life back together he would be considered for discharge, did Tom start to look realistically at where he was. He knew what discharge would mean, what his position would be if he found himself out on the street, and the possibility of being alone suddenly changed his outlook. He was aware of his jeopardy. Now his rational mind began to look at what had caused it.

He started to listen to the lectures and to read the literature, and in doing so, became aware of the commonality he shared with those around him. The terrible loneliness and sense of isolation and uniqueness began to leave him, and he welcomed the companionship he found on the unit. It was suddenly good not to feel alone anymore, and he realized how alone he had felt for a long time. He began to see and appreciate the concern and empathy his alcoholic counselor was offering him, the kindness of the rest of the staff. A loving letter from Sue brought sudden tears, and he found himself talking with his roommate about the guilt and self-condemnation that swamped him. Bit by bit, the alcoholic defenses broke down. He found relief in talking to people about feelings he had kept bottled up for years, slowly and cautiously at first, and then with growing confidence because he was heard and understood as he felt he had never been before. These men, though he had known them such a brief time, were friends on a level he had never experienced. He could play cards with them, and he could also tell them about the growing, horrible fear he had felt at the office, about his flare-ups at home and the remorse that followed, about the feelings of impending doom that had haunted him and the desperation with which he had wanted alcohol.

Most important of all, he was learning about his enemy. As he heard the echoes of his story in the stories of the other patients, and as he heard his symptoms described in lectures, saw his life reflected in films, the realization came with increasing clarity that the villain in each and every one of those stories was not the alcoholic, but the alcohol. The alcoholic was only the helpless vessel that held the illness, becoming more powerless as his life slipped further and further out of his control and his dependency for relief from his fears grew on the drug that was causing them.

Tom worked hard to accept his alcoholism as a fact of life, learning all he could about it and often talking with his peers until far into the night. With them, he shared the feelings that he felt could threaten him with relapse, going over the steps he felt he could take to prevent being overpowered by them. Realizing that he was depending on these men for support and understanding that he felt he could get from no other source, he saw that he would be foolhardy to ever try to go it alone and that he would find an extension of that closeness in A.A. He felt deeply about the problems they were facing and found gratification in trying to help by offering to others the empathy that had been shown to him, aware of a bonding that affected him deeply—the unique caring of one alcoholic for another, linked together by their mutual experience of pain and hope.

He found strength as well in the visits of his family, sensing their joy in seeing him as they had hoped he would someday be, and in a visit from his boss and the personnel director, who took a Sunday afternoon to come and see him. Apprehensive about how he would be viewed when he returned to work, he was touched and encouraged by cards from people at the office. His life was coming together again. People distanced by his disease were coming back, as insecurity and loneliness receded.

He listened carefully, as his discharge date approached, to the cautioning words of his counselor, who warned him that his freedom was new and fragile, and that he would always have to keep in mind that it could be lost again, that relapse was one of the hallmarks of alcoholism and that no one was immune. With him, Tom carefully worked out his aftercare plan, accepting a referral to an individual counselor as a backup and reviewing the strengths and weaknesses he had found in himself, aware that he was embarking on a lifetime project. Sobriety is never a fixed, immovable possession, guaranteed maintenance-free for a lifetime. As we shall see, it is the sole responsibility of its possessor; just as he alone held the key to let himself out of his prison, only he can once again unlock the door to let himself back in.

10. Aftercare: The Re-entry Process

As the end of his treatment experience approaches, the newly recovering alcoholic may be surprised to realize that he has undergone a certain reversal of feeling. After struggling against the idea of going to a facility to come to grips with his drinking, he may very well find that he is not at all eager to go back to the world that he left with such reluctance. In fact, the prospect may fill him with anxiety, or even panic, often mixed with guilt at "feeling this way" about going home and rejoining his family.

The treatment staff is very familiar with this reaction, and understanding of it. The patient has become very used to his surroundings, and is aware that it is a protected environment. All the usual stresses of day-to-day living have been lifted from him for a four-week period, and he is suddenly very much aware that he is returning to all that goes with his job, his home and the complexities of moving about in today's society. He is going to have to deal with a variety of people with whom he interacts on different levels: spouse, children, boss, co-workers, friends, acquaintances, relatives and incidental contacts. He is going to have to take responsibility again, as well, also on a variety of levels. He will be required to make decisions about his personal and social life, decisions on his job, decisions over a spectrum of areas that will affect others as well as himself. In short, he is going to have to function as a responsible adult in the various roles that we all have, and the reality of this rapidly approaching and unavoidable moment is accompanied by the knowledge that he is expected to do so on his own resources, without the familiar backup of his old "friend."

What he is really seeing is that he is going to have to put into practice all that he has been talking about in recent weeks, and this is coupled with the realization that it has been a long time since he has faced his life situation, whatever it may be, in the clear, cold light of reality. He may feel that he has *not* been functioning as an adult, and be panicky at the thought of attempting to do so. The self-confidence that he has been working to regain may very abruptly slip away from him, and everyday activities may suddenly loom as towering obstacles that make him doubt his ability to deal with them. After twenty-eight days in a totally different atmosphere, far removed from his old existence and surrounded by caring and supportive people, it is his previous life which begins to look alien, and the challenges it presents to his new sobriety may well make it appear unfriendly or even hostile.

Fortunately, at this juncture his feelings are shared by others who are also facing re-entry, and an important part of the new knowledge he has gained is that talking about his emotions makes them more manageable. There is comfort and reassurance for him, as there has been throughout his therapy, in knowing that he is not unique in what he is feeling and that he is not facing things alone. It is to be hoped that the alcoholic, by the time he is preparing himself to return to his real, everday world, will have become aware of his old habit of internalizing whatever is troubling him, and that he will be training himself to react differently and to seek out an understanding ear. He must see that bottling up his insecurity or resentment or hurt and dealing with it alone — the famous "my way" — has fed into his physiological addiction and kept him drinking. By the same token, to revert to that old pattern of keeping things to himself and mulling them over and over will not only be unproductive, as in the past, but may well lead him eventually to obey his conditioned response and return to drinking.

This is a very real threat to the newly sober man or woman, and it has been hammered home by staff and fellow-patients throughout his time in the center, not just as a vital component of his treatment, but as an essential change that must be followed through on after discharge. It is emphasized to the patient that there are two outlets available which are often preferable to the possible awkwardness involved in this sort of self-disclosure to family or friends. These are individual counseling and a support group, usually A.A., and the point is stressed that A.A. can provide an extension of the kind of understanding and support that the treatment process has afforded him or her.

Reassuring as this may be, there are still, of course, issues to be faced that vary widely from patient to patient and that are uniquely his or hers. No one aftercare plan can be applied in a blanket fashion to each individual, and the patient needs to sit down with a list of the areas in his life that need attention, identify them specifically and write out precisely what it is that needs to be done and how this will be approached. Such a detailed plan will serve as a checklist later to remind the patient of what were perceived as crucial areas at the point of re-entry and can be invaluable in putting that person back on track when the rush and complexities of living have momentarily swept them to one side. It will be emphasized that it is very easy to lose sight of goals that were previously set and to slip away from good habits, such as regular A.A. attendance or a consistent counseling schedule, when the pressures of one's daily routine tempt one to use the old tried-and-true rationale of "deserving" that time off to relax. A strong element of self-discipline and purpose, widely at variance with the disorder of their lives before achieving sobriety, is one of the major changes in the lives of newly recovering people that will spell the difference between being able to sustain their new well-being and sliding back into active addiction. A plan that is there for them to use, set forth simply and covering only the basics, can be used not only to refer back to, but also to keep their resolve strong by reminding them that this was what they saw they needed to do at the crucial time of going home. Without it, it is all too easy for old patterns of thinking and behavior to reassert themselves.

Setting Priorities

Among the first considerations in making plans and setting goals in recovery is that of deciding what one's involvement is going to be with a support group (Alcoholics Anonymous, Narcotics Anonymous or possibly both) and how the matter of individual counseling is going to be approached. Going to Al-Anon as well may be called for if there is going to be an alcoholic spouse or relative to deal with, and this is not at all unusual.

Closely tied to a realization of the need to be in contact with others who have gone through the same fire is the new awareness that one has of oneself and of what one's relationship is going to be with that newly emerging individual. This, of course, is tied closely to a variety of resolutions about what kind of relationships are going to be established and maintained with others, and this will encompass both intimate, family ties and those with friends, co-workers and people who are met on a business or casual basis. This leads quite naturally to a consideration of making a commitment to oneself as far as the job is concerned, among other obligations that may well have been neglected while the alcoholism was active. For some, there will be as well a return to some kind of religious affiliation or observance, and this can make a great difference in sobriety, not only is assuaging guilt feelings, but often in filling a void that their disease created in their lives and of which they are suddenly and acutely aware. Finally, there are the odds and ends, the items that have been put off and have nagged at the back of the mind. Paramount in finding peace within is the necessity of establishing order in one's life, of having things in place and under control, as opposed to the chaos of the drinking alcoholic's existence. When it is decided, with a clear mind, what courses of action will foster a sustained sense of well-being and order, the newly sober man or woman needs only to keep those resolves in the form of a definite plan and to make sure that a checking process exists as a buffer against goals being lost in the pressures of daily living.

All These New People
One of the intimidating things about coming onto a rehabilitation unit is, quite naturally, the fact that everyone there is a total stranger. The usual response of the new patient is to withdraw protectively, either by keeping a distance physically or by putting on, and keeping on, the masks that he has felt were successful in keeping his inner self from public view while having others see him as he wants to be seen. This may be the Macho Man, the Jokester, the Supernice Guy or the Injured Victim, to cite some of the most often used. All are worn to conceal what is really underneath, and some are worn interchangeably. What they are intended to hide will very commonly be fear, anger, guilt, a low self-concept, shame and remorse, emotions that are too painful to bring out and which have been dealt with in solitude by a wheel-spinning process which has left the patient exhausted and exactly where he started.

An integral part of his early recovery is the realization that he shares this burden with most of those about him, and this gives him the permission he has needed to begin to acknowledge and talk about it. This, incidentally, is one of the reasons that treatment is a fairly lengthy process, that people are optimally removed from the stress and confusion of their everyday lives, and that no one has ever attempted to achieve results by correspondence. The dynamics that take place in a secluded and protected setting produce a commonality and a bonding that remove the sense of uniqueness and isolation characteristic of the alcoholic and enable him to rid himself of emotions that up until then have given him no peace.

Quite simply, he starts to talk about them and thus to start to find solutions for them, with the help of others. These "new" people very quickly become friends and confidantes on a level that is totally new to most patients, and one very strong reason for the panic that may be felt as discharge approaches is the imminent separation from people who have become so close to him and who will not be there for him when he returns to the world he left.

Wrong. There exists for him a very strong extension of what he has found in treatment. It will always be there for him in Alcoholics (and/or Narcotics) Anonymous. The difference is that he will have to seek it out; it will not come ready-made for him, as it did in the treatment center. But the components will be the same. All of the people he hasn't met yet, whether they have been well for a month or for twenty years, will have exactly the same things to offer him; empathy, understanding, patience, a willingness both to share and to listen.

Now, however, it will be his responsibility to form and sustain those relationships, to take the initiative rather than having it thrust upon him, and it is to be hoped that he will have acquired enough of that responsibility to do so. What it will involve for him is using the A.A. booklet that lists meetings in his area — time, place, type of meeting — to begin the process of shopping around for groups in which he feels comfortable and at home. It will have been told him that meetings vary as to membership and ambiance (naturally — they are made up of people who feel at ease with one another) and that deciding which groups he wants to be involved with should be a selective process. Thus, he is cautioned not to go to a meeting simply because it is close to where he lives, but to make the effort to visit different groups.

He will also need to decide how many times a week he feels he should go. It is suggested that initially he go fairly often, so that he can acclimate himself as quickly as possible to being an A.A. member and a *former* patient. In instances where it is felt that the patient needs a good deal of support in readjusting to living without the escape hatch offered to him by his drug or drugs, he will undoubtedly be urged to go very frequently, or perhaps even to use the concept of 90 Meetings in 90 Days to assure maximum "immersion" during the first three months. The latter is not customaril advised upon leaving treatment unless the risk of relapse is seen as very high. For one thing, it may have the opposite effect from the one intended and sour the new member on the program. For another, it is felt that while a fairly intensive exposure is desirable initially to accustom the newcomer to meetings and to enable him to select which meetings are for him, it is best for him to have a balance in his life and not to feel coerced into going to meetings, to the exclusion of spending time with family and friends or of being involved with leisure activities that he enjoys. After all, the purpose of freeing himself from alcohol was to be able to live a normal life and to function well as a family member and as a member of society. For most people, this clearly does not mean spending seven evenings a week at A.A. meetings, and while an individual who is newly sober may feel a strong need for that contact and support, it is expected that as he becomes used to living without alcohol and more confident of his ability to do so, he will begin to tailor his attendance at meetings to his own particular needs and to the needs of those close to him. It should be pointed out candidly that while spouses suffered greatly during the active phase of the illness, they can become resentful of a recovery program that in their eyes deprives them nearly as much of their partner as the alcohol did. Moderation and balance in all areas of his life should be the eventual goal of the recovering person, and he should be aiming at participation in a variety of spheres and wary of becoming involved in his support program to the extent that family, friends and other interests are excluded. Ideally, that program should be a means to an end, the end being sobriety and reintegration into the mainstream as a productive and well-rounded person.

Nonetheless, frequent attendance at meetings upon leaving

treatment, and for as long thereafter as the individual feels is called for, is certainly strongly urged. Otherwise, the patient stands at great risk of losing the threads of communication with similarly oriented people that he acquired in treatment and of finding himself once again on his own, without the empathy that meant so much to him in the center. As in the center, he will at first feel very much the newcomer, but although he is not living twenty-four hours a day with the people in A.A., he will quickly rediscover what he felt he was losing when he was discharged. It will take him a little longer, but it is up to him to take the initiative and to respond to the welcome he will receive. Unlike treatment, no one is going to pressure him to participate, and what he gets out of the program will be in direct proportion to how much he is willing to enter in and be a part of it. Basically, it is a sharing and mutually supportive effort, much as his treatment was. In it, he will find new friends and associations, new people in his life, and through them, a continuation of the process that first began to make him well.

An important part of the A.A. experience is being a member of a group, and this should be done at an early date. Once the shopping period is ended and the newcomer has selected the meetings that he will attend regularly, he should consolidate this association by joining the group to which he feels closest. This entails nothing more than saying that he would like to be a member and signing the book. There are no membership qualifications, and no vote is taken or dues required. There is great truth in the A.A. adage that it has been the most expensive club in the world to get into, but that no one has ever been blackballed. Membership in a group will give the newcomer a sense of belonging that will be augmented by taking responsibilities. They are small ones, but they separate him from the transient participants: making the coffee, setting up before the meeting, greeting new people, running small errands for the group, doing a stint as treasurer, attending the monthly "business" meeting after everyone else has left to discuss any suggested changes in procedure or issues such as whether regular or decaffeinated coffee should be served. Small things, but the feeling of being a part of something is there, and important.

Finally, it is strongly advised that he have a "sponsor." The term is misleading, since no one is sponsored for A.A. membership, but it is clearly here to stay. A sponsor functions as a sort of big brother/sister, and selecting this person is an important decision, for this will be a closer relationship than the new member has with the rest of the group and one in which there is a high level of trust and sharing. A sponsor is in many respects a mentor, keeping a watchful eye on his charge to see that the direction he is taking is in his best interests and that he is not falling into any of the pitfalls of which his experience has made him more acutely aware. The sponsor is frequently the recipient of confidences that are not shared with others and is thus able to advise with more perception and understanding. Obviously, the choice of a sponsor should not be made lightly, but rather after careful observation and evaluation, and it should fall on someone with solid and fairly long-term sobriety and sound experience in staying sober. Many newcomers feel that it is an urgent matter to get a sponsor immediately, rather as if there were a time limit on making a selection, and this is not the case. What is important is that the right choice be made, and this can be allowed to take as long as is required, although it should not be put off indefinitely. The sponsor can be invaluable as both friend and guide in the often confusing and intimidating business of staying sober.

This latter finds its focus, for the majority of A.A. members, in the Twelve Steps of recovery that the program suggests. In fact, they *are* the program. Deceptively simple to the casual reader, they constitute in practice a subtle and involved introspection into one's relationship with the self and with the world that surrounds that being. In his efforts to explore himself, the recovering alcoholic is seeking answers that will insure his sobriety; it is as simple and as complex as that. Presented with simple home truths, he feels a need to apply them to himself, and to do that, he feels he must first acquire a better and more honest understanding of who he is and why he feels and reacts the way he does. Once this becomes clearer to him, he is able to find the perspective he needs on his relationship to the people and events around him, and this is necessary for him to achieve the balance and sense of proportion that he is convinced are necessary for him to survive as a sober alcoholic. This is an activity in which most feel they will be involved for the rest of their lives, and it is both a painful and exhilarating process. Self-delusion about who he really is will be stripped away layer by layer, and he will be obliged to confront all of his weak points; at the same time, he will experience the joy of freedom from the necessity to maintain that elaborate charade which his sickness fed on and perpetuated. The Steps of A.A. become an increasingly absorbing project for those who are engaged in practicing them, and they make an immeasurable contribution to the goal of living rationally and in harmony with all aspects of the life that has been given them.

How Do I Deal With Me?

This is certainly the logical starting point for someone confronted with returning to, and facing, the "real" world. First and foremost, it is to be hoped that his treatment has brought home to him the necessity of being *honest* with himself. This is an enormous change for a man or woman who has run from reality by refusing to accept responsibility for his or her actions (regardless of the fact that those actions were drug-induced) and has fallen into the subtle trap of rationalization, always finding a means to place the blame on "people, places and things," and managing to cap the performance with a wallow in self-pity that they believed was entirely justified. It was frustrating and infuriating behavior for those who witnessed and attempted to cope with it. For the alcoholic who has only recently come to see it and to understand that it is a classic manifestation of the active illness, the need to call a spade a spade and to accept responsibility for actions that were entirely his or her own becomes abundantly clear.

The same honesty can apply to motives. Why am I *really* doing or saying this? What are my actions and statements *really* all about? The same comfortable blanket of self-delusion has probably hidden these for years, as well, and the alcoholic has felt the discomfort of the subconscious knowledge that he or she is a sham without knowing the source of that uneasiness and self-contempt. Getting honest is a growing-up process, and one that most alcoholics find difficult and painful. Yet it is essential for them if they are to rise above the need for their drug and to start feeling good about themselves. Dishonesty has been one of the root causes of the low self-esteem that is so much a part of their illness, but it is an old, familiar pattern as well, one that has always afforded them an out when it was buttressed sufficiently by alcohol. The one always blended very smoothly with the other, and as has been noted earlier, alcoholics, like small children, are unreceptive to change. Clearly, ''Be honest with myself'' needs to be incorporated into their aftercare plan, and this will be made far easier by having the understanding and support of others who have reached the same conclusion and are making the same effort.

An area in which the alcoholic has a freer rein and in which he can utilize both his imagination and his gift for self-indulgence is summed up in the advice he will be given to ''Be good to yourself.'' Obviously, the better he feels, the less likely he will be to feel drawn back to alcohol, and how good his life looks to him is going to depend in large part on how good he makes it. Being good to oneself covers a wide spectrum. The alcoholic can counter the effects of a bad day by giving himself something to look forward to. Earlier, of course, that was a drink. Now it can be planning to go out to dinner, or to do something with a friend, or to buy something that will please his wife or children. One alcoholic smoothes the day's edges by going out and buying something that she wants but doesn't really need. Another will plan to spend some quiet time in a favorite spot, like taking a walk alone on the beach. For this man, solitude is not a lonely thing; it is necessary for him to restore calm and relax; and it is his choice, not a condition forced on him by his disease.

Basically, these people have learned to compensate by giving themselves small pleasures instead of rushing to a sedative drug that will anesthetize them. With practice, it can be refined into a skill that will never fail them and that will very successfully replace the substance that they once saw as the only solution to feeling bad. Alcoholics who learn to be good to themselves also become adept at removing themselves, if at all possible, from people and situations that make them uncomfortable, and this is an acquired skill indeed. It is also a very necessary one for an individual who is determined to maintain his balance and to feel as good as he can about his life and about the world around him. With sobriety, he will realize that it is not always going to be possible for him to put distance between him and people or situations that go against his grain. This is a step toward the maturity that his disease has blocked him from achieving in the past, and he will recognize and speak of it. At the same time, he sees that he has options, up to a certain point, about what he can or cannot do and about what the things are in his life that he must endure. The little serenity prayer stands him in good stead by providing the solution to many situations in which he must accept what he cannot change, have courage enough to change what he can, and enough wisdom to know which is which. Recognizing that he is clearheaded enough to do this kind of reasoning makes him aware of the progress he is making and of the change that has taken place in the way he conducts his life, and this provides him with great validation and encouragement, which in turn he is glad to share with others who are gauging their own progress.

He learns to deal with himself through his reason, drawing on his past experience and on the new understanding he has of what the various elements are in his own nature that make him tick. The focus is by no means always on his flaws and foibles. He also allows himself to give himself credit where credit is due. This wasn't always possible when he was drinking, and probably for some time in his early sobriety, because of the crushing load of guilt and self-condemnation he was carrying. As he regains respect for himself and for his own integrity, the necessity of seeing and utilizing his strengths becomes clear to him, and in balancing the various facets of his nature, he becomes more sure of what is the right direction for him to pursue.

Being good to oneself will often involve self-discipline and doing things that one would rather not. Going to the dentist regularly is a case in point. Few people look forward to it, but in the long run, it is a benefit to them. On another level, visiting someone in the hospital or a nursing home is not high on most people's list of leisure activities, but the reward is in knowing that one has done a kindness and that feelings of guilt later on are thus avoided. These are mature thought processes, and most alcoholics have to learn them, often through trial and error. What puts the lessons solidly in place is that he feels *good* about himself, and this can only be the result of having *been* good to himself. That this is often just as much a process of doing things that he doesn't want to do as it is one of giving himself little pleasures and luxuries is new knowledge for most alcoholics. It is closely tied, as well, to the growing awareness of the order that he is establishing in his life, both materially and emotionally, and with the resulting absence of the guilt that had for so long been his constant companion. The sense of wholeness as a person, difficult to describe, is one of the great rewards of his lengthening sobriety.

Now Where Do I Stand With Others?

One of the most difficult things facing a patient who is in
the re-entry process is the thought of returning to a world that
saw him in his drinking period. With most, visits from family
and caring friends have mitigated much of the anxiety they
felt about whether they would be able to restore relationships
damaged by his alcoholism. The guilt is by no means completely dissipated, but the alcoholic is allowing himself to hope
that he will be able to build back the respect and trust that,
he feels strongly, was removed through his actions. He is wary,
unsure about the extent of the damage and afraid that others
may be masking their real feelings about him. This is a tormenting state of mind, and it is often difficult or impossible
to reassure an alcoholic that time and conscious effort will
in all likelihood succeed in putting important relationships
back together. In typical alcoholic fashion, his imagination
will run away with him, and a great deal of time will be spent
silently brooding and going over and over episodes that fill
him with shame and remorse.

Candor, not polite minimizing, is called for here. Reassur-
ances of the "Don't worry about it" variety are useless and
will often, and with justification, irritate the patient. He can't
help but "worry about it" as painful recollections persist, and
they may bring with them a panic that he will not be able to
withstand the urge to drink if his worst fears are realized and
he does in fact find that the harm done cannot be undone.
That damage must not be waved aside or any attempt made
to paint a rosy picture of amnesia on the part of significant
others in his life. On the contrary, an essential component of
his continued sobriety will be for him *never* to allow those
memories to recede and fade away as time passes. The fear
of having them happen again is a very healthy one, and it need
not be in any way a hindering or crippling one. Time will
remove the pain that he is presently feeling, just as the pain
of a child's first burn subsides eventually. What is important
is that an alcoholic remembers what *caused* the pain, as the

child learns to stay clear of fire. However, there is a difference. Most children do not need to repeat the lesson of what getting burned is—how it happens and what the hurt is like. One such experience last people the rest of their lives, and if it happens again, it is by accident. It would certainly save a great deal of grief and heartache if the same thing were true of alcoholism, but that is not the nature of addiction, and a newly recovering alcoholic has to have the fact register that in this respect, time, the great healer, works against him. As the memory of his unhappiness is softened and blurred by time, the addiction that will never leave him will begin to reassert itself and remind him of the good times that it gave him, of the solace and comfort it provided, of its magical ability to soothe. Without the memory of the hideous price he paid and of the bondage in which he found himself, the day will almost certainly come when stress, or a combination of stresses, will make him dare to drink again. Thus, he must keep that memory green (one of the things that conscientious A.A. attendance will do for him). It is helpful if he can see that relapse, regardless of whatever length of sobriety he achieves, will be a threat for the rest of his life, that he has a genie, imprisoned in a bottle, that will wait forever for him to remove the top. It is enormously helpful if the patient can be made to see that the acuteness of what he is presently feeling will diminish and leave him, and that it is required only that he place his fear of alcohol in with the other healthy fears that he has—the ones that make him look before he steps off the curb, use his rearview mirror, and not put his hand into cages in the zoo. These are instinctive fears that keep him safe and enable him to survive; so, too, should a conditioned response to the idea of a drink protect him, and this will be impossible without a clear image of pain remembered.

However, he must accept the fact that this pain is going to be remembered by others as well, and that time is needed to heal their hurt, too. It would be a great disservice to let him go home expecting anything else. Nonetheless, encouragement can and should be given that with consistent effort and patience on his part, relationships can be repaired and restored to full functioning. He must understand that it is no longer what he *says* that will accomplish this, but what he *does*, and that there will almost certainly be times when he feels discouraged, frustrated and resentful because he sees that people are still uncertain and fearful despite his best efforts. This is where a sponsor is useful for ventilating those emotions and where an A.A. group can provide empathetic support. They will understand as no one else can and they will give comfort by sharing their own, similar experience. Above all, they will impress upon him the great need to develop an ability to put himself in the other person's shoes. Without that talent, he will find himself again as thwarted and bewildered as when his drinking had forced him into an interior world in which he dealt only with the jumble of his own emotions and could not make real contact with those around him.

The re-establishment of communications on a rational and realistic basis should be one of the first goals in recovery, but it is not achieved without first gaining a sound perspective on oneself and a willingness to try to understand what another human being is experiencing. Patience has never been the strong suit of an alcoholic. The compulsive nature of his illness is reflected in the obsession he will frequently have to see immediate results: "I want what I want when I want it." A corollary to this has been put into words by A.A.s who have had the benefit of long-term sobriety: "I'll get what I need when I get it," and this reflects a far more accurate and realistic appraisal of what the fruits of sobriety will be in an imperfect world. To seek perfection is a lofty goal, but A.A.s have found it wiser and more down-to-earth to strive instead for progress. Few relationships ever attain perfection, and our newly sober alcoholic will find it far more comfortable and rewarding to focus simply on making his better. This is an attainable goal, and one that he can pursue with a reasonable expectation of success if he is willing to give it time.

While all of this may, it is hoped, give the patient some comfort, as well as food for thought, it does not seem to apply itself to the thorny and disturbing area of how the world outside his home is going to view him. He feels embarrassment at the thought of facing people at work again, or friends outside of the close circle that has come on visiting days. He is afraid of whispers behind his back and of pressure that he feels certain will be put on him to drink. He sees himself as conspicuous in social gatherings because he is the one drinking a Coke, and is fearful that this will single him out, that "they'll know about me." All this, of course, reflects the fact that his sense of self-worth has not yet been restored. It is understandable and should be expected. It is also very hard to dispel while the patient is still in the treatment facility. However, some suggestions can be made. He can be advised to stay away from his old drinking places and companions. If he feels that he will be rejected because he no longer drinks, it can be pointed out to him that in that case, that was all that there was to that "friendship" and that it is not much of a loss. He can also be reminded that it is his choice to go and drink with his old cronies any time he wants to, and this will usually startle him and elicit the response, "But, I *don't* want to," and he will have answered his own question. In making his plans, it is important for him to know that no one has taken his "friend" from him, that no one *can*, except himself. It is available to him any time he wants it. In short, the choice and the responsibility are his, and his alone.

Armed with what may be a very new realization that it is entirely up to him to decide whether or not he will reactivate his alcoholism, he may also be receptive to the idea that the only thing that really matters is what *he* knows. It is not up to him to give a crash course on his disease in order to justify not drinking. He does not really need to explain himself. His urge to do so is the manifestation of how important his not drinking is to *him* (and how conspicuous), and he needs to realize that it doesn't have much meaning for most others;

the plain fact is that while he is very important to himself, he is not really all that important to them. As long as they have what they want, it is largely a matter of indifference to them what is in his glass. He is probably not going to accept this until experience teaches it to him, but he can be made aware that the choice is his and that, by the same token, it will not affect the rest of the world very much if he begins getting drunk again. They have their own concerns.

At the same time, there are those to whom it matters a great deal, and he is well aware of that. That is certainly his responsibility, and again, it is what *he* knows that matters. Experience will also show him that the people who like him will always like him, that they will feel respect and admiration for what he has done, and that they would be sorry indeed to see him return to drinking. But it is hard to convince him of this at the point of re-entry. His feelings of guilt and shame are still too active, and not drinking will be for a while a humiliating statement that he "couldn't handle it, and had to go away." Time, once more, will ease his embarrassment, as will the reaction of most people to what he has done. As he will probably be incapable of accepting that prediction from the staff, or from anyone else, it is best to advise him to focus on the positive elements of his situation. There are plenty of these, and it should be noted to him that concentrating on what is wrong, and pushing the good things to one side, is an old habit of his, and that his plan should include a conscious effort to readjust his thinking as part of being good to himself. It is going to be all too easy for him, for a while, to slide into feeling abused and sorry for himself, separated from the rest of the world, and he needs to be reminded that drinking with people is never the basis of a true or deep relationship. Rather, it is a cover-up for the absence of it and makes real and honest communication impossible for an alcoholic. Again, the choice is his.

"I Am Responsible"

The maturation process that takes place in a recovering alcoholic varies in proportion to a number of factors. There is the degree to which his emotional growth has been stunted, and this depends upon the age at which his illness began and the length of time the active phase lasted. There is also the degree of motivation he has to make changes in himself and his willingness to accept and work for long-term goals. These will be reflected in an honest aftercare plan, and of course, they can cover a very wide spectrum of priorities that he sees and sets for himself. No one can ever coerce an alcoholic into a permanent course of action that truly goes against his grain, just as no one can ever succeed by force in making him abstinent for a lifetime.

This will come only from his own sense of responsibility; responsibility to himself, to those he cares about, and to those to whom he has obligations. If he continues to drink, it will eventually be impossible for him to be responsible in any of those areas. He will lose every trace of order in his life, and the mastery of alcohol over him will be complete. An aftercare plan is intended for both the short and the long run. It should be a basic design for living that will encompass all areas with a few fundamental precepts, and the most fundamental of these is responsibility. As acceptance of the fact of having alcoholism is the key that will set him free from it, so acceptance of responsibility is the key to staying free and to making the rest of his life a productive and reasonably contented experience. It means growing up in his relationship with himself and with others, at home and at work, to the best of his ability. The promise of sobriety is not one of endless joy in living. It is rather that of never again experiencing or inflicting that particular kind of pain, of the opportunity to grow, and of reaching out for his full share of the peace and fulfillment that his God will grant him.

Conclusion

The scope of this work has been necessarily limited by its intent, which was to present an overview of the alcoholism syndrome for lay people who are, for whatever reason, confronted by the illness in their day-to-day lives and who feel a need for a basic understanding of it.

We have dealt here with the nature of the illness itself and then with the ramifications of it which we see as primary and affecting the largest number of people. As stated earlier, it has been intended only to offer a primer. Thus it is hoped that a basis of understanding may be acquired from reading it, and that some of the more hampering misconceptions which have historically surrounded the disease have been dispelled.

It is our strong feeling that over the last twenty years, this long-misunderstood affliction has slowly but surely begun to come out of the closet and into the light of day, to be seen for what it really is. For those of us who have been working to help its victims, this has been an exciting time, a time of hope and optimism. Many of us relive daily in memory, our own struggles with addiction and can remember that in those days, not so long ago, it was still shrouded with ignorance (our own, as well as that of others) and shame. This has added a great sense of urgency to our labors, for we have seen in the struggles of others a reflection of our own past, of the time when we were searching for the key to the dark and lonely place in which we were imprisoned.

That the key was in the door all the time is one of the first things that newly recovering people learn. Their search has led them everywhere but to the right place, for the miasma through which they have been groping has had centuries in which to thicken. What we are seeing now in the field of addictive disease is truly the dawn of a new time, one in which it is to be hoped that a tremendous number of people who have been very fittingly described as "the walking wounded" will no longer find themselves relegated to the outer edges and the back wards of society, much as other afflicted populations were. There is a distinct parallel to the shunning of the leper and the epileptic in ages past in the treatment that has been accorded the alcoholic, even in recent times. All have been innocent victims of physiological forces beyond their control, and have been the objects of revulsion, pushed away from their more fortunate fellows. The alcoholic is now rejoining them, in the sense that his affliction, too, is now being recognized for what it is and is starting to be treated with compassion and understanding.

Accompanying this great change in perception has been a tremendous amount of study, specialization in particular areas of the disease and, of course, published material. There are many who recall very well a time when alcoholism was, if not precisely a taboo topic, certainly a somewhat distasteful one and something that tended to be brushed aside as a phenomenon peculiar to a murky and alien segment of society. Most people felt that it was not an area with which *they* had to be concerned. Today, people *are* feeling concern. It is an expression of these times that caring is shown for those who have been thrust outside the pale through no fault of their own and that an effort is made to bring them in. More widespread acceptance of the disease concept has played a great part in removing the stigma of alcoholism, and the result has been an impetus to explore the subject and to examine the ripple effect of its impact on the lives of almost everyone: carnage on the highway, billions lost to industry, far-reaching effects on children growing up in alcoholic homes, repeated hospitalizations that can be directly attributed to alcoholism and their effect on insurance costs, divorces and other court matters, welfare costs, the burden placed on police and fire departments — the list is a long one. Many insurance carriers have now been obliged through legislation to cover alcoholism in specialized facilities, rather than limiting treatment to psychiatric hospitals in which the vast majority of alcoholics don't belong and in which what is offered is very likely to be ineffective. Even "60 Minutes" got involved and presented a devastating documentary on the fallacy of thinking that alcoholics can be conditioned into becoming social drinkers and the cruelty of such experimentation.

There still remains, unquestionably, a long way to go before alcoholism will be accepted by the general public as a medical illness to which blame is not attached. Still, it is a measure of the progress made that recovering alcoholics are so much more open about their illness and willing to share their experience than could ever have been dreamed of even twenty years ago. And who in the 1960s had ever seen a television advertisement for an alcoholism treatment facility? Industry has done a significant about-face in dealing with alcoholic employees in referring them to employee assistance programs (EAPs) instead of firing them, and the EAPs, in turn, are showing their recognition of the fact that alcoholism is a disease, not a symptom, by sending those employees to alcoholism centers, rather than to psychiatric hospitals. Indeed, one of the most encouraging aspects of the changing views on providing effective treatment has been the very noticeable diminution of the control that psychiatry and psychiatrists once exercised in the field, both in direct patient contact and in the direction of such bodies as the National Institite on Alcohol Abuse and Alcoholism (NIAAA) and the Alcohol and Drug Problems Association (ADPA). The signs certainly seem to point to the approach of a new day in treatment in which alcoholics will finally be guided by people who are equipped for the task with empathy, sound and practical knowledge of what they are dealing with, enthusiam for their work, and a firm belief that there is a way that works.

Finally, we would like to suggest a beginners' list of publications that address the illness as an entity and specific areas of concern within it:

A.A. itself has a large list of useful publications, including *Alcoholics Anonymous* (the "Big Book") and *Twelve Steps and Twelve Traditions,* which outlines the A.A. recovery programs. Requests for a publications list can be sent to the General Services Board of A.A., 468 Park Avenue South, New York, N.Y. 10016.
Loosening the Grip,: Handbook of Alcohol Information, Kinney & Leaton
The Disease Concept of Alcoholism, E.M. Jellinek, Hillhouse Press, 1960
New Primer on Alcoholism, Marty Mann, Rinehart & Co., 1958
The Biology of Alcoholism, Kissin & Begleiter, Plenum Press, 1974
Is Alcoholism Hereditary?, Donald Goodwin, Oxford University Press, 1976
I'll Quit Tomorrow, Vernon E. Johnson, Harper & Row, 1973
Available (often at discount) from Hazelden Educational Materials, Pleasant Valley Road, Box 176, Center City, Minnesota 55012-0176 (Tel. 1-800-328-9000):
Alcoholism: a Treatable Illness, Strachan
Adult Children of Alcoholics, Woititz
It Will Never Happen to Me, Black
Families, Alcoholism, & Recovery, Dulfano
The Woman Alcoholic, Lindbeck
The Employee Assistance Program, Updated, Lingeman
Drugs from A to Z: a Dictionary, Lingeman
How to Live with an Alcoholic, Jorge Valles, M.D.
Guidebook for the Family with Alcohol Problems, Burgin
Another Chance: Wegscheider
The Invisible Alcoholics, Sandmaier (women alcoholics)